DOUBLE
TROUBLE

Also by Greil Marcus

Mystery Train: Images of America in Rock 'n' Roll Music *(1975)*

Lipstick Traces: A Secret History of the 20th Century *(1989)*

Dead Elvis: A Chronicle of a Cultural Obsession *(1991)*

In the Fascist Bathroom: Punk in Pop Music 1977–1992 *(1993)*

The Dustbin of History *(1995)*

The Old, Weird America: The World of Bob Dylan's Basement Tapes
 (formerly Invisible Republic, *1997)*

GREIL MARCUS

DOUBLE TROUBLE

*Bill Clinton
and Elvis Presley
in a Land of
No Alternatives*

Picador USA
A John Macrae Book
Henry Holt and Company
New York

Picador® is a U.S. registered trademark and is used by Henry Holt and Company
under license from Pan Books Limited.

www.picadorusa.com

For information on Picador USA Reading Group Guides, as well as ordering,
please contact the Trade Marketing department at St. Martin's Press.
Phone: 1-800-221-7945, extension 763
Fax: 212-677-7456
E-mail: trademarketing@stmartins.com

ISBN 0-312-42041-2

First published in the United States by Henry Holt and Company
First Picador USA Paperback Edition: September 2001

10 9 8 7 6 5 4 3 2 1

FOR HOWARD HAMPTON

Contents

Part Three

You laughed at me walkin', baby
But I have no place to go
Bad luck and trouble have taken me
I have no money to show
                    —Otis Rush, "Double Trouble," 1958

Every time I think that I have finally got it made
Some losing cards are played
Just can't make the grade
    I got
    Double trouble
    I got
    Double trouble
    I got
    Double trouble
Twice as much as anybody else oh yeah
                    —Elvis Presley, "Double Trouble," 1967

Katie Couric: The entertainer of the century?
Bill Clinton: For me in my lifetime . . . the early Elvis
                    would be the best.
Katie Couric: Your favorite Elvis song?
Bill Clinton: "I Want You . . . I Need You . . . I Love You."
                    —*Today,* NBC, December 20, 1999

He was an accident waiting to happen
Most accidents happen at home
                    —Warren Zevon on Elvis Presley,
                    "Porcelain Monkey," 2000

Now the stage is nearly bare, but he's still standing there
    —headline to story on Bill Clinton's last year in office,
                    New York Times, January 19, 2000

Introduction

I rooted for him during the impeachment process, of course, because fanaticism and puritanism in any form are my enemies," movie director Oliver Stone said in April 1999, two months after President Bill Clinton's acquittal by the Senate on charges of perjury and obstruction of justice. At issue was Clinton's testimony regarding an affair with a White House intern, originally given during a deposition in a later-dismissed sexual harassment case brought by one Paula Jones, a secretary employed by the State of Arkansas during Clinton's time as its governor; now, after more than a year of leaked and manipulated testimony meant to drive Clinton from office through extralegal means, Independent Counsel Kenneth Starr had lost the formal battle, and the crusade on the part of Republicans in the House of Representatives to expel Clinton from Washington had destroyed not their chosen enemy but two of their own leaders. Not that the victory ennobled the victor, Stone said: "He reminds me so much of Nixon. The pathology. The need to lie. A President who says, I smoked but I didn't inhale. A President who refuses to be proud of, or even to acknowledge that he didn't go to Vietnam for reasons of principle, and makes it sound like he's running away from what he did. Total pandering to the right wing. Clinton and the teenager. Like an Elvis movie. The poor man couldn't even get laid well."

A month later, in an interview with journalist Jack Newfield, *New York Times* columnist Frank Rich was trying to make ordinary sense of the same bizarre series of events and found himself speaking the same language—a language in which a metaphor that at first seems transparent is almost immediately opaque. "Do you think the far right hates Clinton more for cultural than for political reasons?" Newfield asked. "Do they just see him as the avatar of the 1960s with sex, drugs, and rock 'n' roll?" "Yes," Rich said, as if nothing could be simpler. Not that he wanted anyone identifying him or his generation with Clinton anymore than Stone did, just because they were all about the same age: "In some ways it's absurd because many people who still believe in the Left of the 1960s would find Clinton a very poor example of it." Rich recited the litany: "He wasn't really a serious Vietnam war protester; he was an opportunist even then. We know he smoked marijuana, but he's hardly an exemplar of the Ken Kesey LSD generation. Even his taste in Sixties music, I would say, is extremely suspect . . . It's kind of preposterous. It's like if you hated Elvis Presley, choosing Dick Clark as the person to focus on. I'm not a Clinton fan, but he's just not worthy of the kind of hatred that everyone has for him."

Why are these two interesting people drawn so helplessly to the identification of Bill Clinton with Elvis Presley? Trying to pull a usable metaphor out of the air, why are they drawn to that identification so imaginatively? The idea of Clinton's presidency as an Elvis movie (presumably the 1967 *Double Trouble,* where nightclub singer Guy Lambert is pursued both by a smitten seventeen-year-old heiress and a calculating woman his own age) is almost irresistible. The idea of Bill Clinton as Dick Clark creates an archetype that could rewrite Constance Rourke's unsurpassed 1931 classic *American Humor: A Study of the National Character.* But the momentum in the identification of Elvis and Clinton isn't about ideas—why are Stone, who as a Hollywood moviemaker can get more women than the president, and Rich, who during the year of impeachment came perhaps too close to crossing his newspaper's line of tolerance of Bill Clinton, drawn to this identification so personally? In the moment in the conversation when Elvis arrives—like Superman or a bad conscience—to dramatize or mystify what is otherwise a string of unexamined assumptions meant mostly to establish that the speaker is better than Bill Clinton, one can glimpse a piece of each speaker's life story: his attempt, in the 1950s or 1960s, to define himself by and against Elvis Presley, and how uncertain each is about how the story may have turned out. They are almost saying: What if Bill Clinton *is* Elvis Presley's true inheritor?

Gallery owner to Jesse: You think you can waltz in here in your cheap shoes and pass yourself off as an art critic?
Jesse: I want you to know that these shoes were not cheap! They cost fifty bucks! And what about *your* shoes? You look like you mugged Elvis!
Diego, artist with Jesse, attempting to ingratiate himself
with gallery owner: The early, *cool* Elvis . . .

—*Jesse*, NBC, November 5, 1998

Like Jesse and Diego, Oliver Stone and Frank Rich are playing with the Good Elvis and the Bad Elvis. Their Clinton is opposed to the Real, Good Elvis; he's the Bad Elvis, or the Fake Elvis—but somehow the equations don't hold. Apparently simple, the equations are in fact complex; seemingly fixed in cliché, they are unstable. Both Elvis and Clinton are alive in the common imagination as blessed, tawdry actors in a pretentious musical comedy cum dinner-theater Greek tragedy about their country's most unresolved notions of what it means to be good, true, and beautiful—and evil, false, and ugly. Americans are caught between the truth and falsity of performance (or art) (or culture) or of art (or politics) (or culture), caught along with the countless people all over the world whose response to the likes of Elvis Presley has made them, in Leslie Fiedler's phrase, "imaginary Americans"—people like Boris Yeltsin (who in 1991, after standing on a tank in Moscow to rally democratic forces against a fascist coup, returned alone to his office to listen to Elvis sing "Are You Lonesome Tonight?," to hear him say, "You know someone said, the world's a stage, and each must play a part . . ."), Sinéad O'Connor (who, having named Bill Clinton "the sexiest man in the universe" in late 1998, then wrote the *Irish Times* asking, "Does impeachment mean they're going to turn him into a peach? If so, can I eat him?"), or Salman Rushdie (who in 1999 insisted on both Presley and Clinton as familiars: Elvis's music, heard in India in 1956, "didn't seem foreign," he said, and he spoke with pride of the reply Clinton sent him when Rushdie wrote offering his support: "Bill Clinton, c'est moi!"). We are as attracted to the falsity as to the truth—both because we are never sure which is which ("The early, *fake* Elvis"—what if the later, helpless Elvis was the real person?), and because truth is final. That's its satisfaction and its alienation. Falsity is open: its future is always unfixed.

As fans and spectators imagining ourselves on stage—as Oliver Stone and Frank Rich are, for all their notoriety and circumspection, fans and spectators imagining themselves on a far greater stage than they actually inhabit—we play tricks on ourselves in this game, just as the actors play tricks on us (do you think Elvis or Clinton was ever fooled by his audience, either by the applause or the contempt?). We can't tell where the promise shades into betrayal, or the betrayal dissolves the promise for good.

Thus, in the second and third decades after his death, is Elvis reconstructed—randomly, it seems, but relentlessly—as a figure of sadism, domination, mutilation, waste, and ruin. He is a hate crime, his name sprayed along with Ku Klux Klan code signs by racist police officers in Cleveland in 1999. He is the devil, walking side by side with the shade of Robert Johnson in Ace Atkins's 1999 detective novel *Crossroad Blues*—or side by side with Idi Amin Dada, the former Ugandan dictator and sometime cannibal, the two of them scanning the shelves of a supermarket in Saudi Arabia: "A number of my friends say they have met him there in the frozen food aisle," an American lawyer reports in 1996. "They say it was just like meeting Elvis." He is the nightmare of a present-day Dr. Van Helsing, ruminating in the 1995 film *Nadja* over the death of Count Ceauşescu Dracula on the Lower East Side of New York: "He was tired, he was lost. He was—he was like Elvis in the end. Drugs; confused; surrounded by zombies; just going through the motions. And he knew. I didn't kill him. He was already dead." He is a house forever divided against itself, to the point that neither he nor anyone else can get from one room to another and back again; most crepuscularly he is a haunt in Rudolph Giuliani's Gracie Mansion, as critic John Leonard imagines the New York mayor as "Richard Nixon, alone in a darkened wing of the White House, as if Watergate had been a play by Beckett, listening on tape to himself or maybe Elvis"—which, with the year not 1974 but 1999 and Leonard's Nixon not a man about to leave the White House but a man who imagines that he will one day occupy it, makes the tape in question as likely Clinton's testimony to Kenneth Starr's Grand Jury as, say, "Reconsider Baby."

Bill Clinton is a man able to effortlessly convince whoever is speaking to him that it is only that person's voice he hears—just as Elvis convinced so many that, from a hundred rows away, he was singing only to them. Though remade through the Internet as a mass murderer ("I have seen the list," informant Linda Tripp told Starr's Grand Jury darkly), in vast fields of public discourse as a monster destroying all values and decency in his path ("The man in the Oval Office is a rapist, a war criminal, a psychopathic liar," journalist Christopher Hitchens told followers of the Free Republic, a right-wing Web site, as they rallied across from the White House in July 1999), that is not the bad guy's role Bill Clinton plays in the common imagination. He comes forth rather as a perfect version of the American type Herman Melville chased in *The Confidence Man: His Masquerade*—with the Oval Office as the ultimate Big Store and a never-ending parade of good people lining up to be fleeced. "Our father who art in Washington," Memphian Jim Dickinson intoned in 1993, leading off Mudboy and the Neutrons' "Money Talks," "Slick Willie be his name / He taken me off Rabbit Track tobacco / And put me back on Novocain." He is the southerner who goes north to read the law, who returns home, and then to the nation at large, as the Yankee Pedlar—without ever having lost, as country singer Robin Lee put it in 1990 with her Elvis tribute "Black Velvet," "that slow southern style." The fear Bill Clinton inspires is not, as the right has warned the country ever since it woke up to the fact that he had somehow been elected president, that he will steal you blind and corrupt your morals; it is that he will do all that and more, and make you like it. For both Elvis and Clinton, one dead, one back from the dead, behind all the hysterical and gaudy obloquy is the suspicion that each could have been everything he ever promised he would be—and, in the common imagination, still can be.

The unknowableness, or unseeableness, of Elvis Presley and Bill Clinton is part of their common status as outsiders in an America rewritten in the 1950s by means of a newly magical, newly dominant, and altogether unitary media, which from 1945 rushed in to fill the huge gap in the nation's public life, its sense of purpose and definition, left by the death of Franklin Roosevelt. It was an era when images of the good, of what it meant to be American and to be taken seriously as such, were framed by a very few sources: *Life* magazine, daily newspapers, three television networks, and advertisements for cars, refrigerators, and Scotch. As white male southerners without family money (hillbillies, no 'counts, white trash—the source, of course, of much of the identification made between Bill Clinton and Elvis Presley, and of Clinton's own heartfelt or cynical identification of himself with Elvis), Presley and Clinton always had to prove themselves—and they never could, not without abandoning themselves in some essential way, some way that one or the other or both could perhaps desire but never master. "Bush didn't believe the country would throw out the commander of the Gulf War for this cracker governor from Arkansas," Republican Party operative Ed Rollins said in 1999. "He actually told people that." Many still can't believe it, any more than in 1956 they or others, those horrified and those thrilled, could believe what a twenty-one-year-old from Mississippi and Tennessee was doing in their living rooms.

Both Elvis Presley and Bill Clinton reaped all the rewards available in American society except one: moral citizenship. Both remain figures by which that quality can be defined, which is to say that it is defined by, among other things, the degree to which one can believe he or she is better than either or both. Our attraction to both is inseparable from our need to prove to ourselves that we are different from them—to prove that if we will never rise so high, we would never sink so low. Because this is a tricky case to make, it has to be made again and again, and more and more cryptically; that is why for Elvis the story remains untold more than two decades after his death, and why for decades to come the nation may wish Clinton would, like Elvis, have the grace to surrender his right to tell his own story to the rest of us. That is unlikely. As *New York Times* columnist Maureen Dowd put it, when in 1999 rumors surfaced that Clinton was considering a run for the Senate from Arkansas in 2002, "Elvis will *never* leave the building."

This book is a collection of pieces, published from 1992 to 2000, that means to trace the footprints Elvis Presley left in the Clinton years. Some pieces are about Elvis, some about Clinton; some are about the symbiosis of the two, and some, mentioning neither, are local maps of the cultural landscape the two shared in the last decade—but all, I hope, give some voice to the Elvis-Clinton identification that began as a joke and has not quite held that shape.

The book starts off in an election year that saw an increasingly intense and playful conflation of the two figures, as the media and the country tried to fix a positive identity for a man who at first seemed like a candidate carrying more rumors than news, then a nominee all but excluded from the election, then a natural winner who could not be stopped. The Elvis-Clinton identification was an attempt by the country to make sense of an unknown man, then Bill Clinton's attempt to ease the fear of the unknown, then a confident man playing a role that since 1956 so many others had imagined and even tried out for themselves. It worked. VOTE FOR ELVIS ran the full-cover headline on the election day issue of *LA Weekly*. It was a joke but not an irony, or rather a giddy hope that Bill Clinton could give the sorry, horrible climax of the Elvis story a new and better ending, that he might begin the story all over again, and change the country in the bargain: after twelve years of rule for the few, returning it to another America, as if to prove once more, as the sleeve of *Elvis' Gold Records Vol. 2* proclaimed in 1960, that *50,000,000 Elvis Fans Can't Be Wrong*—a figure just barely more than Clinton's 1992 plurality of forty-five million votes.

But once this new, happily impostorous Elvis took office—once Clinton-as-Elvis, or Elvis-as-Clinton, had been, if not accepted, by virtue of the magnitude of his office institutionalized—the recreation of Elvis Presley that in the common imagination had begun with his death all but stopped. The cultural noise made between 1977 and 1991 by those who still found a dead Elvis an unsolved mystery quieted to whispers from the wings and talk of angels, and was stored in meticulously annotated boxed sets of CDs and serious biographies. For Clinton, the Elvis identification vanished when his mastery as a campaigner could not translate into mastery as a chief executive. The Republican party denied the legitimacy of his election—as if it were a trick, like payola—and refused him the prerogatives enjoyed by his predecessors. With majorities in both houses of Congress, Clinton's own Democratic party took him under suspicion as a man who had yet to learn the rules, let alone suggest he would play by them, and as such denied his legitimacy as well, demanding that he prove to them his fitness to govern, as if his election were not an electorate's decision but a phase to be outgrown, like teenage hysteria.

When Republicans took control of the House of Representatives and the Senate in the congressional elections of 1994, Clinton was banished to the wilderness of redundancy. No one had ever asked Ronald Reagan or George Bush, when they faced Democratic majorities in Congress, if their presidencies were irrelevant; Clinton was asked, immediately, at a press conference, point-blank, and he had no answer. Some Republicans announced that they had "cut his presidency in half," claiming that as he was meaningless in 1995 he would be gone by 1997; in the *New Yorker* political writer Michael Kelly conveyed the common assumption, or hope, that the time would soon come when the elders of Clinton's party, the real elected, would make the journey to the White House, as the elders of the Republican party had once done with Nixon, to tell Clinton that he had to go, that he could not run again, that he would bring all of them to ruin, that his time in the light had been an illusion, and that that time had passed. Elvis kept his own counsel. He too receded. No one pretended anymore that he was still alive. He became a narrow story, fit for niche marketing—a thing that had all but given up its now merely Halloween-costumed ghost.

Clinton's reelection in 1996, unimaginable two years before, only confirmed a public discomfort with the megalomania of the Republican majorities. It said nothing about him, and, as he ran, he said nothing himself. He was still president; no one joked anymore that he was Elvis. It was only when Clinton faced impeachment that the Clinton-Elvis identification came back to life—and in a manner that could barely be translated. The seemingly mindless identification of the dead Elvis Presley with a host of demons and fiends in the 1990s was a testament to his exile in his own culture; it was also a replay of the assault this son of the Great Awakening had faced in 1956, when a preacher, speaking for millions, famously declared him "morally insane"; and it was, perhaps, a matching with his sometime Döppelganger, a usurper holding to his office as he was brought forth before the nation as an immoralist and a criminal. So two people from nowhere waited out their enemies—two people who against good evidence believed they belonged in their own country, as their enemies were sure they could prove that belief in the country was nothing against their certainty that they owned it.

That is the story this book tries to keep up with. It is not as funny as the story told in *Dead Elvis,* my first attempt to chronicle the persistence of Elvis Presley in American life, but the stakes are higher.

Berkeley, January 8, 2000

DOUBLE
TROUBLE

Part One

THE ELVIS
ELECTION

★ *1992–1993* ★

Flyer posted in Berkeley, California, on election day,
November 3, 1992

A Moral Crisis

In late February and early March I went from London to Dublin to Amsterdam to talk about a book on the culture that's grown up around Elvis Presley since he died—you can say promote, or flog, but most of the time that's not what it felt like. Newsbreaks included the *National Enquirer's* Dee Presley explosion: HIS OWN STEPMOM REVEALS SHOCKING TRUTH AT LAST—ELVIS AND HIS MOM WERE LOVERS. The U.S. Postal Service announced a primary-season vote to decide which of two artist's-rendering Elvis head shots (more or less '56 vs. '73, both looking fine) would be chosen for the long-awaited Elvis stamp. (With George Bush singing Presley's praises on a campaign stop in Memphis and Molly Ivins rating Paul Tsongas "minus-zero on the Elvis scale"—despite, or because of, his win over Bill Clinton in the New Hampshire Democratic primary—the timing of this election was sublime.) Meanwhile, an Irish high court judge refused to allow a fourteen-year-old girl who, her family told police, had been raped and impregnated by her best friend's father, to travel to England for an abortion.

The theme I carried in my head was "That's Someone You Never Forget," a 1961 Elvis number I'd heard for the first time a week before, on the radio—a ghostly, passionate, infinitely more personal version of his 1955 "Blue Moon." The disc jockey announced the performance as a previously unreleased take from the latest RCA grave robbery, a.k.a. a three-CD box called *Collectors Gold* (the budget apparently didn't allow for an apostrophe). The number wasn't there, but the set did include something just as far away: a moment of studio dialogue worth more than the rest of the music. It's 1968: "PAPA OO MAU MAU papa oo mau mau," Elvis announces to his assembled musicians. "Be talkin' in unknown tongues here in a minute." Before the band can stop him, he slides into a distant second of "I Got a Woman," and you can imagine he is going to take the song all the way home, all the way back to the glossolalia from which both he and the song came, to the primal swamp of deliverance and revelation. Well, of course not: there's work to do, they've got a typically throwaway ballad called "Going Home" to cut. But there is a reach for that deliverance in "That's Someone You Never Forget."

"It's credited to Elvis and Red West—you know, one of his bodyguards," said Ger Rijff, former head of the Dutch Elvis Society, in Amsterdam. "Elvis came to Red West with the title and asked him to write a song from it. About his mother, it's said"—Gladys Presley, who died in 1958, at forty-six, after, if Dee Presley is right, years of bliss with Elvis in her bed, or she in his.

"It makes sense," said Adrian Sibley of the BBC's *The Late Show*. "America has brought Elvis up to date: now he needs therapy just like everybody else. Don't they have twelve-step programs for incest survivors?" "It makes sense," said Jip Golsteijn, pop critic for the Amsterdam *Telegraaf.* "It's what I heard again and again in Tupelo, years ago. Nobody meant it as a condemnation. Given the way Elvis and Gladys were about each other, it was simply the conclusion everyone drew."

In Dublin, Joe Jackson of *Hot Press* looked over the Elvis stamp choices, noted that Elvis was still being shot from the waist up, and mentioned that among Irish intellectuals, it was only the revelation that Elvis, too, was a drug addict, like Charlie Parker or Chet Baker, that made him cool. The day before, Sinéad O'Connor had told a Dublin abortion-rights rally that as a mother she herself had had two abortions—and that if there were to be a new referendum on Ireland's nearly absolute ban on abortions, passed by a two-to-one vote of the populace in 1983, only women of childbearing age should be allowed to take part.

Just as in Amsterdam it was strange to be in a great city without people sleeping in doorways or begging on every corner, in Dublin it was strange, after months of listening to presidential candidates evade the political crisis that is turning the U.S.A. into a nation of scapegoaters, to be in a city in the grip of a moral crisis, where it really made no sense to talk about anything else. People everywhere had their radios on for bulletins on the Irish Supreme Court's hearing on the fourteen-year-old's appeal; as the government spoke of possible exceptions for this "special case," one heard the story of another raped teenager, who had hidden her pregnancy from her family, and who died along with the baby, giving birth in a churchyard, alone.

The papers read tensely. The *Irish Times* alternated hard news with a series of riveting editorials, superbly reasoned, carefully worded. The tabloid press played up accusations by anti-abortion leaders that the raped girl had almost certainly seduced whoever got her pregnant, while a Catholic priest claimed that abortion-rights groups had conspired with the girl to create a "test case" to overturn the abortion law. There were marches in the street, and biting satire on television. RAPED? read a cut-in on *Nighthawks,* an interview show filmed in a studio made over into a crowded Dublin pub: PREGNANT? DISTRESSED? IRISH? FORGET IT. With a cut back to the pub, a woman spoke into a pay phone: "Yeah, this is Sinéad O'Connor," she said, in a good imitation of O'Connor's thick snarl. "You tell the prime minister I'm hangin' on this line until he picks it up—I don't care if I stay here all week." O'Connor was taking a lot of heat in Dublin—for pop-star arrogance, for "divisiveness"— but people missed the point. Singing or talking, she stands up to say what she thinks, to piss people off. Like Madonna, she means to make everyone uncomfortable in their turn. She's a punk, not a politician.

So was Elvis, in a different way—in the clothes he wore, the way he moved, not what he said. No, you can't imagine him in O'Connor's shoes, even if he helped put her in hers; that's why it remains so easy to write him off. "American history doesn't look the slightest bit different for the presence, or the art, of Elvis Presley," I read in the *London Review of Books* as I arrived in the U.K. "Presley is a distraction, a placebo," the writer went on—unlike, he said, the "feral" Howlin' Wolf. The pictures of Elvis in almost every London newspaper and magazine, marking a William Eggleston retrospective at the Barbican Art Gallery—"Colour Photographs Ancient and Modern"—were not an answer. Every publication used the same shot from Memphian Eggleston's Graceland portfolio: the only one that included a portrait of Elvis himself. But the reference was to nothing. In the service of publicity, this Elvis was less a recognizable symbol than a symbol of recognizability.

So I tried to talk around such ciphers, and I was lucky to get back more than I gave. Ger Rijff had been at one of Elvis's winter 1976 concerts, and remembered it with horror: "I knew it couldn't go on." Jip Golsteijn had met Presley after being ushered up to his Las Vegas suite with presidents of various international fan clubs. "I got his ear somehow," Golsteijn said. "I said, 'Was this your ambition? Did you ever think you'd get so far?' He just looked at me. 'If I had any ambition,' he said, 'it was to be as good as Arthur Crudup'"—the bluesman who wrote "That's All Right," Elvis's first record. "'I wanted to be as good as Arthur Crudup when I saw him, back in '49. Arthur Crudup—you know that name?'"

Yeah, he knew it.

Interview, *May 1992*

Contribution to *LA Weekly Advice to Bill Clinton Symposium*

The next church is Union Missionary Baptist on Chicago's Westside
. . . with a congregation that is black working class and poor and
that practices religious rituals not far removed from its members'
Mississippi roots. The music, though, is pure Chicago: organ, piano,
electric guitar, drum kit . . . "The church is not a place for saints,
but for sinners," [Clinton] begins, "but all of us are called to do the
Lord's work." Amens echo again—and the organ and drums, too;
apparently, they will accompany Clinton throughout . . . He omits
his statistics on rising income inequality and conveys their sense in
short rhythmical sentences: "It is honestly true, more people are
working harder for less." He cites experiments in tenant-managed
projects, model schools, community development banks. After
each, he says "If it can be so, why can't it be so everywhere else?"
The drums roll, the guitar and organ riff for a second, the amens
rise. "We are tired of being divided by race!" (Music and amens.)
"We are tired of being divided by gender!" (Music and amens.)
"We are tired of being divided by income!" (Music and amens.)
And then, raising his voice, he closes with scriptural passages
about faith and redemption; he shouts it over the music and
the congregation's own shouts, and he leaves the crowd
in ecstasy.

—Harold Meyerson, *LA Weekly*, March 20–26, 1992

At this stage Perot is irrelevant. You can't hit what you can't see,
what isn't there. Two things need to be done now, and through
the conventions: make yourself real and Bush unreal.

The second is easier. Bush in New Hampshire: "Message: I care." He doesn't care, and people know this, just as they know he is not a leader. Your job is to hammer away at these truths, again and again. In every locality, with local details, and then at the convention, with national scope and national examples, bring forth what the caring leader who does not care and will not lead has to offer: when faced with a disaster, sell something. L.A. riots? Sell the airport. Hurricane in Florida? Sell the waterways. Sell roads, parks, fire departments . . . the list is endless. This, you say, is the politics of the future under George Bush. Behind these easy answers, you say, is a familiar slogan: "BUY NOW! GOING OUT OF BUSINESS!" It's just that the name on the store didn't always read "U.S.A."

You cannot ignore the fact that there remain powerful reasons to vote for Bush. He is a demagogue and none of us are immune to his demagoguery. He is the national guardian of certain hates, fears, divisions, and privileges. People know this as surely as they know he truly believes in only one thing: cutting the capital gains tax. Never forget why people will vote for Bush, but throw bad words and good against him, incessantly, with carefully increasing disbelief and outrage, so that voting for Bush becomes not the act of patriotism that voting for Reagan was made to seem in 1984, but an act of shame, cowardice, and self-hatred. Bad and good words from everywhere (always credited!), from the daily papers (*San Francisco Chronicle,* May 21: UPROAR OVER QUAYLE COMMENTS— "MURPHY BROWN" DEFENDERS FIRE BACK—BUSH NEUTRAL) to the whole of our past ("The things that will destroy America are prosperity at any price, peace at any price, safety first instead of duty first, and love of soft living and the get rich quick theory of life"— Theodore Roosevelt, 1917).

Making yourself real is another story. You have to take a leaf from Jesse Jackson's book (this time uncredited—this is politics— and in your own words): you must present yourself as an unfinished man, as in "God is not finished with me yet." If you don't confront the doubts people have about your actions, behavior, and truthfulness the other side will do it for you, until all you can do is apologize. Be frank: you are not perfect, you have done things you would like to undo, and if you are elected you will do more of them. The difference, you say, is this: *I will take responsibility for what I do, and let you, the people, be the judge. You will not find me, you say, blaming the future on long-dead presidents or TV stars. If you elect me, you say, and you don't like what I do, then don't vote for me again. If you don't like what I'm saying today, don't vote for me now.*

As for what you stand for—well, who knows, really? There are vague intimations, in your campaign talks, in your old letter about the draft, in a few speeches you've made in churches, of decency, thoughtfulness, and the capacity to learn, change, and decide. If you can make the prospect of voting for you the prospect of a venture into an unknown but nevertheless real future, you might win.

LA Weekly, *May 29–June 4, 1992*

How the Heartaches Began

Continuing the grand tradition of titling all Elvis Presley product simply *Elvis,* while at the same time acknowledging that the son of Tupelo deserves a musical accounting more or less as respectful and possibly as renumerative as that recently accorded dead blues singer Robert Johnson, RCA has delivered the first in a series of monuments: *Elvis: The King of Rock 'n' Roll—The Complete 50's Masters.*

It's a five-CD box; depending on how you count them, 116 to 119 of the 141 cuts are "masters," meaning either the official, released version of a song, a unique studio performance of a song previously unreleased, or an alternate version of a released song so different from the official version as to constitute a separate, autonomous assault on the Zeitgeist. The fifth disc contains "Rare and Rockin'" material, which ranges from ancient, never-before-heard artifacts to recordings that are rare only because they have never-before-been-released on CD, which means they have been released. Not all extant 1950s Elvis is here—missing is almost all of the 1956 Million Dollar Quartet session with Carl Perkins and Jerry Lee Lewis, plus numerous live recordings and alternate takes.

All of which, given what's at issue here, is merely consumerist and manifestly trivial. The real question is this: faced with a new configuration of a cultural story that, like it or not, almost everyone in the United States (and billions more beyond it) now lives out in pieces, what is there to hear? Where's the drama? When do the heartaches begin?

The drama begins straight off, with "My Happiness," track one on CD one, and with "That's When Your Heartaches Begin," displaced to the top of "Rare and Rockin'." These are the two sides of the fabled acetate an eighteen-year-old Elvis Presley made in Memphis in 1953 at the Sun Recording Service, the hear-your-own-voice subsidiary of Sam Phillips's Sun label. Long believed lost, the single copy (it cost Elvis four dollars—according to the official story, it was a birthday present for his mother) turned up some years ago, and RCA released "My Happiness"—to overwhelming public indifference—in 1990. But "My Happiness" is an astonishing performance, not only fully realized but fully *stylized*—gentle, swooping, caressing, beyond ghostly, almost pre-posthumous. The feeling the kid brings to this ballad, a 1950 Ink Spots hit, wouldn't be out of place in "Barbara Allen" or "Long Black Veil." Writing in *The Wire*. Hopey Glass hints at something similar, at the confusions of gender and identity hiding in so many of the old mountain songs: "Sung to Gladys or himself, or the young Gladys in himself." Glass hears this teenage Elvis as himself a mother, a cultural mother; he ends up speaking in the same lost tongues William Carlos Williams found for Abraham Lincoln, closing *In the American Grain* in 1925: "The Great Rail-splitter's All I am or ever hope to be I owe to my angel mother; the walking up and down Springfield on the narrow walk between the two houses, day after day, with a neighbor's baby, borrowed for the occasion, sleeping inside his cape on his shoulder to give him stability while thinking about coming speeches . . . The least private would find a woman to caress him, a woman in an old shawl—with a great bearded face and a towering black hat above it, to give it unearthly reality."

This is the unearthly Elvis so many have heard reaching out to them over the years, or from beyond the grave. But it's only one Elvis. The flip side—the teenager's 1953 recording of "That's When Your Heartaches Begin," another number associated with the Ink Spots, among others, and, as Elvis rerecorded it for RCA, a huge hit in 1957—could not be more different. This is a foray into the netherworlds of cool, into the bohemian, white-on-black demimonde that Sun music was already signifying, and that Elvis, with his pink-and-black Negro hipster's outfits, was already inhabiting. Here, in this distant performance, is the self-invention of Elvis Presley—of the mythical Elvis, in any case, the rebel, the boy who had to do what he had to do. The performance is all attitude, the sneer curling for the very first time. It's strange, and it can make you uncomfortable. This is the stance no one was ready for. Elvis himself isn't quite ready for it: compared to "My Happiness"— which against "That's When Your Heartaches Begin" one can hear as Elvis's self-discovery—he's posing, adjusting his clothes in the mirror, still more likely to be written off as a nobody than to take over Memphis, never mind the world.

Throughout the official Sun recordings of 1954–55 and the RCA releases from 1956 to June 1958 (when, because of Army service, Elvis's '50s recordings ceased), the tension of this drama—between the submission in "My Happiness" and the resistance in "That's When Your Heartaches Begin," between socialization and self-creation, mother and the world, wanting to be loved and wanting to be noticed—is constant. Sometimes, as in Elvis's first single, "That's All Right," from July 1954, it's active in the same song. Elsewhere you can hear Elvis slip back into the creamy warmth, the nostalgia, in moments the passivity, of "My Happiness," but in an even more extreme manner. You can hear it right from the start, with "I Love You Because" and other terrible Sun ballads, or you can hear it in his RCA covers of then-current hits, his version of Carl Perkins's "Blue Suede Shoes" now sounding like the first example of corporate rock, his version of Little Richard's "Tutti Frutti" not a lot better than Pat Boone's. And you can hear the cool that lurks in "That's When Your Heartaches Begin" exploding into the glamorous adventures of "Good Rockin' Tonight," "Baby, Let's Play House," "Hound Dog," "Jailhouse Rock"—adventures in lust, anger, refusal, fun, humor, good times, don't-look-back.

The most thrilling moments on this set, then, come when the tension between these two sides of Elvis Presley is gone: not just missing, as in a crummy movie tune like "Poor Boy," but transcended. And it's here—in the great RCA ballads, aching with melodrama, in "Love Me," "Anyway You Want Me," "Playing for Keeps," "First in Line," "Young and Beautiful," "Don't"—that you can hear someone big enough to take the name "the King." Yeah, he sounds like a king, in his own domain, a domain for a time shared by so many: the emotive utopia of his own desire. The kingdom of teen.

I don't mean you had to be there—not at all. There is an event taking place in these songs, and just as you can have your heart broken by events that took place hundreds or thousands of years ago, you might reinhabit this event, and fully. You can bring your own novelty to it and make it new. What I hear is time-specific, historical, but not time-bound: the passage of time, not its prison. When you hear the passage of time, you feel the weight of the past; you also sense that there are new things under the sun. Maybe it's this—the weird heroism of "Love Me," the lack of fear in the voice, or the way the voice slides into an oceanic sensuousness after the line "I would beg and steal," or in the word "just"—that was new. Or still is new—a sound that remains, in its entirety, to its unmapped borders, unheard.

SF Weekly, *August 12, 1992*

Images of the Present Day

There's an image of present-day rock 'n' roll that I've been unable to get out of my head since I first bumped into it on MTV a few years ago. It still runs on the channel, but with the set on or off it comes back to me all the time, without warning, capable of tingeing any musical thrill with nausea.

It's a video for Poison, one of L.A.'s blond metal bands—the clip for "Every Rose Has Its Thorn," a good ballad. In slow motion, you see singer Bret Michaels striding through backstage corridors on his way to the stage, where cameras, visible in the video itself, will soon make it appear as if infinite numbers of fist-thrusting boys and weeping girls want nothing more than to sacrifice themselves on the altar of the band's life force. Backstage, adoring fans, looking at once giddy and scared, are huddled against the wall, as if pressed back by vibrations emanating from Michaels's forehead.

He's flanked by two bodyguards—mountains of flesh with heads so blocklike they barely seem human, no expression on their faces, just a readiness to smash evident in the way that they move. Though nothing is really happening, tension builds. The disdain on Michaels's face, in his walk, is precise and studied, a parody of every rock star swagger from Elvis Presley to Mick Jagger.

The pose is too obvious. One more gesture is called for.

Michaels is carrying a drink in a big paper cup; he tosses it against the wall. There's no anger in his movement, merely contempt; in your mind's eye you can glimpse the bottomless well. Still in slow motion, the drink splatters and drips down the wall.

As in almost any video, symbolism is the currency. As the clenched fists will symbolize self-affirmation, the tears submission, and the visible cameras that what you're seeing is very important— important enough to be filmed—here the meaning is equally plain: the star pisses on his fans and they are blessed.

This tableau of worship and hauteur is staged, an advertisement carefully constructed out of clichés that have been pretested and presold. They need only to be rearranged to produce the proper re- sponse: Bret Michaels, in his role, could be his contemporaries Axl Rose of Guns N' Roses or Vince Neil of Mötley Crüe as easily as he is himself. The demonstration is riveting nonetheless. It is a pornography of money, fame, and domination, all for no reason outside itself, and all based in the magic of music.

If rock 'n' roll is real—not simply a balance sheet, but a matrix of voices and values—then here in this video is something real about rock 'n' roll. For this is, today, a sign, as complete as Little Richard's pompadour in 1956 or Jimi Hendrix's blasted "Star- Spangled Banner" in 1969, of the liberation rock 'n' roll has always promised: I can go where I want, do what I want, say what I want. There are no rules. Freedom's just another word for a mess some- one else has to clean up.

This is my image of the death of rock—or of rock as something that ought to be killed.

The question of the death of rock comes up again and again these days, and not just because of falling record sales, a collapsing con- cert market, major labels consolidating to the point of monopoly, or desperately profligate, rear-guard superstar contracts. Sony Music's

$33.5 million for ancient hard-rock warhorses Aerosmith, for example—a deal that will take the boys into their fifties, if they or Sony lasts that long, a kiddie-toy version of Wall Street's '80s leveraged buyouts, debt-financing, Milkenesque "compensation" at the top, massive layoffs below. The death of rock is not a question because of growing censorship of songs and shows, damaging as that is. (Speaking in March at an American Enterprise Institute conference on popular culture—a forum that included Robert Bork, Irving Kristol, and William J. Bennett—one Walter Berns, a professor of constitutional law at Georgetown University, called for censoring not only the music but "the musicians themselves, the rockers, the rappers, and all the Madonnas"—there's more than one?) It isn't even that the music is empty. Put last year's most interesting platinum albums against the year's most celebrated hit movies and best-selling books—pit *Metallica* against *Bugsy,* or Ice Cube's *Death Certificate* against Julie Salamon's *The Devil's Candy*—and it's clear that there's more life and less formula on the charts.

The question of the death of rock comes up because rock 'n' roll—as a cultural presence rather than a catchphrase—no longer seems to mean anything. It no longer seems to speak in unknown tongues that turn into new and common languages, to say anything that is not instantly translated back into the dominant discourse of our day: the discourse of corporatism, selfishness, crime, racism, sexism, homophobia, government propaganda, scapegoating, and happy endings.

There is an overwhelming sense of separation, isolation: segregation. There might be a vague awareness of the early and mid-'50s, when street corner doo-wop by African- and Italian-Americans, rockabilly by southern whites, and urban rhythm and blues from Chicago on down struggled for a name to mark the new spirit the different forms seemed to share. There might be a memory of *The T.A.M.I. Show,* the 1964 concert film with Jan and Dean, the Supremes, Gerry and the Pacemakers, Chuck Berry, Leslie Gore, the Miracles, the Beach Boys, Marvin Gaye, James Brown, and the Rolling Stones all sharing the same stage and, indisputably, whatever the word meant, all *rock*. The myth of the '60s that today serves as such a beacon and a burden for people in their teens and twenties is, among other things, a myth of wholeness—a wholeness that people who never experienced "the sixties," as fact or illusion, sometimes still feel as an absence, like the itch of a limb amputated before they were born. It's a myth less of unity, or even rebellion, than of a pop lingua franca—that's what brought more young people into the theaters for *The Doors,* a movie that allowed them to imagine themselves dressed up in their parents' clothes, than for *Pump Up the Volume,* a movie in which they could have seen people like themselves seizing the voice Jim Morrison once seemed to have found.

The rock audience began to break apart as far back as the early '70s. As the center of pop gravity, the Beatles had validated every form of the music both as commerce and as art; with that force gone, listeners and genres spun out in all directions. Still, the lines between sounds and audiences have never been so hard or so self-justifying—as commerce and as art—as they are now. Today "rock" refers to—what? Nirvana? Sinéad O'Connor? Michael Jackson? Bruce Springsteen? Prince? Ray Charles for Diet Pepsi? Rapper Ice-T, with or without his thrash band, Body Count? Public Enemy? Carter the Unstoppable Sex Machine, two former London buskers transformed into world-class Jeremiahs? Rosanne Cash? Madonna? Aging and unbowed punk troubadours the Mekons? The Fastbacks from Seattle, Pulnoc from Prague, the Vulgar Boatmen from Florida, Heavens to Betsy from Olympia, anyone's favorite breaking group or nowhere indie band? Some people would withhold the name "rock" from some of those performers, and some of them would withhold it from themselves.

The pop music audience is bigger than ever, despite fifteen-dollar CDs and thirty-dollar concert tickets. Such prices are paid, when they are, because the audience has been organized, or organized itself, into market segments—complex and recombined segments of age, race, class, and gender—efficiently predictable, containable markets that can be sold identity, or anyway self-recognition, packaged as music. As culture the segmentation is so strict that any public violation of its boundaries—say, white fraternity boys blasting N.W.A.'s ho-bitch rap spew—can seem less a matter of outsiders crossing into the mainstream than a privileged raid by the colonists on the colonized. There is no central figure to define the music, or against whom the music could be defined, no one everybody feels compelled to love or hate, nobody everyone wants to argue about (what is pop music if not an argument anyone can join?), unless it's the undead Elvis Presley, dripping almost fifteen years of rot—and, according to the Geto Boys, Houston rappers, deserving winner of the Grammy for Most Appearances Made After Death. "The King couldn't be here due to illness," mouths a white-bread voice on the Geto Boys' "Trophy," "so to accept this award on his behalf we have—Grateful Dead."

Ah, yes, the Grateful Dead, from the Summer of Love in 1967 to . . . the number-one concert draw of 1991. "I've had a few too many, so this might sound strange," Rick Rizzo of the guitar-based Chicago foursome Eleventh Dream Day leads off on "Bomb the Mars Hotel": "To see something that gives pleasure to so many / And want to take it all away." But he does want to take it away, and anyone who's seen too many Deadheads, or heard too much "Classic Rock" while punching buttons in search of something new, knows how he feels. "Bury the righteous monolith," Rizzo shouts. "And kill the sleepy myth / No more traveling microbus hordes / Taking over my town / No more tie-dyed underwear / No more dancing bears."

This is where talk of the death of rock starts: with pointlessness surrounded by repetition. As two Paris critics put it in 1955, writing about the art world, it starts with the feeling that you're trapped in "a dismal yet profitable carnival, where each cliché has its disciples, each regression its admirers, every remake its fans." It's as if the source of the depression is not that rock is dead but that it refuses to die. Far more than Elvis, really, a clone like Bret Michaels, so arrogant and proud, is of the walking dead. It's just that, as Theodor Adorno once wrote, "news of their not-quite-successful decease has been withheld" in the interests of production, which is another way of saying the money's too good to quit.

I believe all that, but as with any fan there are times when I couldn't care less—when, as in the last hour, running a few errands, I can hear the guitar line ripping through John Mellencamp's "Get a Leg Up," the radio shock of the drums kicking off Tom Petty's "Out in the Cold," voices growling in the background of ZZ Top's "My Head's in Mississippi"—times when the question of the death of rock seems like the most tired repetition of all.

Rock 'n' roll fans have always been waiting for the death of rock. Plenty of people will tell you the question is long since answered: rock 'n' roll died in 1957, or 1969, or 1976, when the Sex Pistols, lacking anything better to do, announced they had come to destroy it. From the start, the new music's followers were told *It will never last* so often and so loudly a distrust of the music, a distrust of one's own response to it, was all but built into the sound. Though the music began to argue against its own demise almost as soon as it had a name to trumpet, a belief in the music's end was coded into every one of its early artifacts, from Chuck Berry's "School Days" to the Monotones' "Book of Love." *The music was never meant to last*, fans were later told by critics who came not to bury but to praise, *and that's the fun of it!* The death of rock was a fait accompli by 1960, with the founders missing (Elvis in the Army, Chuck Berry on his way to prison, Buddy Holly dead, Alan Freed driven from the airwaves by the payola scandals, Little Richard in God's arms), Lawrence Welk ascendant (with "Calcutta," his only number-one record)—and Motown, the Stax-Volt Memphis sound, the Beatles, the Rolling Stones, Aretha Franklin, and Bob Dylan (in the crowd at Buddy Holly's last show) all waiting in the wings. In 1971, a year after the Beatles broke up, Don McLean's "American Pie" was number-one record as coroner's report, with the bodies of Brian Jones, Janis Joplin, Jimi Hendrix, and Jim Morrison for evidence. The stone was all but set by 1974, when pop dinosaurs ruled the earth and the likes of Johnny Rotten scurried beneath their feet, wondering what to do with their rage.

By 1979, Danny and the Juniors' unconvincing 1958 anthem "Rock and Roll Is Here to Stay" had been replaced by Neil Young's utterly convincing "Hey Hey, My My"—"*rock and roll will never die,*" he chanted. The song was convincing in its ugly, assaultive fury, but more so in its irony—a doubt so sardonic it froze the song's subjects, the dead Elvis and the by-then ex–Sex Pistol Rotten, into the history they'd already made. Young sang his song about the death of rock with such power that the great event seemed at once irrefutable and impossible. His irony has the kick of life to it—perhaps more now than years ago. Sometimes you need irony to breathe—to filter the stench of a corruption that can pop up anywhere, even in the casual act of a rock star on MTV.

There's a hint of that corruption, in the form of undifferentiated loathing and decay, in the video for Nirvana's "Smells Like Teen Spirit," the most surprising hit of 1991—and irony may be the currency in the five minutes that pass as the band grinds out its slow, corroding punk chords. Late for that, you might think: the death of punk was announced with great fanfare as far back as 1978. Living in Aberdeen, Washington, about a hundred miles southwest of Seattle, Nirvana singer-guitarist Kurt Cobain missed the funeral; for that matter he missed the birth. Born in 1967, he first heard punk, the first sound of walls falling in *his* life, when a friend played him a tape of scavenged punk songs, already old but news to him. It was 1983, the same year Danny Rapp of Danny and the Juniors killed himself, unable to stand one more oldies tour.

Eight years after that, "Smells Like Teen Spirit" begins as if on Jupiter, where body weight has hideously increased, the music pressed down by fatigue, lassitude, why-bother: "Never mind," as Cobain says to kill a line. On Jupiter, bell boy Cinqué Lee tells hotel clerk Screamin' Jay Hawkins in Jim Jarmusch's film *Mystery Train*, at the time of his death Elvis would have weighed 648 pounds, and words take a long time to emerge from this gravity, from Cobain's hoarse, seemingly shredded throat. It might be months on the radio or MTV before you begin to catch what's being said in Nirvana's songs—"sell the kids for food," "I don't mind if I don't have a mind," "I feel stupid and contagious," "I'm neutered and spayed," "at the end of the rainbow and your rope"— but the feeling of humiliation, disintegration, of defeat by some shapeless malevolence, is what the music says by itself. In the video, when you first glimpse Cobain, bassist Krist Novoselic, and drummer Dave Grohl, they seem more than anything to be going through the motions for a crowd as sick of the ritual as they are.

Everything about this video, though, is slightly off. The band is set up on the floor in a high school gym; there are kids in the bleachers against one wall, and pom-pom girls, as if somebody got the dates of the concert and the basketball game mixed up. Everybody plays along; they don't care where they are. The crowd is dressed in an indecipherable motley of styles from the '70s through the '80s; the musicians look like '60s hippies who had to hitchhike for three days to make the gig; as the girls lift their pom-poms, stretching to the roof even more spookily than Cobain expands his fuzztone, they could be in the '50s, except that they look old and hardened, with tattoos curling like snakes around their upper arms.

As in the Poison video, the drama is made of clichés—but what's

dramatic about them is that they don't work as such. They don't return the song to any recognizable cultural or economic shape.
There's red gas in the gym, but it seems less the result of the usual
video smoke machine than disease flaking off the listeners' skin or
floating out of their mouths. Slow motion is used but it feels like
real time. Kids snap their heads back and forth to the music but
they don't give off any sense of pleasure. As a pom-pom girl bends
backward, you follow the curve of her body, which reveals an Ⓐ
stitched into her uniform where her school insignia ought to be.
Cobain communicates not abandon and let's party but hopelessness
and mistrust of his audience. A string comes loose on his guitar, he
hangs sound in the air while he fixes it, and you lose all sense of
performance.

The kids begin to tumble out of their seats and onto the basketball court. As the musicians disappear into the surrounding crowd,
Cobain rails out a blank curse: "A denial! A denial! A denial!" Of
what? By whom? Moments before, he'd named the irony the song
comes from. He's screaming, but still carrying that same sense of
difficulty, as if he'd damn you to hell if only he could summon the
will to get out of bed: "Here we are now, entertain us."

He's trying to say that whatever it is he's doing, it's not entertainment. He's saying that the noise he and his friends are making
is entertainment only insofar as it fails, only to the degree that their
vague intimations of utopia and annihilation—"our little group has
always been and always will until the end," the ending of each word
dragged into the beginning of the next, the whole phrase
smeared—mean nothing, to him or anyone else. *Entertain you,
fuck—we'll set you on fire or drag you down. You want entertainment, the basketball team'll be back here tomorrow night.* The
moods and talismans of five rock 'n' roll decades are in the little
play, and as it finishes, implodes, scatters, it seems as good a death
as the music could ask for.

Sometimes, though, you need to speak without irony—and the

irony in *Smells Like Teen Spirit* can't really filter the corruption in
rock 'n' roll, perhaps because this is only a song, perhaps because
the corruption it speaks for is just too innocent. I have in mind a
corruption that is not limited to pop music, that is not in any sense
innocent, and that irony can't touch.

"The citizenry has been lulled into perceiving government as a
private corporation with no responsibility for the common good
rather than as a democratic mechanism that exists solely to serve
the hopes and hungers of those who need it most," Timothy White,
editor of *Billboard*, wrote earlier this year. The words are so plain,
so direct, that they can make you turn away or rant on in turn, but
let White continue: "The Reagan and Bush administrations have
actively reversed nearly forty years of gains in civil rights while fos-
tering racial demagoguery that destroys the powerless by pitting
them against each other . . . The principle of divide-and-conquer
starts with the power structure cunningly implanting fear and hatred in a society—and then stepping in to 'rescue' the populace
with the sort of massive, heinous repression that can take a century
to undo. In ominous times like these, ordinary people desperately
need the support of each other to endure against such sweeping
and terrible odds, and music can help provide the necessary solace,
public truth, and social strength."

Even if you were with White as he summed up the state of the
nation—and I was; if George Bush vs. Bill Clinton is a choice between tyranny and betrayal, the choice seems easy enough to me—
chances are he lost you with his last lines. Against all that, *music*?
Rock 'n' roll? Hey, take your good times where you find them, later
for that save-the-world shit. White's voice loses its hardness and
dissolves into sentimentality. The speaker who begins in complete
candor and follows his lines where they lead ends up sounding like
a fool. But any attempt to talk about the death of rock must finally
be made without irony, even if that ensures fool is the only role left
to play. For there is no way to talk about the death of rock without

facing what, exactly, is being consigned to the scrap heap—without recognizing what is being given up.

In his recent book *Rythm Oil: A Journey Through the Music of the American South*, Stanley Booth writes about a record made in 1956 by a white rockabilly singer:

It has been suggested that Carl Perkins's "Blue Suede Shoes"—the first record to reach the top of the pop, rhythm and blues, and country charts—represents one of the most important steps in the evolution of American consciousness since the Emancipation Proclamation. Perhaps it was an even more important step, because the Proclamation was an edict handed down from above, and the success of "Blue Suede Shoes" among Afro-Americans represented an actual grass-roots acknowledgment of a common heritage, a mutual overcoming of poverty and lack of style, an act of forgiveness, of redemption.

At a distance of thirty-five years, a generation, it can be seen as the prelude to a tragedy, the murder of Martin Luther King, one of the '60s assassinations from which the country has not yet recovered.

There's a lot going on in those few sentences—about race, democracy, fame and money, multiculturalism, shared language, social destruction. Placing questions of style and redemption on the same plane is remarkable in itself. But perhaps most striking is the displacing shock that Booth's words can deliver. Think of how unlikely Carl Perkins's gesture and the response that greeted it would have seemed in the very moment before they occurred—and think of how impossible such a gesture and such a response seem today. Booth's claims are big. They're as big as any claims that can be made for rock 'n' roll, or any form of culture, or any form of art. Very gracefully, as if casually, he offers a ditty about "a country boy proud of a new pair of blue suedes" (as Carl Perkins once put it) as a wedge in history, as a breach that opened up new roads—a road to utopia and, from there, a road to annihilation.

It's this sort of sweeping affirmation that always brings forth a chorus of skeptics happy to forsake the mysteries of art and culture for the facts of entertainment: *How can you make so much of a song?* The answer is: because it isn't simply a matter of the right notes in the right place at the right time that makes a song like Tom Petty's "Out in the Cold" so thrilling—or rather it's a matter of hearing the notes with a vastly enlarged sense of place and time. It is the echo those notes carry of a promise and a threat as vast as one can find in "Blue Suede Shoes"—even if, today, it is only an echo, and a faint, distorted echo at that. Whatever it is that "Out in the Cold" distantly promises, it is self-contained: a few minutes of pleasure swiftly returned to the strictures of a segmented format. If the sound seems explosive, unstoppable, out of control, it promises first and last that maybe it will be a hit.

In 1956, when "Blue Suede Shoes" momentarily suggested that all sectors of American society could sing the same song—suggested it because, for a moment, they did—there was no pop market, no pop America. Such territory remained to be made. Today the pop market is made: it's cut up like a kiddie-toy version of the electoral market, with stars and genres targeted like politicians' sound bites. There is little access to mass culture—to the risk of dissolution that entering mass culture entails, or to the chance of reaching everyone—and none of the peculiar energy of that fundamental pop journey, the leap (as with Carl Perkins, a balding married man from Tennessee) from nowhere to everywhere. Today rock 'n' roll exists in mass culture only as recycled commercial jingles for products everyone recognizes; the music itself is recognized only in its parts. The pop market, the pop world, is a thing in itself, complete in itself. The idea that music can travel outside its borders, into the larger world, where such promises and warnings as those in "Blue Suede Shoes" were fought over, seems childish.

It's often said that rock 'n' roll, like any popular art form, reflects or mirrors society at large; this is not interesting, and not to the point. Certainly it is not if one buys even a fraction of what Stanley Booth says about "Blue Suede Shoes." That record—coming two years after the Supreme Court's decision in *Brown v. Board of Education,* which mandated the integration of public schools, and decades before that mandate would be, as Timothy White writes, wrecked by the new Reagan-Bush Supreme Court—did not merely reflect. As a novel cultural event—part of its time, but speaking a new language—it did something very different. With preternatural intensity—with a new kind of humor and drive—it absorbed events in the world at large and sent them back into the world altogether transfigured and disguised, in a form that deflected any refusal. The song took in the social energies of change, desire, fear, jeopardy, of hatred of difference and ambivalence toward it too, and said: a new day is dawning. Now, without embarrassment, we can all dress up in new clothes.

The energies of absorption and transfiguration power the most indelible rock 'n' roll. "Dylan exhibits a profound awareness of the war and how it is affecting all of us," Jon Landau wrote in 1968 of *John Wesley Harding,* that oddly quiet, paradoxical reversal of the psychedelic '60s. "This doesn't mean that I think any of the particular songs"—among other things, a paean to an old-west mass murderer, a lament for Tom Paine, a meditation on St. Augustine, and a tune in which Dylan rhymed "moon" with "spoon"—"are about the war or that any of the songs are protests against it. All I mean to say is that Dylan has felt the war, that there is an awareness of it contained within the mood of the album as a whole. . . . Dylan's songs"—which seemed to ask, what is the country made of, where did it come from, which roads are open, which are closed off?— "acknowledge the war in the same way that songs like 'Magical

Mystery Tour' or 'Fool on the Hill' ignore it. They acknowledge it,"
Landau concluded, quoting *John Wesley Harding*'s "All Along the
Watchtower," "by attempting not to speak falsely."

The same spirit may be at work in Nirvana's sound, which can
seem so adolescent, so *hormonal*. "When we went to make this
record," Krist Novoselic has said of the sessions that produced
"Smells Like Teen Spirit," which took place during the Gulf War, "I
had *such* a feeling of us versus them. All those people waving the
flag and being brainwashed, I really hated them. And all of a sud-
den, they're buying our record, and I think, *You don't get it at all*."

When rock 'n' roll fails to absorb the events of the larger world, it
does reflect—and that's all it does. Then you have such famous scandals as a Guns N' Roses number denouncing "immigrants," "faggots," and "niggers"; an Ice Cube cut threatening to burn Korean
grocers out of Los Angeles; and Public Enemy's Chuck D recount-
ing his crucifixion at the hands of the tribe that "got me like Jesus,"
or explaining that unfortunately, not his fault, homosexuality remains
a crime against nature: "The parts don't fit." You get, in other words,
no more than a blank, glamorized reflection of the daily newspaper.
You get Axl Rose translating his lyrics into an explanation that "nig-
ger" merely refers to people he doesn't like as surely as David Duke
insists that all he's saying is that white people deserve an even break.
You get critics rushing to provide the apologies the performers can't
or won't make, just as Patrick Buchanan's talk show colleagues come
forth to assure the nation that, when you get him alone, Pat's as nice
a guy as you'd ever want to meet. And you get, as on a breathless National Public Radio report on the release of Guns N' Roses' *Use Your
Illusion I* and *II*—the albums went on sale at midnight, September
23, 1991, stores stayed open, fans lined up, eager to testify—an exit
poll, as it were, confirming that for the Guns N' Roses campaign,
"immigrants," "faggots," and "niggers" were not a problem, but selling points. As a stockbroker, new CDs in his attaché case, told the
NPR reporter, *At least Axl has the nerve to say what everybody's*

thinking. Look in this mirror and you see a person, like Axl Rose or Bret Michaels, who is just like you, except that he, unlike you, seems empowered. So you give him your money—hoping that, in the course of the transaction, some of that power is passed over to you.

By their definition of a single rock 'n' roll event, Stanley Booth's words on "Blue Suede Shoes" measure the progress of the death of rock. It is an ongoing story that cannot quite be contained by an insistence on how old a story it is. Along with the presumption of the death of its form, encoded in any rock 'n' roll song is the promise that the music will, in some barely definable way, impinge upon the world that presumes to contain it, or take its profit, or write off its loss. Without that promise, there's only profit and loss—and, soon enough, merely loss.

Against all that I offer a fantasy, sparked by a real song. In 1990, the Geto Boys' second album was scheduled for release on Geffen Records; mostly because of "Mind of a Lunatic," a tune about rape, murder, and necrophilia, Geffen, which had had no problem with Guns N' Roses' "niggers" and "faggots," refused it. *The Geto Boys* came out instead on the Def American label, with this blaring public safety advisory: "Def American Records is opposed to censorship. Our manufacturer and distributor, however, do not condone or endorse the content of this recording, which they find violent, sexist, racist, and indecent."

The Geto Boys were fixed, in that segment of the public imagination that was aware of their existence, as a Willie Hortonism, as vandals occupying the furthest extremes of capitalism and the First Amendment, as the scum of the earth. Last year, on the Rap-a-Lot label, they released the album *We Can't Be Stopped,* led by the single "Mind Playing Tricks on Me." The single was a hit on stations that play rap—black stations. It wasn't heard on Contemporary Hit Radio, on the stations formatted as Modern Rock or Rock of the

'90s, or on many college stations, the refuge of the avant-garde in pop music: as the singers' name suggested, the song was ghettoized. In my fantasy, though, the new song is heard as a new "Blue Suede Shoes."

The tune opens lightly, with pretty little notes sweeping up a theme, as if reprising a dream already dreamed too many times before. Those same notes, on a guitar or a synthesizer, remain constant throughout the piece, changing in tone according to the story set against them: comfort turns into mockery, mockery turns cold. The echoes here are very deep: "Mind Playing Tricks on Me" shares the fatalism of Robert Johnson's 1936 "Me and the Devil Blues," the otherworldliness of the Orioles' 1948 "It's Too Soon to Know," the dead-end introspection of Sly and the Family Stone's 1971 "Thank You for Talkin' to Me Africa"—dead-end, because Africa isn't talking, and the only one who'll listen to you is yourself.

The narrator—his part taken in turn by Willie D., twenty-five, Scarface, twenty-two, and Bushwick Bill, twenty-five—is a dope dealer in Houston's Fifth Ward. You can stay tuned to that fact and keep the song corralled, or you can forget it; chances are you'll forget it. Beginning in specifics of time and place, the song moves past them, almost refutes them, looking for a way out. There's something horribly small and humiliated about the way the man tells you what a big shot he is, how he's like a movie star, and something enormous about the way he says "I often drift when I drive." Moving easily through the streets he owns, he says, he thinks about killing himself. Scarface has the vocal; he's fluid, soulful. You believe him. The music has moved just slightly away from realism. The speaker's mind is playing tricks on him, but so far he can solve them.

It's with the last section of the song that the story breaks up. Bushwick Bill's speech is hesitant; you can't quite follow him. He doesn't sing, he recites. He's not soulful; he tries to distance himself from what he's saying. Day and night, sleep and waking are scrambled. He doesn't understand. He testifies. The music in the background says, *Yeah, I've heard it all before.*

> This year Halloween fell on a weekend
> Me and Geto Boys were trick or treatin'
> Robbin' little kids for bags

A cop appears; the men run; he catches them. The pettiness—the pathetic, bizarrely automatic account of men stealing candy from children (you don't have to want it, it's there, you take it)—wars against the bravado that follows when the gang turns to face the cop.

They jump him—but here the narrative dissolves. Who the cop is, and who they are, is suddenly unclear. Why they've done what they've done, which a minute before was set out with all the inevitability of manners, is now a mystery. Boundaries break up; characters who moved through the earlier moments of the song move on; specters take their places. The devil who starred by name in Robert Johnson's song, and in Sly and the Family Stone's, returns, no name needed. Those songs are about a struggle to see clearly; the Orioles' "It's Too Soon to Know," with its delicate, fading doo-wop moans, is about the impossibility of seeing clearly; "Mind Playing Tricks on Me" faces Robert Johnson's nemesis through the Orioles' haze. The devil is the cop; he's the singer. The singer is the cop. He kills himself. The headless horseman rides again.

> He was goin' down we planned
> But this wasn't no ordinary man
> Now that's a creep I'll be seein' in my sleep
> So we tripled-teamed on 'im
> Droppin' those Fifth Ward B's on 'im
> The more I swung the more blood flew

Then he disappeared and my boys disappeared too
Then I felt just like a fiend
It wasn't even close to Halloween
It was dark as death on the streets
My hands were all bloody
From punching on the concrete

If you can hear the Geto Boys not as Houston rappers, or even as African-Americans, but directly as exemplary Americans with a story to tell and the means to tell it, then metaphors suggest themselves as quickly as, in its most intense moments, the music in "Mind Playing Tricks on Me" seems to slow down, the car door opening, a hand beckoning you inside. That drifting, swirling sound, those tinkling notes—almost a merry-go-round sound, after a bit—make room for anyone's displacement, confusion, terror, despair. The way Bushwick Bill mutters, "Ah, man, homey, my mind is playing tricks on me"—yes, you've felt that, maybe the last time you turned on the news. Is the way he says that line, is anything in the song, redemptive, as the response to "Blue Suede Shoes" might have been redemptive? "Mind Playing Tricks on Me" as a record on the top of every chart is just a fantasy; the song has yet to find the response it deserves. Maybe it never will. It's too soon to know.

In a time when it has been definitively pronounced that we have reached the end of history, the death of rock may appear to be a very small thing. Certainly it is if you believe that rock 'n' roll and history have nothing to do with each other—if you believe that rock 'n' roll cannot help make history, and that history cannot help make good rock 'n' roll. If you believe that, though, you may have to accept that rock 'n' roll never existed at all.

Esquire, *August 1992*

The Roger Clinton Experience

I can't look at Bush," said Linda Perry, singer for 4 Non Blondes—three women, one man, and, on the night of August 15, a huge Uncle Sam hat on Perry's head. "Have you ever looked at that guy? Clinton—I could look at him, maybe three years."

That seemed an apt summation of the mood you might have expected at a Bill Clinton benefit staged at the I-Beam, a seedy-glitzy postpunk nightclub in the Haight-Ashbury district in San Francisco. A plainly suspicious audience wouldn't have been a surprise in the place, let alone a sense of hipper than thou. There wasn't much of that around, though. People seemed happy to be there for the chance to save the country—there's no cool way to say that. And, along with a slew of local bands, there was the top of the bill, Roger Clinton, Bill Clinton's black-sheep younger brother. You got the feeling this might be the closest any of us in the I-Beam might get to the next president, or the last blown chance. Attitude was in short supply. The place was packed, and there was a long line outside that didn't go away even after the doorman said his last no.

Two fantasies ruled the night for me. First, that this was some sort of GOP dirty-tricks masterpiece, using double agents in the Clinton campaign to set up hapless Roger for videotapes of him posing with Buck Naked (of Buck Naked and the Bare Bottom

Boys, performing this night with Pearl Harbour) and God knows what other San Francisco demimonde atrocities. (In fact, when a photographer tried to shoot Clinton with Enrique, the two-man drag team emceeing the show, a Clinton handler tried to call a halt.) The second fantasy perhaps touched the sentimentality that lies behind both rock 'n' roll dreams and electoral politics. As I was heading for the I-Beam, the radio turned up Foreigner's "I Want to Know What Love Is"—still, after eight years, an expanding universe of a song, passion bleeding out of the corn, the finale of Jennifer Holliday screaming "ONLY LOVE IS REAL," making you believe the story that when Ahmet Ertegun first heard the record he wept. Well, then, why shouldn't Roger Clinton, a thirty-six-year-old white R&B singer with a demo tape, hit the stage, fill his lungs to bursting with "I Want to Know What Love Is," and send everybody home with the certainty that not only can the world be changed, it will be? Hell, stranger things have happened.

Inside the I-Beam, I tried out the scenario on a friend. "Well," he said, "maybe that, or maybe he'll be the political version of the Elvis impersonator: people will act like he's *Bill* Clinton."

"Maybe he'll be the new Lee Atwater," I offered hopefully.

"Yeah," said my friend. "Or the new karaoke."

There was a feeling, as Mordred finished its set and Roger Clinton walked through the crowd on his way to the stage, that the happy idea of the night—that the country would change, that it would be fun to see Bill Clinton's brother sing—was about to collapse. The undercurrent of bitter determination that seemed to power most of the talk I heard—talk that went, *I don't like Clinton much, I don't like Tipper at* all, *but I'm not gonna live through four more years of this shit*—was about to slam into the crowd's inability to sustain the night's illusions, or Roger Clinton's inability to extend them.

What actually happened may not predict who will win in November, but it did suggest that people are no longer as embarrassed as they used to be to say that they want to live in a different country. Backed by the Limbomaniacs, an expert white soul band with a good horn section, Clinton opened with Traffic's "Feelin' Alright," followed with Rufus Thomas's "Walking the Dog," produced a reggae version of Blues Image's "Ride Captain Ride," which he opined had hit potential, and then went into Gino Vannelli's "Down with Love."

The material was as bland as could be, with edges coming only from the band. Clinton looked like Mickey Dolenz, mugged like Francis the Talking Mule, and oozed smarm. ("That Clinton trait," someone said, "wanting to be liked.") Clinton fluttered his fingers at the wrong moments and everyone in the crowd grinned without boredom. When, for his last number, Clinton tried Sly and the Family Stone's "Thank You (Falettinme Be Mice Elf Agin)," he left the crowd wanting more. He didn't seem to understand the song, which is about fatalism and defeat—"Thank you for the party / I could never stay"—but he made it work, and the audience didn't care whether he understood the song or not. They cared whether he was putting whatever it was he had into it, and clearly he was.

Because, you see, the Bill Clinton for President benefit at the I-Beam was at once infinitely important and not a big deal, and everyone seemed to understand that. It was a small, congenial moment in a very large, unwieldy story—a moment in which people turned out mainly for themselves, to attest that they too had reason to take part. There was anticipation in the room, eagerness, friendliness, attentiveness—when Ann Powers, a columnist for *SF Weekly*, gave a speech about censorship, Tipper Gore, and the First Amendment, the noisy crowd cheered in all the right places—but no tension. Maybe it was the human scale of the event; maybe it was that the person representing Bill Clinton, who may soon be forgotten but who this night seemed very big, was someone as small as you or I.

Interview, *October 1992*

Flashback: The Music Playing Outside Bill Clinton's Oxford Dorm Room

People called Donovan a genius, but nobody ever said he was smart. Hear him now in his heyday in 1967, still warm from the Summer of Love, in the pages of the first issue of *Rolling Stone:* "We are magic. It is magic that we're walking around . . ."

"You're a rarity and you're aware of it," says the interviewer, with nice internal assonance. "Yes, I'm very aware of this," Donovan says. "Yes, the more aware I get the more I can understand how big it is, how big it'll get . . . To say to somebody that God lives and is everything that lives and that ever has lived and . . ."

He sounds little different today, a forty-six-year-old grandfather who gets his name in the papers as the father of actors Ione Skye and Donovan Leitch. "The heartfelt longing to discover the truth within," he burbles in the notes to *Troubador: The Definitive Collection 1964–1976,* his new boxed set (everybody gets one these days). "This quartet of movements in my life I attribute to four powerful influences," Dad, Mom, wife, and, "In praise, I raise my voice to the great and glorious spirit . . ."

Yeah, right. Can't argue with that. But you can argue with *Troubador.* It sounds so depressingly time-bound, inert—while his two signature albums, *Sunshine Superman* (1966) and *Mellow Yellow* (1967), remain full of generosity, curiosity, play, and surprise, leaping into a future that vanished almost as quickly as it came into view. For all the story-goes-on lilt of the essays in *Troubador*'s requisite illustrated booklet, the discs mainly remind a listener of how easily Donovan can be summed up—which is to say, even though he is performing today, dismissed. Donovan had his first hit single in 1965 and his career as a pop icon was wrapped by 1969. He was a Scottish Woody Guthrie transformed by the smoke and mirrors of Swinging London into a visionary in caftans, a flower bearing gifts for your garden—and then the pop world turned its back on him as one. *Go away! Please! Don't embarrass us! Don't you know it's 1970?*

Pop fans were embarrassed by Donovan's fey silliness, but also by the shame they felt when the promise of their time, a promise he and they had shared, failed to turn into real life. It may have been Donovan's essential dumbness that allowed him to fulfill that promise in a few of his songs, a spinning handful: "Season of the Witch," "Guinevere," "The Trip" (included on *Troubador*), "Legend of a Girl Child Linda," "Celeste," "Young Girl Blues," "Hampstead Incident," and "Bert's Blues" (not included). Invited to a '60s party that was never going to end, that guaranteed more glamour and wonder every time he turned his head, Donovan didn't think, he just opened his eyes. Unlike Bob Dylan, skulking in a corner, doubting everything, Donovan doubted nothing. He was going to go all night.

You can hear this best in "Bert's Blues," from 1966, as good a proof as any there is of the right of pop music to do whatever it pleases. It's that all-night party, and now it's about four in the morning. Some of the revelers have fallen asleep, the rest are happily halfway to oblivion. Someone starts singing. It's an odd, off-the-mark hipster shuffle, jazzed up, hilariously fake, the singer's diction clipped and stilted (*Who invited this clown?*). He doesn't say "It ain't for me to say," he says "Ih t'aint for me." It's pure narcissism. He's in love with the sound of his own voice, with the way he can play with it, and just as you're laughing at the pose, you're charmed. But what's that *harpsichord* doing—playing *blues?*

With utter grace—a natural shift, somehow—the song flies away. A cello comes up, and now it's as if the singer has nodded off on his feet and you're dreaming his dream. Something about fairy castles, kings, queens—flutes and more strings finish the scene with chilly elegance. A sense of privilege, chivalry, nobility—a sense that you are privileged to be present in this moment, even though it is your right of birth—settles on the room. The cello rises higher, pursuing a minor chord, signifying danger. "Sadly goes the wind on its way to Hades," the singer's dreaming voice says; you don't believe him. But then there is only that harpsichord, moving with stately slowness through a harsh, severe solo. The cello and the flutes return, "Lucifer calls his legions," the singer says, and now you do believe him. The music seems to draw a breath, and in that tiny suspension the song is swept back to its opening theme: blues again, but harder. The party is over, now you're in an after-hours jazz joint in Soho, the hipster is there, there's a lot of noise, the harpsichord is wailing (the harpsichord?). You finally stumble home, fall asleep, dream—and what you dream is what you heard. You wake up: where, you say, have I been? Can I get back?

The answers "Bert's Blues" give are these: where you were was in the middle of a Pre-Raphaelite painting, in Edward Burne-Jones's *The Tree of Forgiveness* or *The Beguiling of Merlin,* in Dante Gabriel Rossetti's *Beata Beatrix* or a thousand cheap knock-offs of the like. You were in a state of grace where there was no noise, only a dance of seductive gestures, an instant before desire overcame all fear. And can you get back? Of course you can, because the past is in the present, the present opens onto the infinite past. Time is a trick you need no longer play on yourself. You can be whoever you imagine yourself to be: Soho hipster, Arthurian maiden, '60s pop star.

You can still hear the leavings of this state of mind—not an idea, but a sensation—in "Season of the Witch," Donovan's most piercing, most indelible recording. He looks in the mirror: "So many different people to be," he says. But the rest of the song—cut up with unfriendly guitar chords, rumbling organ, and terribly hesitant, uncertain movement—turns the face of Beata Beatrix from the instant before ecstasy to the instant before murder. It sounded funny in 1966: "Beatniks out to make it rich," what a laugh. Now, though, you hear the reveler awake in his hangover, shaking: "You got to pick up every stitch," he says again and again, but he can't even pick up the coins on the floor. He can't close his fist around the nineteenth-century Arthurian detritus that in 1966 and '67 flared up like new clothes.

Donovan didn't think, but he drifted through the signs and symbols that were common coin in his time. Because he had the sense that those signs and symbols were very old, the best songs he made of them are now no more tied to the time of their making than Pre-Raphaelite paintings are to theirs. So, oddly, the weird shifts in "Bert's Blues" now sound less contrived than those in the Beatles' "A Day in the Life" and "Season of the Witch" sounds meaner than Bob Dylan's "Like a Rolling Stone." All are at least a quarter-century old, but none has been off the radio since it was made, save for "Bert's Blues," which has never been on it.

Interview, *November 1992*

Pop Music Saves the World Again

Take a day when the Lemonheads' unhurried "It's a Shame About Ray" sounds as soulful as Al Green's "Look What You Done for Me"—or when the Ramones' pained "Poison Heart" seems up to the Yugoslavian civil war—and you've got a day that's out of joint. The claims of the world are too big and pop music is in a stall. Most of what you're really hearing with the Lemonheads or the Ramones or Tori Amos or Shinehead, or whoever it might be that touches you, is *relief*—and everything else is irritating, clichés locking into one another until you know the radio's not giving up anything you want to hear.

Stuff that otherwise might just be room spray turns venal. You can begin to hear Axl Rose's arching whine as the sound of the times, infecting Anthony Kiedis's crooning ballads until you can't tell the Red Hot Chili Peppers from Journey—until you realize the Red Hot Chili Peppers *are* Journey. Then "Under the Bridge" fades and Rose is back with "November Rain," making insincerity a transcendental value, the value against which all others are measured. If you're very lucky, you might then hear Vanessa Paradis, recently four-paged in *Vanity Fair* as "the French Madonna." Hey, why stop there, why not the French Bob Dylan? Vanessa Paradis— I checked the CD to see if there was a credit for whoever made up her name. Move on to the singing, and you can write the whole thing off as a hoax. But next to Paradis, anything halfway decent sounds infinitely better than it is. Sinéad O'Connor puts a lot into the standards and neo-standards on her *am I not your girl?* ("Gloomy Sunday," "Don't Cry for Me Argentina," "Love Letters"), but it's not clear she's put anything of herself into them. These may be, as she testifies in the liner notes, "the songs I grew up listening to," but now she's somebody else, and, with luck, she's somewhere else. She sings brilliantly on "Bewitched, Bothered and Bewildered"—powerfully enough to make the line "I'll worship the trousers that cling to him" turn your stomach. *No*, you might want to yell back, *you're not "our girl," that was Paula Abdul!* You're the person who tears up pictures of the Pope on TV! Well, she's sure as hell herself on the cover of *am I not your girl?* with her six-inch heels: on O'Connor they still look like Doc Martens.

What else? Maybe Mike Oldfield's *Tubular Bells II*, a follow-up nineteen years after the fact to the album that may be remembered less for inventing New Age music than for getting Richard Branson on his way to a seat in the House of Lords; look, this is history, you don't have to listen to it. It'd be tempting to say the same thing about Neil Young's *Harvest Moon*, billed as the follow-up to *Harvest*, his only number-one album, making it a full *twenty*-years-after-the-fact follow-up—tempting, but no one's faked out Neil Young since he fell for Ronald Reagan in 1984. And Young has a trick. At forty-seven, he can sing with the same innocence, the exact same wounded timbre he was using at twenty-two. Even Joey Ramone's voice is thick and beaten on "Poison Heart" (it makes the song), but Neil Young does not age, and that's what makes *Harvest Moon* as weird as anything else he's done. Rather than offering the catchy blandness of the original *Harvest, Harvest Moon* is as off-key as *Tonight's the Night*—save for the title tune, which is so craven it's hilarious.

Yes, a stall. Maybe it's the music of the moment, and maybe it's a memory of the last verse of an old Bob Dylan song: "And here I sit so patiently / Waiting to find out what price / You have to pay to get out of / Going through all these things twice." George Bush, twice. I'm writing this on October 3rd, one month before the elections. Greetings to us all in the future.

Interview, *December 1992*

Contribution to City Pages
Artist of the Year Issue

In a simple pop year Sinéad O'Connor would take the prize. There she was on October 3, on *Saturday Night Live,* in a long formal gown, Star of David necklace, and nose stud, chanting her rewrite of Bob Marley's "War"—his rewrite of a speech Haile Selassie, Emperor of Ethiopia, King of Kings, Lord of Lords, and Conquering Lion of the Tribe of Judah, delivered at Stanford University in 1968. She's singing a cappella, her face shifting by imperceptible degrees from saint to thug, rat to Hedy Lamarr, when for the last line, "The victory of good over evil," she produces a picture of Pope John Paul II, rips it into pieces: "Fight the real enemy!" You could hear it the next day on the radio news, and there, without anything to look at, just sound to hear, it was so suggestive: "Good . . . over . . . *e*vil," then just *switch, switch, switch.*

It was a classic media shock. Even if you were with her all the way—after the fact; there was no way to know what was coming—you had to realize that someone this intransigent will sooner or later put you on the other side. And if the act itself seems cheap, a setup, self-aggrandizing, ask yourself this: Given the chance to say what I wanted to the whole country, would I have the nerve?

Bill Clinton got away without answering. Fast on his feet in New Hampshire, expert at the Sister Souljah/Jesse Jackson double feint, absorbing punishment as the primaries wound down like George Foreman in the twelfth round against Evander Holyfield, then basking, coasting, risking a sneer around the edges of his grin as November 3 got closer, then even closer, then even closer than that—Bill Clinton is performer of the year because he seemed to enjoy performance more, to let it bring him to life more quickly, to share that wealth more readily than anyone else.

Two memories of the campaign I doubt will fade, no matter how cold a president Clinton turns out to be: first, from June, in one of the Twin Cities dailies, a poll with Clinton trailing both Bush and Perot. By a lot. A *state* poll. A Democrat, running third, in *Minnesota?* Second, on the second-to-last night of the campaign, a live feed from CNN, Clinton at a rally in the midst of his insane forty-eight-hour Ohio-to-Pennsylvania-to-Denver-to-Little Rock marathon, voiceless and wrapped tight against the cold, brandishing his sax like a flag, pulling notes out of his horn so fast they tumble over and over, for an instant only *this* momentum real.

I can't remember what town it was. Maybe it was the night's stop in Cherry Hill, New Jersey, when Clinton shared the platform with the Dovells; maybe the tune was "You Can't Sit Down," the Dovells' only hit (#3, 1963, Dovells lead singer Len Barry was twenty-one, Clinton was seventeen) that needs a sax break. Maybe it wasn't. Whatever it was, though, it signaled a turnaround, from last to runaway, that so far no one has come close to explaining. "In rock 'n' roll," as Sonic Youth bassist Kim Gordon once said, "many things happen and anything can happen."

City Pages *(Minneapolis), December 30, 1992,*
with material from Artforum, *December 1992*

Bill Clinton: Hound Dog
or Teddy Bear?

This is the mystery of democracy, that its richest fruits spring up
out of soils which no man has prepared and in circumstances
where they are least expected.

> —President Woodrow Wilson, dedicating the
> birthplace of Abraham Lincoln

Today, the steelworker and the stenographer, the teacher and the
nurse, had as much power in the mystery of our democracy
as the president, the billionaire, and the governor. You all spoke
with equal voices.

> —Bill Clinton, election night,
> November 3, 1992, Little Rock, Arkansas

Nine days ago, on January 8, 1993, the Postal Service issued the
Elvis stamp; three days from now Bill Clinton will be inaugu-
rated as the forty-second president of the United States. This confluence of circumstances is not exactly an accident.

Even before election day, people were wondering what sort of
Elvis a President Clinton might be. "Clinton's Elvis has little to do
with the transcendent aspects of the King," Richard Goldstein
wrote in October for the *Village Voice*, "and much to do with what
made that cat from Tupelo a star. Elvis played to the girls with his
hips, his hair and his eyes. He set a style for male sexuality that was
at once ecstatic and needy—a far cry from the strong, silent type."

For that matter, some people were wondering if a President
Clinton would be any kind of Elvis at all. Waiting for Clinton's vic-

tory speech on election night, Steve Perry, editor of Minneapolis's *City Pages,* was drawn into a fantasy that can hardly have been his alone. "The statehouse doors open," Perry thought, "and here's Bill—in a *white jumpsuit! . . .* I imagined him stepping to the microphone, that trademark Elvis curl around his lips, hinting at once at an arrogant faith in his own power and a secret available to all who believed." Perry went on to see Clinton stripping off the disguise, as it were, that he'd worn throughout the campaign, revealing the conservative "New Democrat" as in truth "a bold progressive"—as if beneath the jumpsuit were the old rebel threads of the '50s rocker. But then Clinton *does* appear, in the flesh, "spouting the same old neo-liberalisms," and Perry hits a bum note as the dream ends (so soon!): "He's no Elvis." Aw . . .

It's unlikely the rest of the country is going to give up on the metaphor so easily. Not long ago, Ian Shoales named Elvis Presley "America's secret angel." If he's right, that means there must be a certain unspoken understanding of Elvis as the embodiment of everything good about the country—and of Elvis as the devil in disguise. It's about *time* a president was judged on the Elvis standard.

The metaphor of Clinton as Elvis is powerful because of a sense that we may be able to catch what we want from this man, what we hope for and what we most fear, if we think of him as a version of Elvis Presley rather than merely as himself. But which Elvis? Elvis contained multitudes; he contradicted himself every time he opened his mouth or took a step. He was the boy unafraid of his difference from everyone around him, ready to claim his own territory and stand his ground; he was the man who would do anything to win the acceptance he could never have. He broke every rule, then begged Richard Nixon to make him a narcotics officer. He embraced the values of family, clean living, faith, and charity, and rotted from the inside. He was the sexiest thing America had ever seen, and pleased to play the sap, a toy, your teddy bear.

Elvis Presley is the country's most extreme embodiment of possibility and disruption, of renewal and defeat. Surrounding Elvis is an aura of irreducible glamour and desire, an American mirror, a mirror that gives back horror and grace, success and failure, pride and shame. It's no wonder that, in one way or another, America now asks if Bill Clinton will be singing "Anyway You Want Me (That's How I Will Be)" or "Hound Dog." But with the answer in the future, it's worth looking back on the strange roles Elvis Presley has already played in the election just past. After all, though columnist Dave Barry is surely right when he says that "If Elvis were alive today, he'd probably be dead by now," in no presidential year was Elvis Presley so inseparable from the action as in 1992, a neat fifteen years after his death. It was as if the whole affair was only an echo of the most unnerving Elvis recording of the year: "Can't Help Falling in Love" as covered by Bono of U2, from the soundtrack to *Honeymoon in Vegas,* a film that ended with Nicolas Cage getting into an Elvis impersonator's costume to win back the heart of Sarah Jessica Parker. A twisted reading of the ultimate Presley show-closer was accompanied principally not by instruments, but by an old Elvis interview running in the background. As Bono climbed the golden ladder of the song toward a falsetto so desperate it was all too obvious who he couldn't help falling in love with, the man himself—or the boy: the Elvis one heard sounded very young and completely guileless—talked about a book called *Poems That Touch the Heart.* After a couple of minutes Bono faded into the ether, and from out of it came that familiar voice: "Yessir, I'll be looking forward to coming back. Yessir, I'm looking forward to it."

Following the conventions, a George Bush sample record—presidential speeches cut up and fitted with a rhythm track—was released under the title "Hard Times," and credited to "Fresh Bush and the Invisible Man." Framed by alternating choruses—a harsh male chant of "Hard times, hard times" and a rhapsodic female "We can change the world, we can change America"—the phantom president offered such nostrums as "Take two aspirin and call me after the election." It was funny, but when Bush cried "I SAW ELVIS!" (the source was Bush's 1991 State of the Union address; he was quoting a Desert Storm GI), it was spooky, because by the time the record appeared you knew Bush had seen him—with a new face.

The Elvis year and the presidential year began on separate tracks that soon converged. The February titillation of the *National Enquirer* headlining Elvis's stepmother's charge that the dead Elvis and his dead mother engaged in incest was more or less matched in August by Dayton *Daily News* cartoonist Mike Peters, who rendered Bush campaign faxes on Clinton's supposed fear of "bimbo eruptions" as the headline on the latest issue of the "GOP Enquirer": CLINTON CARRYING ELVIS' LOVE-CHILD. By the spring, though, interest in the Postal Service's Elvis-stamp election seemed to overwhelm public concern for the primaries themselves. What the intensity of the national-joke-cum-struggle over the choice between older and younger Elvis images demonstrated was, among other things, a profound dissatisfaction with the presidential candidates actually on view: the Elvis election was more fun, and in some distant way more meaningful, than the real one. Thus when Ross Perot emerged to fill the vacuum Elvis's ghost had revealed, Perot was not only himself, steely-eyed Mr. Fixit; he was also the weirdest Elvis stand-in anyone had ever seen.*

The weirdest, but not, in this political year, the most eager. In March, the press corps nickname for lifelong Elvis fan Bill Clinton was a human interest joke on a slow day (the *Washington Post's* "Elvis with a calculator on his belt" was one of the better variations); as the primary season wound down with Clinton, far behind

---

*Not that Perot's campaign workers missed the joke. When the boss exited headquarters at the end of the day, the word among the staff was always the same: "Elvis has left the building."

both Bush and Perot in all polls, seemingly the winner of a worthless prize, a wan version of the Big E's lazy grin seemed nearly all
Clinton had left. When he offered a verse of "Don't Be Cruel" to
close a TV interview, it sounded like a loser's plea.

Then came the great shift. Perot's campaign collapsed, Bush fell
back, and Clinton surged, as if truly warming to his alias. By mid-
July, one "Elvis Aron Presley" was listed in press handouts as "Entertainment Coordinator" of the Democratic Convention in New
York ("He reportedly died in 1977," read the official convention
bio). Senator Al Gore began his speech accepting the vice-
presidential nomination with the confession that he'd "been
dreaming of this moment since I was a kid growing up in Ten-
nesee—that one day, I'd have the chance to come here to Madison
Square Garden and be the warm-up act for Elvis."

When Bush accepted his own party's nomination in August, his
attacks on his rival were themselves couched in bizarre Elvisisms.
Clinton was on all sides of every issue, Bush complained: "He's
been spotted in more places than Elvis Presley." "I guess you'd say
his plan really is 'Elvis Economics,'" the president continued:
"America will be checking into the 'Heartbreak Hotel.'" Out on the
hustings, Bush repeated the lines for weeks—even as the GOP
hired an Elvis impersonator to dog the Clinton-Gore campaign bus
with offerings of baloney sandwiches—but they had a petulant,
vaguely jealous edge, like 1950s bluenoses sniffing at "Elvis the
Pelvis" and "jungle music."

Even in early October, with Clinton holding a strong lead and
press references to his campaign plane as "Air Elvis" now not exactly a joke at all, Bush could not let go. His Clinton, or his Elvis,
had turned into a tar baby. "I finally figured out why he compares
himself to Elvis," Bush said of Clinton, though Clinton never had.
"The minute he has to take a stand on something, he starts wig-
gling." The tone was sour, you could almost hear Elvis's ghost ob-
jecting (Elvis always hated the word "wiggle"), and even Clinton

finally felt free to join the conversation, as much fan as candidate. "Bush is always comparing me to Elvis in sort of unflattering ways," Clinton said on October 12. "Well, I don't think Bush would have liked Elvis very much."

It was a charge Bush couldn't pork-rind, and it raised the question of why Bush would risk alienating masses of working-class white southerners (that is, Reagan Democrats) with remarks that in fact disparaged Elvis Presley far more definitively than they did Clinton. The answer is at once simple and mysterious.

The simple part is this: slap Elvis on anything and you'll be noticed. Elvis in a campaign speech is a guaranteed sound bite on that night's news, maybe even a small headline in the next day's papers. But if Elvis is a hook, he—or it—is a hook already lodged in millions of hearts. You're guaranteed a response when you pull the Elvis cord, but there's no guarantee what the response will be.

For Bush it may have backfired, in a small way. For Russell Feingold it exploded—in a big way. Running third in a three-way primary race for the Democratic senatorial nomination in Wisconsin, he ran a TV ad featuring an *Enquirer*-style ELVIS ENDORSES FEINGOLD! headline. The idea was to counter charges the other two Democrats were making against him ("Don't believe everything you read"); the spot turned Feingold into the Elvis candidate.

The next day everyone in the state suddenly knew Feingold's name—and that he had a sense of humor. Feingold won the primary in a landslide. His new opponent, incumbent Senator Robert Kasten, a down-the-line Reaganite, swiftly got on the air with an Elvis impersonator lounging in the back seat of a Cadillac, denying that he'd ever endorsed Feingold. Kasten missed the joke; Feingold went into the final stretch of the race with a slight lead in the polls. Appearing with Feingold at Milwaukee's Mecca Arena a few days before the election, Clinton brought the crowd to a hush: "The next to last concert Elvis ever sang was right here in this arena. Now, it's well known that I commune with his spirit regularly, and just as I walked in here today, he said, 'I'm for Russ Feingold, not Bob Kasten.'" A few days after the election, Feingold was asked whether Elvis had truly supported him. "Well, he never said otherwise," said the senator-elect, whose favorite Elvis song is "Don't Be Cruel." "I think Mr. Presley, to the extent that he's involved with politics, stayed with us to the very end."

And there is Clinton himself. Back in June, when an Electoral College survey divided the map of the states between Bush and Perot, with the flat notation that "Gov. Bill Clinton is currently not a factor in the race," Clinton had nothing to lose. He took his saxophone onto the Arsenio Hall show, put on a pair of dark glasses, and blew "Heartbreak Hotel." I think this incident will ultimately come into focus as the moment in which Clinton turned the race around, stepping forward as if to say, *All right. Who cares. Let's rip it up.*

It was the first time in the campaign Clinton was more Elvis than calculator. The spirit of freedom in Elvis's best music is a freedom of self-discovery; this night, Clinton accepted the gift, or seized it. Playing the old song as best he could, he was more fan than star, more himself than Elvis, but perhaps just Elvis enough.

> Image (San Francisco Examiner), *January 17, 1993,*
> *adapted from "The Elvis Strategy,"* New York Times,
> *October 27, 1992*

Part Two

TRACES OF
EXTREMIST
CULTURE
IN A TIME
OF BROKEN
POLITICS

★ *1993–1997* ★

Bob Dylan Argues with Himself
at the Inauguration

The very old ballads and prewar blues standards that make up Bob Dylan's *Good as I Been to You*—the collection of solo vocals set to acoustic guitar and harmonica that he released last November 3, which just happened to be election day—are "other people's songs," but the authority with which Dylan sings and plays them makes them as much his as anyone else's. "Little Maggie" is always taken up for its melody, but Dylan goes for its drama, the drama of a weak, frightened man in love with an unfaithful drunk. The music is cut up, stretched, snapped back: each line opens with a stop, and at its end just fades out. With such eighteenth- and nineteenth-century chronicles of fraud and deception as "Canadee-I-O" or "Arthur McBride," Dylan inhabits the first-person narratives as if he lived them twice—and it's only after a time, when the melancholy and bitterness seem too great for one voice, that you hear them as history, as more than one man's plight. As the rough, tested character of the voice and the fatalism of the melodies found on the guitar links the undatable past of "Blackjack Davey" to the early twentieth century of "Sittin' on Top of the World," you hear the old songs resolve themselves into a single story: variations on the tale of innocents setting out for long journeys into the unknown and the terrible betrayals they find when they reach their destinations. Finally all of the story is shared, the singer only its mouthpiece, a medium for private miseries within the great sweep of the disaster; these songs are yours as much as anyone else's. It's only the pleasing cynicism in the singer's voice that leaves you to wonder why, at just this moment in time, one person who has in stray moments seen as clearly as Natty Bumppo is offering *this* story as a version of American legacy.

"We Are the World" was sung to close "An American Reunion," the mass pre-inaugural concert held on the Washington Mall, with, standing up and giving voice, Michael Jackson, Aretha Franklin, Bill Clinton, James Ingram, Stevie Wonder, Tony Bennett, Dionne Warwick, Michael Bolton, choruses of children, choruses of adults, and many more. Earlier, Bob Dylan had, like the other stars, sung directly to the president-elect—leaving aside his most recent, querulous recordings from *Good as I Been to You* for the thirty-four-year-old metaphysical protest song "Chimes of Freedom." Clinton beamed, as if he knew just what it meant to have this man even unspokenly dedicate a number to him. Dylan sounded terrible, but his purple jacket with black appliqué was fabulous; he looked like he'd just bought a Nashville haberdashery. Along with Jackson, Warwick, Wonder, and Ingram, Dylan had been present in 1985 for the original, simpering "We Are the World" recording session; now, though, without the star turns of that production, as a singalong the anthem brought forth great good feeling, no matter that at the heart of the performance there was perhaps only a glamorous sheen of communal self-recognition disguising a new leader who may mean to leave the country as he found it. But as John F. Kennedy proved against his own will, or for that matter his own thoughtlessness, false promises can be taken up by those who only hear the tune and don't care about the copyright, If, as Robert Ray of the Gainesville teen-dream combo the Vulgar Boatmen puts it, "the *sound* of Dylan's voice changed more people's ideas about the world than his political message did," the same can be said of Kennedy's voice versus his political acts. The same may prove true of Bill Clinton's demeanor versus his political instinct to pull back at the first sign of trouble. Desires have been loosed in the air and there's no telling where they'll light—even if, at the end of *Good as I Been to You,* with the seven minutes of the children's ditty "Froggy Went A-Courtin'" apparently out of place with all the accounts of double-crossing that precede it, the grand wedding of Mr. Froggy and Miss Mousie ends with the massacre of the bride, groom, and everyone else at the party.

adapted from "Roots and Branches,"
Image (San Francisco Examiner),
January 17, 1993, and "Real Life Rock Top Ten,"
Artforum, *February and March 1993*

The Summer of Love Generation
Reaches the White House.
So Do Their Kids

. . . m eanwhile a tipsy blond woman plays Sixties songs on the jukebox and choogles frantically out of rhythm. Then she has another drink. A couple of guys in suits stand around. I have my last drink for the evening . . . The blond woman sits two seats away yelling at me, 'Purple haze! Is in my brain!' She says over and over, angrily, 'I was *there,* I was there, man. I was a child of the Sixties.'"

So wrote Steve Erickson of his encounter with Tipper Gore in a Manhattan bar in the midst of election year 1988. Well, really it's Erickson's fantasy of running into Tipper Gore, from *Leap Year,* his 1989 book on the campaign. Later Tipper shows up in Erickson's hotel room ("You gonna cry! Ninety-six tears!" she screams at him. "You gonna cry, cry, cry!"), which gives Erickson the chance to wheel Al into the picture. Looking for his wife, the senator comes up to Erickson's room and sizes up the scribbler. "You're a writer no one's ever heard of," Gore says (Erickson had by then published three novels), "and I'm two years older than you, probably younger than some of your *best friends,* and someday I'm going to be president of the United States."

As they say, close enough for rock 'n' roll. Soon the Clintons and the Gores should be sitting around the White House listening to the special deluxe four-CD *Monterey International Pop Festival: June 16–17–18, 1967* boxed set ("I was *there*, man"), while at the other end of the place Chelsea and the Gore kids are pumping PJ Harvey and Babes in Toyland and Sonic Youth and Nirvana and th faith healers. While their parents lick their Elvis stamps and get all misty-eyed over Janis Joplin emoting on that great Monterey version of "Ball and Chain," you can picture their children trying to keep up with th faith healers' Roxanne as she shouts helplessly out of the maelstrom of the generational slam "Hippy Hole": "LOOK AT THE FLOWERS, TAKE SOME OF THIS, SHIT FOR HOURS!" Fabulous. Th faith healers—a London band who claim the *e* from their "the" was stolen by Thee Hypnotics—might as well be singing about the Monterey Pop Festival. Or Woodstock. Or all the dope 'n' mud extravaganzas that followed in their wake.

On the other hand, Kim Gordon of Sonic Youth is a lot closer to Hillary's age than she is to Chelsea's—who's to say Hillary won't be the one to turn Chelsea on to Sonic Youth's "Death Valley '69"? Or that Bill won't hear the noise one day as he passes Chelsea's bedroom, sneak back later, pick up a few discs, and kill the night working on the federal bench while in the background Sonic Youth's Thurston Moore snaps off "Youth Against Fascism"? " 'I believe Anita Hill,' " President Clinton automatically sings along: " 'That judge'll rot in hell.' "

The truth is, people aren't moved according to the cultural clichés that supposedly define who likes what, people are moved by what they hear—and for that matter you can't get all misty-eyed over Janis Joplin's great Monterey version of "Ball and Chain," because she won't let you. She will let you hear Kat Bjelland of Babes in Toyland screaming "Pull my legs apart," though; she'll let you hear Kim Gordon chanting "I'll take off your dress / I'll shake off your flesh." She'll let you hear the way Kurt Cobain stumbles to the chorus of "Lithium," or how Roxanne gets her head above the flash flood of "Hippy Hole." And she'll let you understand how far Polly Harvey is from getting hold of the voice she wants.

On PJ Harvey's *Dry*—with two guys backing her on drums and bass, this twenty-two-year-old Englishwoman writes, sings, and plays guitar—the music is all about going to extremes it never reaches. Harvey comes closest with "Dress," because here she finds the biggest beat. Elsewhere, as on "Sheela-Na-Gig"—it's named for the Celtic carving of a woman pulling the lips of her vagina open, Harvey has to explain in every interview—you're aware of how written the music is, how self-conscious, how distanced. It's not exactly news that wearing one's heart on one's sleeve has never topped the U.K. fashion charts, but if as long ago as 1977 Margaret Drabble was writing that people were becoming "more ironic, more cynical, more amused by more things and less touched by anything," her words define a sensibility Polly Harvey has inherited, like straight hair she'll always have to curl. To *not* sing this way is what she wants; if she gets what she wants, it will be partly because Janis Joplin once defined what going to extremes was worth.

"Ball and Chain," as Janis Joplin, as a member of Big Brother and the Holding Company, sang it at Monterey in 1967, is the only irreducible piece of music she ever recorded, and up against it everything else anyone has ever put out with her name on it is a joke. The song, taken from blues singer Willie May Thornton, was Joplin's big number, the extravaganza. One minute into this performance and she's not wearing her heart on her sleeve; all of her internal organs are draped over her body like a hideous new skin. Blood seeps through her pores; stigmata break out all over, making signs no one can read. Marshaling an array of blues and soul mannerisms, she contrives an act that in certain moments—and you can hear them coming—ceases to be any kind of act at all. The means of illusion produce the real, and the real is horrible, but so vivid you couldn't turn away to save your life, or the singer's. It's thrilling, but no fun: there's an instant in the last chorus of the performance when Joplin's voice goes . . . *somewhere else,* and it's simply not credible that the music then ends with an ordinary flourish people can cheer for. How did she get back?

As everybody knows, she didn't. But there are openings in Kat Bjelland's screams, in the blank, demented momentum Roxanne gets in "Hippy Hole," or in the way Kim Gordon flatly surrenders to "I Wanna Be Your Dog" on Sonic Youth's *Confusion Is Sex,* where the same question comes up.

There's going to be a great need for extremism in the next few years, as a new administration moves with care and caution: extremism in art, certainly, but more than that in public discourse in the broadest sense, as a form of honesty. So in my fantasy, as in Steve Erickson's, everyone in the White House has a role in a great cultural drama. Bill passes Chelsea's room: "What the hell is she listening to?" he says to Hillary. " 'I'll take off your dress, I'll shake off your flesh'?" Chelsea passes her parents' room and with Joplin's sound coming out from under the door hears it happening. "What the *fuck,*" she says, "are *they* listening to?"

Interview, *January 1993*

More Thoughts on the White House Playlist

Writing a few days after the Justice Department said *fuck it* in Waco, and the day after the GOP killed the White House job-stimulus bill in the Senate, I have to confess a continuing anesthetized euphoria in the face of blunt facts and dubious battles—an impervious good feeling despite craven compromises and worse. I'm glad Bill Clinton is in the White House.

My capacity for outrage has been short-circuited. I'm trying to sharpen the knife with David Baerwald's no-hope album *Triage* (cover: gruesomely bloody hands with the flag behind them), but not even that seems to help—or hurt. Our times are less fixed than they were a year ago. I think that Bill Clinton is an unfinished man; that the future, at least in the near term, is now unpredictable; that the next few years will be full of surprises, some of them thrilling. How all this will translate culturally, and musically, is up for grabs.

Ronald Reagan changed the presidency by using cultural power to legitimize his politics. This was something new. John F. Kennedy dabbled in culture—mostly high culture—but it was a sham, just good PR. Reagan came out of popular culture; he understood its language, spoke it every day. He changed the way we perceive the presidency: now, if we cannot see a president culturally, we can't

see him politically. To a certain degree, a president is now powerful politically to the exent that he is real culturally. This was a good
part of George Bush's problem: culturally, he was a cipher. Clinton
isn't. He's no foreigner in pop culture. The excitement in his face
when Ben E. King took over "Stand by Me" at the January 17
Washington Mall concert was as real as it gets.

The White House booking policy already under way is not the
issue. Judy Collins has slept over at the White House; rock 'n'
rollers in their forties (or rock 'n' rollers in their fifties pretending
they're in their forties) are puffed up with a new legitimacy, new
reasons to flog "Teach Your Children" one more time, one million
more times (Clinton likes it). We're going to be seeing a lot more
of Stephen Stills, David Crosby, Jerry Garcia, maybe even such ur-
'60s horrors as Richie Havens, definitely Bonnie Raitt (admit it:
she's a good person, she's worked hard, and she's a bigger bore than
Michael Bolton). From all evidence, this is the kind of stuff Bill
Clinton loves—not mainstream pop, but some bizarrely neutral-
ized "Welcome Back, Kotter" mainstream within the mainstream.

The issue is that Clinton has raised a lot of hopes, a lot of spirits—and one result is going to be a lot of crashes. Along with a blind
optimism that in songs and melodies can lead anywhere, usually
nowhere, we're going to see a rising sense of betrayal. More than
that: just as Clinton's commitment to abortion rights has led to an
intensification of anti-abortion murderousness, and his position in
favor of gay military service will lead to an increase in anti-gay violence, so can we expect an intensification of certain strains of pop
vengefulness. More homophobia in pop culture. More racism, especially from the white side—hip racism, the snort of sneering that
made Jay McInerney's *Bright Lights, Big City* such a Reaganite
classic. More misogyny—the Spin Doctors' "Little Miss Can't Be
Wrong" smirk as modern charm.

Bland, contentless songs will, as almost always, make up the bulk
of pop. But they may not travel as well as they usually do. I think

people are going to demand more out of their music. A desire that pop speech have consequences, *must* have consequences, may rule. You can already hear it happening, in the desperate, unholy fervor Lou Reed found in "Foot of Pride" at the Bob Dylan Thirtieth Anniversary Concert at Madison Square Garden, or in the weird courage shown by Kurt Cobain of Nirvana, beaten up throughout his adolescence as a "faggot," appearing in public in a dress.

It's as if everyone is auditioning for the White House, and why not? James Taylor and James Brown may get the invitations, but the real action may be a spectral battle of the bands, between people poised to talk about the state of the nation on their own terms: Neil Young and Ice Cube, Negativland and Courtney Love, the Geto Boys and Madonna, Eleventh Dream Day and Come. These are smart, thoughtful people. You can imagine them, even rap artists committed to a nation of their own, trying to figure out where they stand with this guy, Bill Clinton, and where he stands with them—because for the first time in American history since Lincoln named "Dixie" his favorite tune the question of whether the president of the United States might or might not like a particular song is actually interesting.

Of course, Bill Clinton isn't going to hear Eleventh Dream Day, isn't going to hear their naked tales of big-city fatalism and hope against hope, but that's not the point. The point is that the fantasy that Bill Clinton might hear Eleventh Dream Day, or anyone else, might animate their music. The fantasy might make the music cowardly, eager to please; it might make the music more daring, as if to prove that even in fantasy a no-health-insurance nowhere band from Chicago can tell a president what he doesn't want to hear, and be heard. That means that even a no-health-insurance nowhere band can no longer claim bohemian ground—where the presidency and the polity are beneath them.

All of this may lead to stronger music. Just as likely, though, is a cynicism as contentless as any happy-ending ballad: a seizure of every defeat, every compromise, as proof that Bill Clinton's quickening of so many heartbeats is just a con. After so many years of brutalization, even a suspicion of better times is dangerous. There are now, and there have always been, far more openings on the right in the United States than on the left; by definition, Bill Clinton has only a fraction of the freedom of action that Ronald Reagan started with. The safest position to take is to embrace every failure and disparage every victory.

What would that sound like? I don't even want to think about it.

Details, *July 1993*

But Not Life

In June I was in England and Germany, giving readings and lectures. The first thing people wanted to talk about was the Velvet Underground reunion tour. By a quirk of scheduling I was chasing the band around the EEC, missing them by a day in city after city. Everybody who asked what I thought had just seen the group, in Edinburgh, London, Hamburg; nevertheless they seemed to want permission to like what they'd already seen, or for that matter already liked. Was this—retrograde? If you could still have fun with the Velvet Underground, was that proof time had passed you by?

It had been a neat quarter-century since bandleader, guitarist, and composer Lou Reed had kicked bassist and violist John Cale out of the group. Formed in 1965 and soon coming under the aegis of Andy Warhol, who for their first album forced the German face Nico on Reed, Cale, drummer Maureen Tucker, and guitarist Sterling Morrison, the band was defunct—no matter who the players were—by 1970. But even before any formal ending, the Velvet Underground was already a legend: of freedom, extremism, self-destruction, rebirth, to-thine-own-self-be-true, of art. The legend always overshadowed solo careers, or even lives. Or history. As one Garth Marat-Trech proved in 1992, in *The Wire*, reviewing Margaret Thatcher's spoken-word disc *Salute to Democracy* (no kidding—it's on EMI Classics), beyond a certain limit a good legend has room for absolutely everyone and facts are utterly beside the point.

Margaret Thatcher, the enigmatic conceptual artist, is probably best known to the general public for her series of "action music" pieces, which "detourned" the mass rallies often associated with totalitarian regimes, but her talents have been deployed in many fields over the years. Legend has it that in about 1963, quitting an early lineup of the Velvet Underground (she played electric violin; Henry Flynt was her replacement), Thatcher effectively retreated from the art world: "There is no such thing as society" became an in-joke at Warhol's Factory (often diluted with typical loft-apartment humor to "There is no such thing as Andy Warhol" or "There is no such thing as Margaret Thatcher").

The legend had other facets, perhaps most gleamingly that avant-garde standby "fleurs du mal," more popularly known as evil. the *New Yorker* used to run cartoons of dumpy, middle-aged couples sitting around their middle-class living rooms: "Darling," the woman would be saying, "they're playing our song!" and coming out of a radio would be "You ain't nothin' but a hound dog" or maybe "Da doo ron ron." Whether or not the Velvet Underground bring their show home this fall, there will be a new live album, and likely a new middle-aged *New Yorker* couple mooning over "Heroin."

The Velvet Underground and Nico, the band's first album, is nowhere nearly so striking as legend has made it out to be. Most of it sounds exactly like 1967, as time-bound as fashions from Carnaby Street. But "Heroin" is still pure terror. The song opens up a void, and one hand invites you in, because there are secrets you'll never learn any other way; the other hand dismisses you, because you're not strong enough to know those secrets. The song is evil because it celebrates death and apologizes for nothing. The fatigue, the weight in Lou Reed's voice at the very end, the flat refusal to explain himself for one word more in the last "I just don't know," are unlike anything else in modern culture, unless it's the way Jean-Paul Belmondo falls down dead at the end of *Breathless*.

I'll never forget the first time I heard the song. I was a college student in Berkeley; the tune was on the radio. I wanted to turn it off, but I couldn't. Near the end, when Maureen Tucker stops playing and Reed and Cale crisscross lines of sound so crazily it seems certain the piece will break up in the air, you can almost believe the song doesn't mean what it says. Then Reed comes back, and with an irreducible subjectivity—an affirmation that he and no one else is telling you the way the world looks to him—nails that last line.

"That was the Velvet Underground," said the disc jockey, the late Tom Donahue. "A very New York sound. Let's hope it stays there." What did that mean, outside of simple snobbery? Maybe this was only art—New York art, but not *life*. Experience is overrated in art, after all; empathy is the test and imagination is the judge. Writing in 1965 to Delmore Schwartz, his first mentor, Lou Reed himself sounded like a tourist:

I've had some strange experiences since returning to ny, sick but strange and fascinating and even, sometimes ultimately revealing, healing and helpful . . . ny has so many sad, sick people and I have a knack for meeting them. they try to drag you down with them. If you're weak ny has many outlets. I can't resist peering, probing, sometimes participating, othertimes going right to the edge before side-stepping. Finding viciousness in yourself and that fantastic killer urge and worse yet having the opportunity presented before you is certainly interesting.

Or not like a tourist: "Interesting," he wrote next, "is not the word."

The first challenge Reed, Cale, Tucker, and Morrison faced in June was get out from under this sort of legend—to reclaim their subjectivity from it. Audiences were expecting them to burst into flames onstage. Playing legendary songs, they had to find a way to do so prosaically, for prosaic reasons—to have fun, to make money. From all accounts, they were able to do that. "The crowd was very young, and the place wasn't nearly full," said a photographer in Hamburg. "I don't know what they wanted—I don't know what *I* wanted. They were having a *good time* playing 'Heroin,' smiling. I don't know what that means." "Did it sound good?" I asked. "Oh, it sounded good," she said. "So good."

That is a great truth about the Velvet Underground the legend obscures, though it's the basis of the legend: by sounding good, songs like "Heroin" give pleasure. Is it free, the way heroin, the real thing, gives a pleasure that isn't free? For people like Pere Ubu's Peter Laughner, who drank himself to death in pursuit of the sound of "Heroin," obviously it wasn't free. For other people, obviously it is, and why not? "I'd just spent the afternoon with my mother," said a film producer from Edinburgh. "She doesn't recognize me anymore. When I got out of the place I felt I was barely alive myself. Then I passed a newsagent's and I saw the Velvet Underground on the cover of *Vox*. It said they were playing in Edinburgh that night. I got a I ticket, I went. I never thought I would get to see them. They were full of life, but it was so ordinary, too—I don't know. When it was over I walked out of the hall and I felt as if I could start my whole life over if I wanted to."

Interview, September 1993

What's New in the Cemetery

For the second time in less than a year, Bob Dylan has released an unproduced, acoustic-guitar-and-harmonica collection of traditional blues and folk songs. A small voice from the sidelines—even the wilderness—in its own quiet manner *World Gone Wrong* traces the renunciations of fame, responsibility, and authority Nirvana tries and fails to enact on *In Utero*, their response to the stardom that followed *Nevermind*, which they now see as a failure because too many people liked it. Dylan won't have that problem.

Good as I Been to You, his 1992 Election Day special, was his most striking music since . . . since the last time he cut the ground out from under your feet, whenever that was. It stopped at number fifty-one on the *Billboard* charts and didn't make the *Village Voice* national critics poll chart at all. Their loss: Dylan came to life in the old clothes of "Canadee-i-o," "Hard Times," "Frankie & Albert." As he does on *World Gone Wrong,* he came to life as a singer; then as now, as a singer, in the hesitations and elisions of his phrasing, he came to life as a philosopher.

On both records, the music is all about values: what counts and what doesn't, what lasts, what shouldn't. The performance is modest, but anything but casual. Finding the fatalism—the foreboding—in the ancient, twisting melodies of "Love Henry" and

"Jack-a-Roe" on *World Gone Wrong*, as he did with "Jim Jones" and "Blackjack Davey" on *Good as I Been to You*, as a philosopher Dylan comes to life as a gatekeeper, a guardian. "I have to think of all this as traditional music," he said in 1966. "Traditional music is based on hexagrams. It comes about from legends, Bibles, plagues, and it revolves around vegetables and death. All these songs about roses growing out of people's brains and lovers who are really geese and swans that turn into angels—they're not going to die. It's all those paranoid people who think that someone's going to come and take away their toilet paper—*they're* going to die. Songs like 'Which Side Are You On?' and 'I Loves You Porgy'—they're not folk-music songs; they're political songs. They're *already* dead."

This is precisely the talk Dylan talks in the liner notes to *World Gone Wrong*, where he says where the songs on the album come from and explains what they're about. "What attracts me to the song," he writes of "Lone Pilgrim" (the only composition on *World Gone Wrong* legally credited to a named author, as opposed to a blues or folk progenitor), "is how the lunacy of trying to fool the self is set aside at some given point, salvation & the needs of mankind are prominent & hegemony takes a breathing spell." Regarding "Stack A Lee," archetypal tale of the black outlaw and perhaps the best-known number on *World Gone Wrong*, "what does the song say exactly? it says no man gains immortality thru public acclaim. truth is shadowy . . . the song says that a man's hat is his crown. futurologists would insist it's a matter of taste." On Blind Willie McTell's "Broke Down Engine": "it's about variations of human longing—the low hum in meters & syllables. it's about dupes of commerce & politics colliding on tracks . . . it's about Ambiguity, the fortunes of the privileged elite, flood control—watching the red dawn and not bothering to dress."

Dylan is claiming absolute and infinite meaning for the songs he's now singing. The challenge is to hear in these songs even a fraction of what he hears: whether it's McTell's 1931 "Broke Down

Engine" or Dylan's, Dylan's "Blood in My Eyes" or the Mississippi Sheiks' '31 original, William Brown's 1942 "Ragged & Dirty" or the same story half a century later. Dylan hears a whole world, a complete millenarian drama, in every tune; the person who buys the record, takes it home, puts it on, is going to hear a small-time drama into which intimations of the uncanny ("roses growing out of people's brains and lovers who are really geese") occasionally, inexplicably, intrude. "Ragged & Dirty," a sly blues, is first of all carnal; the way Dylan slides into the piece, barely speeding the pace, is a one-verse seduction. "Stack A Lee" is quickstep true crime, graveyard humor: "Taken him to the cemetery, but they failed to bring him back." But Dylan hears as much mysticism in these prosaic American jokes as he does politics in the almost Arthurian "Love Henry," where a parrot bears witness against its murdering mistress.

In "Blood in My Eyes" a man is trying to get something going with a prostitute. You can feel the age in his voice; you can also feel he's probably impotent. The weariness, the fear of humilation, the despair in the man's voice as he describes the situation, the way he hopes he'll get what he wants, is almost too painful. Only that moment when he drifts out of the dollars and cents of the day's concern and into the chorus, "Got blood in my eyes / For you," is sweet. It's so sweet, summoning a desire so plainly outside the realm of fulfillment, that the man's loneliness overwhelms anything else he might bring into his life. And yet, when you're as lonely as Dylan has now made this man—as he's made you, if he has—you'll bring anything into your life in an attempt to turn that isolation into something else: an adventure in a foreign land, a lover's murder, God's kiss.

As *World Gone Wrong* plays, with Dylan's scratchy, seemingly disdainful voice quickly growing full, earnest, urgent, then delicate, all these things do turn into one another. The music traces a circle from which there need be no exit. And if you pick up Dylan's cues and hunt down the originals of the songs as he names them—the Mississippi Sheiks' "Blood in My Eyes," on their *Complete Recordings, Vol. 3,* or Doc Watson's "Lone Pilgrim," on *The Watson Family*—you might find a certain discontinuity between the old versions and the new. The older singers often sound eager to please; Dylan doesn't. He sounds as if his goal has been to get all the way into these old songs, and then get lost.

Interview, *December 1993*

Mystery Train After
Thirty-nine Years

Reading *Sweet Nothings,* an anthology of poems about rock 'n' roll, I kept thinking of two scenes in Jim Sheridan's film *In the Name of the Father.*

In the first, the Daniel Day-Lewis character, Belfast petty thief Gerry Conlon, is running from cops and soldiers. As he hurls himself down tiny back alleys, the huge, devouring chords of Jimi Hendrix's "Voodoo Chile (Slight Return)" pursue him like a dinosaur in *King Kong.* Hendrix's guitar might be a mouth with fire coming out of it: his noise, his presence, is all over Conlon, breathing down his back, laughing in his face, tangling his feet. The chase is thrilling, scary, and the music is just right—it adds so much. Still, that's all it does. The use of the Hendrix tune is a simple, conventional orchestration, the sort of thing you can find anywhere. You've seen it before—for that matter, you've seen it in a sequence in *The Harder They Come* that uses the Maytals' "Pressure Drop" on Jimmy Cliff in exactly the same way.

The second scene comes shortly after. Gerry Conlon's stolid, responsible father has decided to get his good-for-nothing son out of Belfast and send him to London. Conlon's all for it: London 1974, still full of hippies and squats, drugs and free love. He can't wait. He boards a ferry out of Belfast, meets a friend. They get beers, drop a coin in the jukebox, and as the first notes of Bob Dylan's "Like a Rolling Stone" come on, they hoist their glasses in a toast to their new adventure, to life in a new land.

Here the music does not orchestrate what the actors are doing; they are orchestrating the music. The chase could exist without Hendrix; this scene could not exist without the sound on the screen. All Sheridan uses is the fanfare that opens the song—that thick, swirling, implacable rising tide of hope and fate, promise and threat. It's just Dylan's band taking its first steps into the song, as Conlon and his friend are taking their first steps; the music is faded off the soundtrack as Dylan begins to sing. The event is so strong, so emotionally lucid, it can take you right out of the story, freezing this perfect moment, this tiny utopia that, over the next hour or so, will be torn to pieces.

There are orchestrations like Sheridan's use of Hendrix among the poems in *Sweet Nothings,* as with Yusef Komunyakaa's "Hanoi Hannah," where a North Vietnamese DJ harangues GIs waiting for the next attack: "Her knife-edge song cuts / deep as a sniper's bullet." When the music is simply used, you get the equivalent of bad rock criticism. It's the instances when poets make room for a song to make its own claims in a new way that make the book sing, that lets it remind you of your own experiences as a listener trying to hold on to one of those instantaneous musical utopias as it vanished. The example I keep coming back to is David Rivard's "Cures."

A man and woman are sitting in their living room, after a fight that's left them disgusted, ashamed, and bored. They've turned the stereo up to drown out their own thoughts; for some reason they're playing "Mystery Train," "where Elvis relates some dark to himself." The scene doesn't develop; it just sits there, like the two people, "each doubt a little larger / than desire."

The poem goes on, but Rivard has closed it with those lines; as the couple listen to this song of movement, of danger, fear, lust, chase, and triumph, it freezes them, shows the depth of their paralysis. Each doubt is a little larger than desire, and the longer each doubt lasts, the larger it grows.

This wasn't why Elvis Presley and Sam Phillips made "Mystery Train" in Memphis in 1955, presumably: to expose people to their own weakness. But people don't use songs according to anyone's intent. In their truest moments, songs, like microbes—without intent, without brains—use people. The real mystery Rivard's poem opens up has nothing to do with a train; it's about the way songs enter people's lives, the way people can't get them out. Their beauty, at its most intense, might be more a rebuke than a promise. In "Cures," it's the passion and the heedlessness of the music that define how much the two people listening have given up, how much they've given up on each other, on themselves—just as the jukebox notes in *In the Name of the Father*, lifting like a curtain in a theater, define the preciousness of everything that's about to be taken away.

Interview, *April 1994*

Elvis and Hermes,
Together Again at Last

Elvis Presley made a tremendous amount of ghostly racket in the last weeks of the 1992 presidential campaign. But after the election of Clinton-code-name-"Elvis"—and that election day flyer can hardly have been calling for anything else—the ghost shut up. It might have been listed as Entertainment Coordinator in the credits for the Democratic convention where Clinton was nominated; when Aretha Franklin, Bob Dylan, Ben E. King, Fleetwood Mac, and so many more came forth at the Inauguration to celebrate the birth of a new era, Elvis was a stamp, and hardly missed.

In this season, then, the serious, elaborate Elvis exhibition that curators Sheila Muto, Rick Rinehart, Kurt True, and Lisa Weber mounted in the Bernice Layne Brown Gallery of the Doe Library at Berkeley seemed both out of place and out of time. Wasn't the story finished? Didn't everybody know the answers, if they even cared about the questions?

As a showcase for hundreds of Elvis artifacts, from a high school yearbook to a simple postcard ("WRITE TO ELVIS IN HELL— Help Feed the King"), the Brown Gallery was odd enough. It's a severe, elegant space, with walls of gleaming gray marble; looking down over two large display cases and a series of flat vitrines are busts of Augustus Caesar, Marcus Aurelius, Homer, and Hermes. As you walked through, you moved from the ordinary to the awful, from real movie posters to a garish painting of a baby Elvis as Baby Jesus—with big sideburns. The conventional, the obscene, the blasphemous, and the worshipful were all mixed up.

Elvis had apparently become a blank slate—wiped clean by his new, government-approved status—or at best a question mark without words preceding it, a brainless affront to all seekers after meaning. Leah Garchik, personals columnist for the *San Francisco Chronicle*, provided a perfect example the month before the Berkeley exhibit opened. She took a readers' poll: "Imagine President Clinton sitting in the Oval Office. He finds that both Elvis Presley and Eleanor Roosevelt are on the line. Whose call should he take first?" There were some predictable responses, from the reasonable ("That's the stupidest question I ever heard") to the pro forma ("Clinton knows that Eleanor is dead, so he'd talk to Elvis"). But the final entry Garchik listed was completely inexplicable, leaping from the margins to some scrambled center of cultural signs. "He'd talk to Eleanor," said the last of Garchik's respondents, "because she *is* Elvis."

The same Elvis—radioactive, with an immeasurable half-life, decaying backward to lay waste to the past as surely as it claims the future—pops up as well in "Culture," a ranting prose poem by the critic and designer Glenn O'Brien. It's a play on Hermann Göring's "When I hear the word culture, I reach for my revolver"; O'Brien wants to see how much mileage he can get out of the line. "When

I hear the word culture," he begins, "I reach not for a revolver but for TCBY, The Country's Best Yogurt." He goes on like that for many paragraphs, reaching for penicillin and Roquefort cheese, riffing off into vegetables and plutonium—and then it's as if he stumbles into the image he's been seeking all along. "When I hear the word culture," he says, "I don't reach for weapons of war, I reach for TCBY. That's Takin' Care of Business, Y'all. Elvis may be dead, but in his head the worms sing Return to Sender and the beat goes on and Elvis lives in the ghost that moves across the TV screen. And the ghost sings a song that Elvis never sang before. There it is on my TV, Elvis singing All Along the Watchtower . . ."

As a complete and ever-expanding American metaphor, that's as spooky as Elvis gets—seeking, truth-telling, banished, trapped in an oblivion that is also a utopia, the new American promise that when we get enough channels, everything will be given to us, an infinity of shows spontaneously generating all the shows we only wished we saw. Reading O'Brien, I want to see Elvis singing "All Along the Watchtower," Bob Dylan's precise, prosaic, soft-spoken account of justice and apocalypse; I almost can see it. You can almost believe that someday—in 2035, maybe, the hundredth anniversary of Elvis's birth, an event RCA must be planning even now—the recording will be assembled and released. Why not? The technology is already there. Elvis broke so many promises that the ones which remain—even if he never made them, even if, like O'Brien or Garchik's reader, we have to think them up ourselves—retain an absolute allure.

With all of that swirling in distant air, the loose-leaf folder for visitors' comments left in the Brown Gallery seemed altogether innocuous. It wasn't. The book was where the action was: the "Secret Exhibition," to borrow the title the Los Angeles assemblage artist George Herms gave to the pieces that in 1956 he installed in a series of vacant lots, "to be taken, destroyed, or to disintegrate." Here, outside of the glass cases, was something you could touch, make, unmake, inscribe, deface; people started arguing with each other on the first page, over racism, class, taste, religion, and didn't let up until the show closed, though for all I know someone broke in after that just to get the last word. The case wasn't closed. Elvis was still a kind of cauldron, a bubbling pot containing nearly every unresolved question he, his music, and his country ever raised. What was Elvis doing in this place, people asked in English, Chinese, Hebrew, Catalan, Spanish, Japanese, Arabic—what were they doing there? Excerpts from the book of the dead:

Elvis is dead! • Elvis is more alive than you will ever be! • I AM ELVIS—David Koresh • Elvis the greatest! He is Jesus! • Elvis is a faget [thoughtfully corrected by whoever added a "g," then again by whoever spelled the word out properly] • "I am not the son of a point"—Elvis • I have found he had been and has been an honest man • An honest dope addict • Dear Friends On the Wheel of Destiny— It was and Is Elvis is Time to Shine! & When it's yo' time Bro'—Its yo time! (PS Cheer up—We all have Our Time on the Wheel!) • I never found him remotely attractive • Dear Elvis—I never put much interest in you until I met my boyfriend. He thinks you are the greatest. I think he loves you more than me. I am jealous • Elvis & I would like to know how do we get out of here? The door is closed •
WE HAVE WOMYN'S STUDIES ETHNO CENTRO STUDIES, QUEER STUDIES, ABSURD MARXIST DADA DERRIDA SEMIOTICS STUDIES WHY NOT ELVIS STUDIES. WOULD ALLOW SOME MORE HACKS TENURE AND CHAIRS. ALL HAIL THE FUTURE OF SCHOLARSHIP •
I am disgusted that the University is spending $ and wasting display areas with this disgusting racist freak. I feel that if his racism is applauded by the country and by the school, then how can we be safe from bigotry in our society. Elvis is evil! • Elvis has become an overbearing and *ridiculous* icon of the 20th cent. He hardly belongs in such a prestigious learning institution as UC Berkeley. Leave Elvis to the

wackos who infest Graceland • Wife beating is cool when they deserve it! I have a newfound appreciation for Elvis. I'm not so keen on the racism • NO? YOU PROBABLY HAVEN'T REALLY GIVEN IT A CHANCE. YOU SHOW GREAT POTENTIAL FOR IT • whoever wrote this . . . • I must comment on the irony of academia embracing Elvis (and, slowly, other rock musicians as well, esp. the Beatles) after years of snobbish putdowns and judgmentalism, which we lovers of rock have put up with for *decades*. Screw you, academia, for taking so long to recognize great music! • The statues would cover their eyes if they had arms • Look closely at the faces of those statues . . . Elvis is in at least one of them •

You'd have to be tougher than I am not to look up at this point. Elvis's pals used to tease him that he looked like Greek gods in the picture books he kept around Graceland; in one of William Eggleston's famous Graceland photos a bust of a Greek god is paired with a bust of Elvis. Up on the display ledge running around the gallery, Caesar, Aurelius, and Homer look nothing like Elvis, but then they were no gods, merely men. But Hermes—he's a dead ringer. On the other hand, that may only mean that they're both Immortal European White Males.

Elvis was a racist!—doesn't anyone remember? Oh yea? Ask *Alice Walker, Muhammad Ali, or EDDIE MURPHY!* • Elvis could spell • WHAT'S UP NEGRÉ? • Elvis was a sleazy ho!! • Elvis likes to suck big Black Dick • [a full page] SUCK MY BLACK DICK ELVIS PELVIS • Why do you choose to glorify the memory & life of a man who did nothing but steal the rhythms of African American blues singers & destroy himself. Let the memory of this racist die • Was it *he* who was racist or the society he lived in? Why didn't black rock and rollers make it? They were just as talented. Can you blame the poor idiot for being a man of his times? Ah, forget it. He's dead now anyway. Who cares? • I cannot believe you people made an exhibit of a racist woman beater. Next time are you going to do an exhibit on the KKK? Elvis is dead bury him and this sick exhibit. If you want to honor a person do it on someone great not an asshole • If you hate Elvis so much you should get to know your enemy • We are a nation of small minds, bad taste and short memories. We are a nation of elvis fans, a nation who can't hear James Brown •

Elvis I like you • I hate Elvis my father made me come • Ann Margarait was gorgeous. I wonder if Elvis "did" her • Of course he did, you idiot! • His sense of humor and grace under fire will always endure beyond the stabs of uncomprehending, money-sucking critics, who can only stand back and have their grotesque little faces illuminated by his fire!!! • Elvis I don't like you • I NEED A JOB! • This book is so hilarious! I've been thinking about stealing it all week!

"I am just about to take an impossible Organic Chemistry Exam," a woman wrote in a flowery hand near the end of the book. "Just by seeing the Elvis exhibition, I feel his spiritual soul taking over me. The King will lead me to do well on this exam—at least I'll pass." I thought this was pure parody until the last four words; if that's not the voice of real life, I've never heard it. Want to bet she didn't make it?

Modern Review (*London*), *May–June 1994*
and Texte zur Kunst (*Cologne*), *June 1994*

Clinton Places Behind Juliette Lewis,
Ahead of Prince in New Poll;
McCarthyism Tops
"Don't Ask, Don't Tell"

1. Martina McBride: "Independence Day" (RCA) Written by
Gretchen Peters, this is one of those ultraprofessional Nashville
songs where all craft is marshaled to burn a tune into your heart.
McBride sings it rangy, loud, and hard, like Trisha Yearwood with
more than a career on her mind. "Talk about your revolution," says
a young girl of her drunk of a father and her battered, broken
mother; by the time her story finds its end everyone's life has
changed, or ended, and the record has joined Van Morrison's "Almost Independence Day" and X's cover of Dave Alvin's "4th of
July" in the thin folio of recordings that expose a legacy nearly too
distant and demanding to think about. It's a legacy that still carries
an echo of Herman Melville's version: "The Declaration of Independence makes a difference."

**2. John McNaughton, director, Samuel Fuller and Christa
Lang, writers:** *Girls in Prison* **(Showtime made-for-TV
movie)** By far the most intense entry in the *Rebel Highway* series
of old-title/new-script remakes of '50s AIP teen-exploitation flicks:
a young woman who's written a song that turns out to be "Endless
Sleep" gets framed for murder. The film goes giddy with glee over
its freedom to push old ideas to the point of explosion: to get its

first two heroines into the slam, they're shown as driven literally berserk by McCarthyism. A famous liberal Hollywood actor and his daughter rehearse a new script; then, as you see it tried out in a little L.A. theater, with the father playing a witness fighting off his McCarthyist inquisitor, the members of the audience rise from their seats and, all barriers between art, life, and propaganda dissolving, beat the father to the edge of death. After that, he can only mumble "Are you a Communist?" over and over; after shock therapy, he says nothing at all.

3. Juliette Lewis: "These Boots Are Made for Walking," in ***Natural Born Killers*, Oliver Stone, director (Warner Bros.)** Out on her feet from snakebite, finally captured, her stomach covered with blood from the crisscrossings of a cop's knife, whispering the words under her breath, she's got rhythm, just barely.

4/5. Bill Clinton et al: ***Bill Clinton Jam Session—The Pres Blows*** **(Pres, available through 1-800-666-5277) and Roger Clinton & Politics:** ***Nothing Good Comes Easy*** **(Pyramid)** For B.C. there's the queer sneer of the subtitle, itself an homage to Lester Young, the first tenor saxophonist to take the name "Prez," and the Mark of the Beast in the 800 number, but put that aside: this seventeen-minute CD is straight cool school, with more soul than Clinton fave Kenny G. Cut at the Reduta Jazz Club in Prague on January 11, with Clinton playing a horn offered by Vaclav Havel and leading a small troupe of Czechs through "Summertime" and a ten-minute "My Funny Valentine," the music meanders at first, with more to hear as themes fade than as they try to take shape. At the end, Clinton gathers Jan Konopasek's baritone sax to his tenor, and there's a stirring moment of peace at the heart of a storm not long in the past. As for the concurrent release of brother Roger's debut disc, it's lounge music, and where was it when the KGB could have used it? Lock Havel back in his old cell, pump this in for . . . oh, about five tracks, and he'd renounce his hero Frank Zappa and the Velvet Underground too if that's what it took to get out.

6. Richard Huelsenbeck, editor: *Dada Almanac*, presented by Malcolm Green (Atlas Press) A long-overdue translation of the still unsatisfied 1920 anthology. Almost three-quarters of a century have not recovered the language Walter Mehring found in Berlin for "Revelations," even if the frame of reference has returned with a vengeance: "Since [the] Balkan division [of the first Dada dynasty] began the Albanian interregnum in collaboration with the Viennese Bankverein and the Italian Banca Commerciale, and launched its missionary activities among the Shiite Bektashiyahs, even simple jobbers at the stock exchange are beginning to realize . . ."

7. Come: *Don't Ask, Don't Tell* (Matador) No matter what dustbin of history Clinton's gays-in-the-military policy ends up in, the phrase will live on. It's a work of genius, a perfect title for anything save what it supposedly stands for—including this moody, cruel album by a band that was previously a dirge factory for singer Thalia Zedek. Admitting light and speed, the sound gets stronger and more whole song by song, until you can almost believe that inside the Gothic clichés some kind of secret is waiting.

8. Prince 1958–1993: *Come* (Warner Bros.) Currently on an avowedly permanent recording strike, the Artist Formerly Known as Prince has announced his intention to fulfull his huge Warner Bros. contract by dumping tapes out of his bottomless vaults for as long as it takes. The first fruit of this bizarre insult is his/its most elegant album since *Dirty Mind,* and that was fourteen years ago. *Come* is super high-concept: the careful, inventive, all but liquid dramatization of a single 48-minute, 46-second fuck. Except for the hokey last track, "Orgasm"—if you believe Prince when he promises "I love you" to the accompanying female vocalist, credited as "partner," he's got an old Warner Bros. contract you might be interested in—the music basks in the kind of ease and luxury that call up Willie Dixon's opening brag on Howlin' Wolf's "Goin' Down Slow," lines you can imagine spinning off the last tape the Kid retrieves from the last vault: "Now, I did not say / I was a millionaire / But I said, I have spent more *money* / Than a millionaire."

9. Beck's Beer Commercial: "Sail Away" spot (Wensauer • D.D.B. Needham, Dusseldorf) I once wondered what would happen if Randy Newman's greatest song, conceived as a slaver's recruiting pitch, were heard anytime, anywhere—part of the noise of any given day. Here's the answer: though only the title phrase and a hint of melody are used, the song is instantly recognizable behind footage of tall ships and waves surging. Why? To catch a vague echo of its evil, to give the commercial just the subliminal edge it needs?

10. Fastbacks: *"Answer the Phone, Dummy"* (Sub Pop) After fourteen years of evading anything resembling professionalism—seemingly abandoning all craft to glance a tune off your heart—bassist Kim Warnick and guitarist Lulu Gargiulo are singing guitarist Kurt Bloch's songs with a new confidence, which doesn't hurt lines like "I learned something today / People don't think the way I do."

Traces of Extremist Culture in a Time of Broken Politics

Marianne Faithfull's recent autobiography and retrospective album have the same title, *Faithfull,* and the same cover art: a stark, black-and-white Bruce Weber photo of a woman in her forties, battered by the years, her dark junkie's tattoo just visible, cigarette burning, her face wistful as she thinks it all through. The book and album each come with an ad for the other, and both raise the same question. If, once, you were at the right place at the right time, what do you do—or what happens to you—when your day is over?

Faithfull may not have been, as Bharati Mukherjee says of the heroine of her novel *The Holder of the World,* "one of those extraordinary lives through which history runs a four-lane highway," but as a Swinging '60s chanteuse and Mick Jagger's consort, her face and voice caught the recklessness, the allure, and the mystery of the cultural revolution that for a few years overtook London and much of the rest of the world. Grainy footage from the forgotten British interview show "Personal Choice" preserves the moment: "If everyone did what you seem to be advocating," an overstuffed interviewer says to a teenage Faithfull, "do you not agree that the whole structure of society would just collapse?" "Yes," she says, her angelic tone summing up a kingdom of indulgence, of pleasure and freedom, of megalomania and acid, her interrogator will never know, "wouldn't it be lovely? I think I'm really powerful. They could—they'll smash me, probably. But I want to *try*." Faithfull left the world slightly different than she found it, and then it cast her out, or she cast herself out of it. Writing about reading William Burroughs's *Naked Lunch* for the first time, on vacation with Jagger in 1967, when she was twenty, Faithfull recalls "a blinding flash. This was something I was going to have to pursue. I would become a junkie . . . a junkie on the street."

"The vibe at Redding was insane . . . It was like goddess worship verging on stoning me to death," Courtney Love said in September of the U.K. music festival she'd just played; the extremes she describes would make perfect sense to a woman whose book is filled with metaphors of all kinds of witchery. Put on the *Faithfull* album, and witchcraft is the first thing you hear. The opening cut is "Broken English," the title song from Faithfull's then-shocking, now-celebrated 1979 punk rant—a song "inspired," Faithfull writes, "by the German terrorist Ulrike Meinhof." The Red Army Faction, a.k.a. the Baader-Meinhof Gang, which all but pulled the rug of legitimacy out from under the West German regime in the 1970s, "had just been arrested, and the phrase 'say it in broken English' came from something that flashed on the TV screen, this mysterious subtitle: 'broken English . . . spoken English . . .' I don't know what it was in reference to, but I wrote it down in my notebook."

Meinhof hanged herself in prison in 1976; once a popular political columnist, with the guileless looks of an ingenue, she had been outside of society since 1970, when she and others broke Andreas Baader out of prison in a shoot-out, and at the end she looked as ruined as Faithfull ever did. The song, these fifteen years since 1979, has lost nothing. The gloomy, harsh rhythm almost promises to take you somewhere you don't want to go; Faithfull, her unstable croak as shaped and purposeful as anyone else's clear voice (hers, say, in 1964, fifteen years before), comes from the far side.

Over and over, her words refuse the challenge, or the temptation, of the song's unnamed inspiration—"What are you / Fighting for / It's not my / Security . . . It's not my / Reality"—but the way the words are sung, and the music behind them, give the demurrer the lie; the piece pulls hard against itself. Listening, you believe Faithfull thinks she knows exactly what the fight is about, and anyway she sounds as if she's already fallen.

Faithfull comes out from behind the song in her book, and it's one of the few times a singer's explanation of what she meant does her song any good. "I identified with Ulrike Meinhof," she says. "The same blocked emotions that turn some people into junkies turn others into terrorists . . . 'I won't have it! I won't stand for it! This is totally unacceptable!' . . . A form of idealism that leads down different paths."

Whether re-creating the time when her first husband, John Dunbar, joined with others to plot the transformation of London into "the pyschic bloody center of the world," "our New Jerusalem," or the years when she did little more than fuck for dope and shoot it, Faithfull's tone is fast, breezy—the horrors and the rage that course all through *Broken English,* the sense of a last chance to say your piece, or anything at all, is altogether missing. Instead there are passages that fix Faithfull's right place at the right time perfectly, and in her own voice. As the Rolling Stones begin to crumble under an orchestrated series of drug raids—Jagger and Keith Richards were due for long prison terms until the London *Times* came to their defense—Faithfull imagines the police rummaging through her dossier: "Let's see, daughter of Glynn Faithfull, well-known crank, runs a cauldron of obscurantist foment called Brazier's Park. Mother, the Baroness von Sacher-Masoch . . . Good God!"

If I'd had those words in my head as I left a show she did some years ago in San Francisco, I don't know that I would have had the nerve to repeat them. That night, plainly nervous, with everyone in the audience having to decide if she was still on heroin before they could begin to respond to anything she did, Faithfull left an impression of struggle and dignity. Self-mocking, she put not the kitsch knowledge of her legend into her music but rather a dramatization of what she didn't know, as if her whole performance was a wish, or a proof, that she still had an unfinished life to lead.

"Ah, Marianne!" said Keith Richards after Faithfull called to tell him she had, she believed, finally kicked heroin. "But what about the Holy Grail?" Someone else will find it, presumably; as she has since *Broken English,* Faithfull continues her search for a sound that will turn the world toward her aged, human face. She has already proven she can wait—that she can wait out the glow of her golden moments, and wait out herself. As she has pulled the years into herself, Mick Jagger, her old lover, has reenacted *The Picture of Dorian Gray,* to the point that he seems as undead as Michael Jackson, his body forever fixed in 1967, his face expiring in its gilded frame. Faithfull could go tomorrow, or she could be the last one standing.

Interview, *November 1994*

Kurt Cobain 1967–1994

APRIL 12, 1994

The word on Kurt Cobain in the days before he killed himself was so awful that every time a Nirvana song came on the radio, I was sure it was only a prelude to the announcement that he was dead. Over and over, for some reason, before the fact, the song was always "Come As You Are." As it played, on Wednesday or Thursday, it seemed to slow down and expand, to drag itself across its own sound, to rub itself raw.

When the news came, the version I got was queer, ugly—mocking, not like the announcement of any other pop death. Several people were talking on KALX-FM, the Berkeley college station. They were back-announcing records by the Raincoats and the Vaselines: ". . . two of his favorites. Yeah, it's too bad about Kurt Cobain's passing"—that moronic euphemism—"but what the hell, it's *his* life." Someone snickered, and then a loud, hyped-up tabloid voice hit the mike: *"He shot himself! With a shotgun! In a cabin next to his house! He left a note!"* "Hey," said the first voice, sarcasm dripping, "we're not making *fun* of this." They went straight into "My Way" by Sid Vicious.

That night I dreamed about a Kurt Cobain funeral procession, with an open hearse trundling down First Avenue in Seattle as thousands lined the street. Every few moments, someone would break out of the crowd, leap onto the hearse like a mosh-pit dancer taking the stage, then lift the lid on the coffin and rush back to the sidewalk, shouting: "No face, man! No face!"

At a small gathering at Booksmith's, on Haight Street in San Francisco, the night before Kurt Cobain's body was found, the subject of Nirvana came up. Gina Arnold, who wrote the book *Route 666: The Road to Nirvana,* spoke bitterly: "People talk about Kurt Cobain's wonderful sense of irony. There isn't any irony."

Driving for six hours from Kansas City to Fayetteville on Sunday, April 10, the day after the story was front page all over the country, there wasn't any Kurt Cobain. Radio is now so demographically segmented its formats are absolutely resistant to events in the world at large; here it's always . . . wherever it is. On Your Favorite Oldies, Best of the '70s, Lite Rock, not to mention 24-Hour News, talk radio, Adult Contemporary, country, or hip hop stations, Kurt Cobain didn't die, and neither was he ever born. Finally, just over the Missouri-Arkansas border, on a station that mixed Michael Bolton, Salt-N-Pepa, and Beck, up came a no-comment "All Apologies." Probably it had been computer-programmed the week before.

It was appropriate, of course. Kurt Cobain wrote too many songs appropriate to suicide. Not murder, though, or anything like it. The violence is always an echo; it's loud only to the one who's shouting. "Sometimes," said guitarist Roy Buchanan, another suicide, "it gets so quiet you could fire a gun inside yourself"—and, he must have meant, no one would hear it.

Was it easy to hear Kurt Cobain, as he made hits full of violence, as he struggled through that sound to do and say those things he thought were right, to stand up and condemn those who, like Axl Rose, he believed were thugs? In that struggle you could hear a belief that to embrace decency in the world at large—to fight homophobia, to aid the suffering, to denounce evil—would be, even if your own soul were a charnel house, to find decency in yourself. Come as you are—when you live your life in pieces, it's easier said than done. The song plays in my head now, with an added line from Laurie Anderson: come as you are, and pay as you go.

Rolling Stone, *June 2, 1994*

CONTRIBUTION TO CITY PAGES ARTIST OF THE YEAR ISSUE

As the year began it grew increasingly difficult to look Kurt Cobain in the eye—to listen to him without flinching. The first four words of *Dream and Lie of Franco,* Picasso's corrosive, blasphemous 1937 comic strip, could in 1994 have been added to anything with Cobain's name on it, or near it: "Dream and Lie of Lithium." "Dream and Lie of the Man Who Sold the World." "Dream and Lie of Polly." "Dream and Lie of I Hate Myself and Want to Die." Dream and lie of the photograph of Courtney Love in that Rome ambulance in March, looking blasted but somehow in control, with Cobain prostrate behind her; dream and lie of the April 8 photo, shot through the door of Cobain's garage apartment, of his splayed sneakered foot.

Since Cobain prepared for his suicide in his music, in the outside world—outside of the world of people who knew and worked with him, or cared about what he had done with his life, or with theirs; that is, people who looked Cobain in the eye without having ever met him, people who had, at one time or another, found Cobain, as they listened to him, looking *them* in the eye—the event of his death settled quickly. A cartoon I saw in the *Arkansas Traveler,* the student paper at the University of Arkansas, showed a grungy bleach-head arriving in cloudland only to be stopped by the heavenly gatekeeper: "I'm sorry, Mr. Cobain, but the self-absorbed, self-pitying rock star section of the afterlife is all booked up right now." For others, though, Cobain's death forced a blunt taking stock—as, for a lot of people, his music had always done. Faced with critic Bill Wyman's terse aside (in a *Chicago Reader* piece titled "Rock Star Blows Brains Out") that "comparisons to lesser lights—Janis Jopin, Jimi Hendrix, or, most frequently, Jim Morrison—are merely quaint," some turned away in disgust, leaving Kurt Cobain, culturally, a sort of merely local hero, and leaving those whose eyes he'd looked through with an even greater sense of exile within their own culture, their own country. They knew the old slogan: you're either on the bus, or under it.

"There really wasn't a stronger dissenting voice in the Reaganist aftermath," critic Howard Hampton wrote to a friend three days after Cobain's body was found. If this was true, as time goes on it will be more and more important to understand just how it was true. For the time being, as Sarah Vowell stated more plainly than anyone else I've read or overheard or argued with, Cobain is the bad conscience of present-day walk and talk: the real, the only new Dylan, if only in death. It was six months later, and Vowell was reviewing Joseph Lanza's much-praised *Elevator Music: A Surreal History of Muzak, Easy-Listening, and Other Moodsong:*

Lanza writes about the way an Easy Listening group called the Alan Copeland Singers turned a song by bluesman Leadbelly into a "sweet suburban incantation." Last New Year's Eve, I attended a Nirvana concert at the Oakland Coliseum. Singing Leadbelly's ballad "Where Did You Sleep Last Night?" Cobain started off with a gently scratchy drawl. For an instant, he sounded like the greatest country singer who ever lived. Suddenly, he was screaming through the rest of it, claiming the words as his own and spewing them out of his tortured belly with more profound passion than I have ever witnessed in my short life. Remembering what that moment meant to me as I read Lanza's statement that "not every musician should be obligated to reassure us that we are not zombies" made me sick.

Anybody else around who can make decent, honest, fair-minded folk seem like the liars they are? Name them, they can be artist of the year instead.

City Pages (*Minneapolis*), *December 28, 1994*

Nirvana After the 1994 Congressional Elections

Soundtrack for the day after Republicans achieved majorities in both the House and the Senate, and the day after that:

> Led Zeppelin, "When the Levee Breaks"
> Fastbacks, "In America"
> Sam Cooke, "A Change Is Gonna Come" (set on
>   replay and leave the house)
> Bob Dylan, "Memphis Blues Again"
> Rod Stewart, "I've Been Drinking"
> Eleventh Dream Day, "It's Not My World" (set on
>   replay and lock the door from the inside)
> Destroy All Monsters, *1974–1976*
> anything by Nirvana

Some of these numbers may be hard to find. The Rod Stewart heartbreaker is a twenty-seven-year-old track from a Jeff Beck album. The Destroy All Monsters material is a three-CD compendium of experiments by a Detroit anti-rock band that included since-celebrated visual artist Mike Kelley—I like the group's sound, but these days what I'm really playing is their name. Listening to Nirvana is no problem, unless listening to someone who isn't here is a problem.

Last April 8, the day Kurt Cobain's death hit the news, a friend's roommates came home to find her sitting on the floor amid what looked like the residue of a party; there were empty bottles lined up all along the wall. "Who was here?" they asked. "Just me," she said. Cobain's suicide left a lot of people feeling that alone—that isolated, stranded in rooms locked from the inside. He committed the ultimate solitary act and, by means of a suicide note addressed in part to his fans, made it a public act. In his note he mapped the void between fandom and stardom, the void that forces each of us to play one role or the other; the only way he could refuse the choice the void demanded, he said, was to choose the void itself. He thus became, as Howard Hampton wrote so cruelly, "for the first time anywhere the self-assassinating rock star, John Lennon and Mark Chapman as a one-man band, doing a command performance of that old Sonic Youth favorite, 'Kill Yr. Idols.'"

"Come As You Are" has been on the radio ever since Cobain died—standing in for everything else Nirvana ever did, it seems—probably because whatever it is that makes a medium a medium can't resist the kick of making Kurt Cobain shout "I SWEAR THAT I DON'T HAVE A GUN" all day long. But now, as with all dead pop heroes, Cobain is back in the front racks.

Recorded November 18, 1993, Nirvana's *Unplugged in New York* is merely as unique as the group was. With cellist Lori Goldstein swaying in the background, the set creates an odd drama of resolute, self-deprecating, almost casual daring—a band daring demons to come down and mess up the music that's being made. The sound on Nirvana's own songs is hollowed out by Cobain and Krist Novoselic's acoustic guitars; it's less that the electric dimension of the the music is missing than that it's been sucked into what remains. On the songs by others Nirvana plays—the Vaselines' "Jesus Doesn't Want Me for a Sunbeam," David Bowie's "The Man Who Sold the World," the Meat Puppets' "Plateau," "Oh Me," and "Lake of Fire"—the music grows, expands, fills any room, and you glimpse a person who plainly believed he could never make anything so good himself, a star who, singing these songs, is their best fan. The last number, Lead Belly's "Where Did You Sleep Last Night," is shattering, one of those performances where you can't imagine the singer escaping from the song, and it seals a certain tone: this song comes from the nineteenth century, but almost every song played this night seems ancient. The Meat Puppets' "Lake of Fire" feels as if it's been retrieved from a cave, not borrowed from another punk band. With its lyric constructed like an authorless folk ballad—each line, each prophecy or joke, at once a literal non sequitur and a poetic link to every other line—the out-of-nowhere reference to "the Fourth of July" suggests that here, as in "The Coo Coo," in America the type case for this kind of song, the Fourth of July is a predestined date, waiting, deep in unknown traditions, to be found and used. In other words, the feeling the music gives off is that, as a talisman, the Fourth of July not only preceded the Declaration of Independence but called it into being. Or as if the song could call it back.

Much cheesier, and finally more powerful, is the video *Live! Tonight! Sold Out!!* ("I think if you make money," Novoselic said in 1992 as *Nevermind* hit the top of the charts, "and you start voting Republican, because you'll get tax breaks and they're the party of the rich, I mean, *that's* sold out.") The tape combines reams of live footage, onstage and in TV studios, with interviews; most of the footage is indifferently shot, on the cheap. For the first half it all seems conventional enough, your basic rockumentary, despite opening with Cobain and drummer Dave Grohl parading in front of a huge crowd in drag, a sequence in which the band is attacked onstage by its own guards, or a clip of Novoselic and Cobain appearing on MTV's "Headbangers' Ball," Novoselic in street clothes and

Cobain in a flowing yellow ball gown. "He wouldn't wear his tux," Cobain complains of Novoselic. "He didn't get me a corsage, either."

By the second half of the video, the accumulation of such apparently ridiculous or inexplicable events makes you see Nirvana's performances differently, and you are given different performances to see. As Cobain, Novoselic, and Grohl speak—as equals, with different points of view, with no deference, with a mutual affection and respect so strong and easy you can't believe it couldn't last— the fundamental Nirvana drama takes on a new shape. Again, it is a dramatization of the satanic gravity that pulls stars toward fans, and fans toward stars, until all cease to exist as people who in any given moment might be able to step out of the parade and say no to anything. With increasing desperation and violence—across a whole montage of the band's onstage destruction of its instruments and equipment, until this old cliché seems like a play about to spill out of the theater and into real life—you see the band seeking that *no,* demanding it, and finding it only in abjection. They're flailing wildly, hopelessly. Singing is turned into half-human squawks, masks are broken in an attempt to appear naked before the crowd, to turn the crowd back into individuals. Onstage, Cobain pulls down his pajama pants to his underwear; Novoselic exposes his pubic hair; Cobain crawls on his stomach like a reptile, in a slip.

The weight of all of Nirvana's songs are on his back; their uncertainties and doubts are woven into the flimsy fabric he wears. Cobain has sung Nirvana's awful anti-rape ballad "Polly" in the voice of the rapist—that's how the song is written, that's why it's powerful—but in a woman's garment, acting out the solidarity of abjection. You can imagine that, someday, he might have sung Lead Belly songs in blackface, in the same spirit. As the sort of people he hated, and who would have hated him, bask in triumph, it's a drama the country could use.

Interview, *January 1995, with material
from* Artforum, *January 1995*

Gladys Love Smith
and Vernon Elvis Presley

In the course of researching *The Life and Cuisine of Elvis Presley*—never mind the title, it's a wonderful book—David Adler, a man with no previous interest in Presley, a hired gun for a publisher looking to ride a trend, found himself in Tupelo, Mississippi, the site of Elvis's birth on January 8, 1935. There he met a woman who told him a story. She had worked at a local garment factory with Gladys Presley, who had married Vernon Presley in June 1933; now Gladys was expecting twins, and as was the local custom, Gladys's coworkers took up a collection to help their friend with birth expenses. In this case, however, Gladys's friends did not want the money—anywhere from $10 to $30, the woman remembered, a great deal of money for a woman who earned at most two dollars for a twelve-hour day—to go directly to the Presleys, "because Vernon would drink it up." So the woman bought two blankets, and took them to the Presleys' tiny house—without indoor plumbing or electricity—that Vernon had built the month before. Entering, the woman saw Gladys on her bed, having just given birth to a live child; on a table she saw a shoebox. She opened the box, and inside it saw a dead baby: Elvis's stillborn twin, Jesse Garon, who would be buried in an umarked grave.

When Adler retold this story on a panel at the 1993 Tennessee

Williams Literary Festival in New Orleans, a gathering of writers and readers mostly from the South, the room was spellbound. I was seated on the panel next to Adler: "That's the most incredible Elvis story I've ever heard!" I said. There were loud, almost religious assents—or Amen's—from the audience. We were all shocked. To some in the crowd, it must have been as if we were in a room with a man who had met a woman who was present at the birth of Jesus; to others, as if we were in a room with a man who had met a woman who was present at the birth of the modern age. "You see," Adler said of his research, "I met all these people who knew Elvis, and it absolutely *flabbergasted* me. Here you have this mythical figure— and people actually *knew* him."

Now, in one sense this story and the response that greeted it are completely ridiculous. There was nothing new in the story; the facts had been public knowledge for almost forty years. There was nothing incredible about the story: women give birth to twins all the time, and often one of them dies. And yet there is no denying the aura, the sense of fatedness, of catastrophe and deliverance, that hangs over this tale. The people in this story are indeed mythical figures, and for the public at large they have never been real. Summoning the ghosts of Gladys Presley, who died at forty-six in 1958, or Vernon Presley, who died in 1979, two years after Elvis, at sixty-three, one must remind oneself that in conventional terms, on the terms of ordinary or even celebrity biography, we know almost nothing about them.

There are of course skeleton details. Gladys Smith was by all accounts a strong-willed, vibrant young woman—she must have been, to run off at twenty-one to marry a boy who had turned seventeen only two months before, right about the time Gladys and Vernon met. They lied about their ages, as Vernon was too young to marry without his parents' consent, and the age difference was embarrassing: Vernon pretended to be twenty-one and Gladys, nineteen (for the rest of her life she pretended, even to herself, to be younger than she really was). It was at the very worst period of the Great Depression, with the American economy in wreckage, and even compared to their neighbors and relatives the young Presleys were desperately poor, often surviving on handouts and government-distributed food. Vernon worked odd jobs—milkman, carpenter, delivery man, grass cutter, truck driver—though none lasted very long. At one point he forged a check, altering a $4 sum to $14 or $40—and was sentenced to three years' hard labor at Mississippi's notorious Parchman Farm, though he was released after eight months. In 1948 the family moved to Memphis; Vernon worked less and Gladys worked more. They lived in public housing. Their son grew up. In 1956 he became world-famous—perhaps the most famous man in the Western world. Forced into the public eye and separated from her beloved son, Gladys began to drink. She got fat; she took diet pills. She drank more. Soon she was a ruin, suffering from hepatitis; a heart attack ended her life. Within eighteen months Vernon remarried.

We know about the preternatural closeness of Elvis and Gladys, especially from the time that Vernon disappeared into prison, when Elvis was three. We know nothing of Gladys and Vernon but that they remained married until Gladys died; that they were poor, and then rich. When we look at a marriage we want to know about money and love; perhaps we know about money. We know nothing about love.

Gladys Presley was a handsome young woman; Vernon Presley, at seventeen and for years afterward, was gorgeous—movie star gorgeous. Yet if she was ebullient, a buck dancer, he was a brooder, suspicious of everyone around him, afraid of life. Not surprisingly, Elvis, who changed the world with his exuberance and died a paranoid wreck, combined both sides. But perhaps there is more, just a bit more that tells an unpleasant story, a story no one has wanted to hear.

Peter Guralnick, likely Elvis's only reliable biographer, believes that before his marriage to Priscilla Beaulieu, Elvis, while wildly active sexually at the start of his career, never had sexual intercourse with a woman he cared about: no girlfriend, not even Natalie Wood. Priscilla herself states in her autobiography that despite living with Elvis in Graceland from 1961, she had intercourse with him for the first time on their wedding night in 1967, became pregnant almost immediately, and after that found his sexual interest in her almost nonexistent.

This is odd behaviour; it is, one might suspect, learned behavior. Whether Elvis was following in the footsteps of his mother or his father there is no telling, but it is hard to believe he was not acting out a life that one of them chose, and together both of them led, for their quarter-century as a married couple. So this is odd; it is unsettling; and finally it is ordinary. There is no aura that adheres to the story if we tell it this way. Is that why the question of Gladys Presley, Vernon Presley, and sex has hardly been asked? Everyone knows it is difficult to imagine one's parents engaged in sexual intercourse; does this mean that in some distant, symbolic way, the countless people who saw themselves in Elvis have imagined these two ordinary Mississippians as the mother and father not merely of an extraordinary individual, but of themselves?

Süddeutsche Zeitung Magazin, *January 27, 1995*

Bob Dylan After the 1994
Congressional Elections

I admit I was thrown by the Bob Dylan segment of the NBC News end-of-the-year wrap-up on December 30. After the requisite Bobbitts-Simpson-Tonya-Michael Jackson montage, and a similar smear of Rwanda-Bosnia-Haiti-Chechnya, there was bright footage of Newt Gingrich and other Republican stalwarts celebrating their November triumph—with Dylan's 1964 recording of "The Times They Are A-Changin'" ("Come senators, congressmen / Please heed the call / Don't stand in the doorway / Don't block up the hall") churning in the background. Despite Gingrich's immediate postelection identification of the seemingly long-gone counter-culture as the enemy within (deriding Bill and especially Hillary Clinton as "counterculture McGoverniks," the unusual suffix meant for automatic, subconscious decoding: first back to beatnik, from there to a source of that word in Sputnik, the first space satel-lite, launched by the Soviet Union in 1957, and thus to the root translation: commie), the song sounded so weirdly apt it was as if Republicans had now seized all rights to it, along with the rest of the country. The NBC orchestration conflated all too perfectly with a new TV commercial Taco Bell began running about the same time, announcing a burrito-plus-CD promotion (you can pick up a sampler with General Public, Cracker, the Spin Doctors: "Some

call it 'alternative' or 'new rock'—we just call it 'dinner music'")
with footage of dancing young people turning Taco Bells into dance
clubs. "Don't let it pass you by," said the announcer in a friendly
voice, which suddenly, unexpectedly, turned hard: "Because there
is . . . *no* alternative."

On the other hand, it didn't bother me at all that Dylan recently
licensed "The Times They Are A-Changin' "—certainly his most famous, catchphrase-ready protest song, in the mid-'60s an in-
escapable affirmation of the power of youth to redeem the nation's
soul—to be used in a TV commercial for the Coopers & Lybrand
accounting firm. I think all songs should go up on this block. As
with the NBC joke (perhaps inspired by Tim Robbins's film *Bob
Roberts*, in which a right-wing folk-singer/politician storms the
heights with an answer-record to Dylan's old hit, "The Times They
Are A-Changin' Back"), it's a way of finding out if songs that carry
people with them, songs that seem tied to a particular time and
place, can survive a radical recontextualization, or if that recontextualization dissolves them.

The Beatles' "Revolution" may never recover from its Nike commercial, but Coopers & Lybrand didn't lay a glove on "The Times
They Are A-Changin'." When Dylan sang it on his MTV "Unplugged" show—taped November 17 and 18, little more than a
week after the elections, it aired December 14—the song was full
of new life. With a lively band around him, Dylan took the lead on
acoustic guitar; following his own cues from *Good As I Been to You*
and *World Gone Wrong,* he made more of the song's inner
melodies, its hidden rhythms, than ever before. He slowed the
song down, as if to give it a chance to catch up with the history that
should have superseded it. Or was the feeling that the song was still
lying in wait, readying its ambush? As he did throughout the performance, Dylan focused certain lines, words, syllables, looking
around behind impenetrable, blacker-than-black dark glasses, as if
to ask, "Are you listening, are you hearing, who are you, why are

you here?" By design, the people in the front rows of the audience were young enough to go from this show to the taping of the Taco Bell commercial without skipping a beat, but if "The Times They Are A-Changin'" had any specific political purpose this night, it seemed to be to break such a rhythm, not seal it.

Emphasis was the motor of the performance, with quietly stinging notes highlighting especially "If your time to you is worth savin'," a phrase that in 1964 felt certain and today can feel desperate and bereft—a deeper challenge. Or perhaps those words, sung and played as they were, were now a challenge for the first time. If Dylan was celebrating anything as he retrieved the number, it was menace. The song took on a new face, and you could hear the song as if it were putting a new face on a new time: instead of Great Day Coming, Look Out. What opened up out of the song was not the future, but a void. It was all done lightly, with a delight in music for its own sake: Dylan's gestures and expressions, like his black-and-white polka-dot shirt, radiated pleasure. You didn't have to hear anything I heard, but what you couldn't have heard, I think, was an old warhorse of a greatest hit trotted out to meet the expectations of the crowd.

This was not in any way the highlight of the show; that was probably "With God on Our Side," also from the 1964 album *The Times They Are A-Changin'*. With its circa-1952 grade school–textbook summary of American wars—the Indian wars, the Civil War, the forgotten Spanish-American War, the First World War, the Second World War, the Cold War—it brought the same displacement the Cranberries play with in "Zombie." There the word "nineteen-sixteen" leaps out, because today the mention of an event that took place before a song's intended audience was born, in this case the Easter Rebellion, is a bizarre use of pop language. It's a strange violation of an art form that sells narcissism more effectively than anything else.

Seven years ago, describing Bob Dylan at the great Live Aid

concert of 1985, Jim Miller, in perhaps the best short overview of Dylan's career, spoke of a "waxen effigy," "a lifeless pop icon," "a mummy." The guy onstage in late 1994 was more like a detective, investigating his own songs—and then treating them as clues, following them wherever they led, to the real mystery, the real crime. For the last year or so, the most ubiquitous appearance of this pop icon in pop media has been that moment in Counting Crows' "Mr. Jones" when Adam Duritz shouts "I WANT TO BE BOB DYLAN!"—and it's a wonderful non sequitur. What in the world does it mean? As it seemingly was not a few years ago, what it means to be Bob Dylan is now an open question; as Taco Bell insists, there may be fewer open questions around these days than one might have thought.

Interview, *March 1995, with material from* Artforum, *January 1995*

Nostalgia

"Real Love" is the latest pseudo-Beatles single—constructed, like last year's "Free as a Bird," out of Paul, George, and Ringoisms added to a late '70s John Lennon tape—and it breaks me in half. When the historical/legal fiction currently trading under the name "Beatles" arrives at the title phrase of the song, a high Lennon voice begins to draw the phrase out, too slowly, too fast— you don't want the moment to end, but you can't wait to find out how it ends—and the sweetness is almost unbearable.

Once, listening to the tune on a bad day, I felt waves of nostalgia sweeping over me like nausea: the feeling was that physical, that irresistible. It was too much. I dug something the poet Robert Hass once said out of the back of my mind, trying to make sense of the moment. Hass was describing himself as a child, discovering a poem by Wallace Stevens: "It made me swoon, and made me understand what the word 'swoon' meant. It was the first physical sensation of the truthfulness of a thing I had ever felt." "Real Love" felt like that—just like that—just like Hass saying he read the Stevens poem again and again, "exactly like the way I lined up for a roller-coaster ride with a dime tight in my fist." But nostalgia is something like a yearning for that first time, isn't it? A yearning for something you probably never experienced, a sentimentalized false

memory. Hass was talking about discovery—isn't nostalgia the opposite? Isn't it worse: a taste for discovery in ruins, an emotional
decadence, the refuge of a crippled soul or an impoverished heart?
Hass spoke proudly; isn't nostalgia embarrassing?

I found myself trying to fight off the truthfulness of "Real Love."
There were some ugly facts behind the doors it opened. As I listened, the historical abstraction of what was lost when that twisted
cretin Mark Chapman shot John Lennon became as immediate as
responding to heat or cold. Somehow, the song distilled the purest
sense of Beatles—the whole new world so many people thought
they believed they were living in when the Beatles ruled their lives,
or when the Beatles simply ruled their own lives, if they ever really
did. This is where nostalgia takes you, into never-never land. But no
feeling as strong as the feeling loaded into "Real Love" can be tri-
fled with. Embarrassment in the face of a song is the reaction of
someone afraid to say what he or she loves, which changes easily
into the willingness to like what you're supposed to like, to do as
you're told. I began thinking about a conversation I'd had some
months before with David Thomas, behemoth singer for the great
punk band Pere Ubu.

We were backstage at a performance festival called Crossing
Border, in the Hague, talking about the old Carter Family song
"Worried Man Blues." We talked about the mystery of the song, the
way the rhythm contained a sense of fate. We talked like fans, our
faces bright. But then Thomas hesitated over a word, and his face
clouded under his tilted fedora. "I was about to say where I first
heard that song," he said. "But I'm too embarrassed." "Don't be
embarrassed," I said. "I know exactly where you heard it. You heard
it the same place I heard it. You heard it on the radio in 1959, when
it was a hit for the Kingston Trio." Easy for me to say; I hadn't
brought up who we'd first heard do the song.

Some time after that, I was walking through my local record
store, and a little box caught my eye: *The Kingston Trio—The Cap-*

ital Years, four CDs. I'd picked up a Kingston Trio best-of a while
before, played it, found it dull as dust, and didn't regret getting rid
of all my Kingston Trio LPs twenty or thirty years ago. But now this
thing in the record store was working on me like a magnet. For a
couple of weeks, I was drawn to its rack, and every time I passed it
by, I wondered how long I was going to be able to resist—altogether, four passes, I think. I bought it, took it home, and played all
107 cuts straight through.

It was the oddest experience I'd had in a long time: a removal, a
going back, a displacement. The Kingston Trio were huge in the
late '50s and early '60s, a collegiate folk trio that remade the pop
landscape. Their first record, "Tom Dooley," a version of a
nineteenth-century North Carolina murder ballad, had the same
effect on hearts and minds in 1958 that Nirvana's "Smells Like
Teen Spirit" did in 1991. Instantly, across the country, people had
to hear it again. They wondered what it was. They wondered why
what had been their favorite songs the day before now sounded
tired and fake.

The Kingston Trio box was like a time machine—a time machine
that, like "Real Love," went to an unreal place with real dates:
1960, 1961, 1962. The phoniness of the New Frontier was in the
music along with its glamour, JFK's beckoning hand along with his
crossed fingers, all blamelessly. Like the unreal Beatles song plead-
ing for real love, there was the delicious feeling of floating in an
overwhelmingly familiar world, a world where all illusions were
served like kings. This was a time when white people, madras
shirts, and good intentions could conquer the world. As the songs
rolled by, the phoniness of the music rose to the top, and turned
into a crust; the crust broke, and far beneath the surface you could
hear wish and regret: real people. Then they vanished, and again
nostalgia ruled: the desire to reach back and touch the perfect person you never were.

It can be hard, listening to music that on the surface sounds so innocent and playful, because the more deeply the well of nostalgia is plumbed, the more intense one's feelings of loss will become, and the listener will be stranded, caught between the embarrassment of mourning the loss of things that never existed and the embarrassment of finding that wounds that should have closed long ago are still open. "Real Love" and the Kingston Trio set are about times of enthusiasm that may have prepared the ground for murder. The records ask a strange question: what produced your deepest reaction, "Tom Dooley" or November 22, 1963? "Eight Days a Week" or John Lennon's killing? And if nostalgia is about deep feeling, what is it that you're truly nostalgic for, the music or the death?

Interview, *June 1996*

Mario Savio 1943–1996

I n the fall of 1964 at the University of California at Berkeley, the United States entered a new stage in its history: in places of privilege, ordinary people once again began to make history. The previous spring, students had helped organize highly effective protests against racist hiring practices in the San Francisco Bay Area. Regional business interests demanded an end to what they considered harassment, and the University—defined by its then-president, Clark Kerr, as a "knowledge factory" meant to serve American productivity—responded by banning all political acitivity on campus: distributing literature, collecting donations, circulating petitions, publicizing meetings. But some students on campus had just returned from Mississippi, where they had spent the summer in an effort to open a new public space where black Mississippians could exercise their rights as citizens; three of their comrades had been murdered. Now they found their own rights in question.

Among those students was Mario Savio, who died November 6, at the age of fifty-three, in Sebastopol, California. In 1964, he was a twenty-one-year-old philosophy major. Savio helped found the Free Speech Movement, whose members ranged from Students for Goldwater to the communist W. E. B. Du Bois Club. As Savio put it in 1965, looking back: "The Berkeley students now demand what hopefully the rest of an oppressed white middle class will someday demand: freedom for all Americans, not just for Negroes!"

That idea was a paradox in those days, when the campuses of great universities were almost all white, and throughout the fall of 1964 the entire university community was convulsed by it. There were fruitless negotiations, sit-ins, daily rallies, and, at the end, with the arrest of nearly eight hundred demonstrators and police violence in the midst of a grand convocation, historic events. Finally, nobody talked about anything else—but everybody talked, many as never before.

From the first, Mario Savio emerged as the principal spokesperson of the Free Speech Movement. There was often a scary rush in his speeches, sometimes a tense, brittle calm, but always vehemence—an insistence that choices were being made as you listened, which meant that you, too, had to choose. "He took the mantle," *Rolling Stone* editor Jann Wenner said when we talked over Savio's death; we were both undergraduates at Berkeley in the fall of 1964. "He rose to it. That probably took five years off his life." Savio seemed to embody not just will but also doubt, and the need to speak and act in the face of doubt.

"We have an *autocracy* which runs this university," Savio said on December 2, 1964, speaking to a huge crowd moments before the beginning of the climactic demonstration of the Free Speech Movement. "It's *managed*. I ask you to consider"—those last five words by now, because of Savio's peculiar sensibility, the common watchword of the Free Speech Movement, forming an invitation to judgment, turning a crowd into an assembly of thinking individuals who might decide to act in concert, and might not—"I ask you to consider, if this is a firm, and if the Board of Regents are the board of directors, and if President Kerr is in fact the manager, then I tell you something: the faculty are a bunch of employees, and we're the raw material! But we're a bunch of raw material that don't mean to be, to have any process put upon us—don't mean to be made into any product—don't mean, don't mean to end up being bought by some clients of the university, be they government be they industry be they organized labor be they anyone. We're human beings!"

Then came the words with which Savio's name will always be linked. "There's a time," he said—with the word "time" extended as Van Morrison might have extended it, rolled out, then pulled back in—"when the operation of the machine becomes so odious, makes you so sick at heart, that you can't take part; you can't even tacitly take part, and you've got to put your bodies upon the gears and upon the wheels, upon the levers, upon all the apparatus and you've got to make it stop. And you've got to indicate to the people who run it, to the people who own it, that unless you're free, the machine will be prevented from working at all."

And that, over the next days, is just what happened. Over the next several years, all across the country, it happened again and again.

At the Thirtieth Anniversary reunion of the Free Speech Movement, in 1994, only a certain bitter burr was missing from Savio's voice. He had long since absented himself from public life; perhaps following the example of civil rights leader Bob Moses, he had understood from the beginning that in public affairs, one's own celebrity only absolves others from having to make their own choices. This day, three decades later, he had been asked, he said with a laugh, to talk about "spiritual values." "This isn't my job," he said. "I know what my job has been, all these years. This isn't my job. But I'm going to try to do it anyway."

Savio didn't explain that day what his job had been; in a way, his death explained for him. His job was never to betray the history he and others had once made. That was the best way to ensure that it was a story that would hold its shape and continue to be told.

Savio's job was never to trade away whatever moral authority had attached itself to him—not for power, respectability, comfort, or peace of mind.

In his last months, Savio was again speaking out—in his own community, at the state university in Sonoma, California, where he was teaching—against Proposition 209, the state ballot initiative that promised to end all affirmative action against discrimination based on race or gender in California. It passed just four days after Savio suffered the heart attack that would kill him; it passed the day before he died.

Had history come full circle? The purpose of Proposition 209 was to inaugurate a movement to roll the country back to the days when, as in 1964 in the San Francisco Bay Area, there was only one form of affirmative action, for white men. To protest the initiative, the day after Savio's death five Berkeley students chained themselves to the Campanile, the campus tower, and were arrested; hundreds more marched through the campus. "We are able to do what we're doing because of Mario Savio," one student, Anthony Weathington, told a reporter. "When he died, he passed the torch on to us."

Rolling Stone, *December 26, 1996*

Allen Ginsberg 1926–1997

GO FUCK YOURSELF WITH YOUR ATOM BOMB."
That's the fifth line of "America," a poem Allen Ginsberg wrote in Berkeley, in 1956, just as he was finding his voice, and if you don't think it's funny maybe you're not an American. Certainly you don't live in the same country that was invented by tall-tale tellers—crafty and sly, indomitable and bitter—like Davy Crockett, Abraham Lincoln, Mark Twain, Sophie Tucker, William Faulkner, Mae West, Ralph Ellison, Cassius Clay, Bob Dylan, and Allen Ginsberg. That was always Ginsberg's country, whether in "A Western Ballad," a still, empty-desert song he composed in Paterson, New Jersey, in 1948—

> When I died, love, when I died
> there was a war in the upper air:
> all that happens, happens there

—or in a not-so-famous line from the famous "Howl," so famously debuted at the Six Gallery in San Francisco in 1955: "The cosmos instinctively vibrated at their feet in Kansas." The line confused me when I first came across it, so I made fun of it (" 'Kansas'?") to a friend who'd seen a lot more of the country than I had, as Ginsberg had. "Look," said the late Sandy Darlington, a writer and folksinger from Washington State, in words Ginsberg's Kansan comrades Bruce Conner and Michael McClure might have used, "anyone can run off to Japan like Gary Snyder and get the cosmos to vibrate at your feet at the top of Mount Fuji. To get the cosmos to vibrate at your feet in Kansas—well, then you know it's really *there*."

Like "Howl," like the 1966 "Wichita Vortex Sutra" (perhaps Ginsberg's greatest poem, certainly his most expansive, his most American-geographical: the cosmos doesn't vibrate at his feet in this Kansas, America itself does), "America" is, among other things, a comic rant. Its cadences are simple, blunt, and in perfect balance, so much so that the lines of the poem seem less made than found, overheard, taken off bathroom walls, one-liners anybody else would have thrown away that Ginsberg had a use for. Whether you hear the poem on the page, or on Ginsberg's four-CD set *Holy Soul Jelly Roll,* as Ginsberg in stand-up comedy drag recited the piece to a laughing Berkeley audience in 1956, or as collected on the three-CD set *The Beat Generation,* in a more somber recording Ginsberg made in 1959, the same qualities are present, and they take the poem out of the time from which it emerged, connecting it to all-American time—to, among other things, Jimi Hendrix's 1969 Woodstock version of "The Star Spangled Banner." There's a bemused but finally baffled—almost defeated—reverence toward the enormity and impenetrability of this thing, this America, this terrible, looming, witch-hunting Godzilla of infinite hope and charm (in 1956 Ginsberg performs the poem as if all of America's crimes against him, the queer-commie-dope-fiend-Jew, against itself, are a kind of shaggy-dog story, just like the poem itself). There's an instinctive, soon-enough cultivated impiety toward any or all of America's priests. And at rock bottom there is embrace, the impossibility of separation or exile or even pulling away: America as the tar baby, and Ginsberg's hand stuck. When I hear Ginsberg say *America go fuck yourself with your atom bomb,* I see him grinning with pleasure—the pleasure of telling your own country to go fuck itself, to be sure, but also the thrill of Slim Pickens riding his hydrogen bomb at the end of *Dr. Strangelove,* wahooing himself and everybody else into oblivion.

If Ginsberg had reformed himself, renounced a few past errors, smiled through a bit of youthful excess, he too might have been present at Bill Clinton's first inauguration, along with such dubious characters as Bob Dylan and Michael Jackson: on that day in 1993 the barriers of legitimacy were very low. As it happened, though, Ginsberg never renounced anything, in the same way that a statement often offered by elders, "There is nothing new under the sun," never passed his lips. When I met him last fall he seemed most excited by plans for his own MTV *Unplugged* special, "with Dylan, Paul McCartney, and Beck!" In all of his gestures of quietude or vehemence, basking in celebrity while at the same time raising old grudges from the dead, he was as he'd always been, spreading the word, promoting the cause, honoring his fellows, casing the room.

Even shaking hands for the first time, Ginsberg was cruising. Not well, moving very carefully, dressed like a retired, respectable Jewish bookseller from his parents' generation, he was a dirty old man in the guise of a clean old man, like the "clean old man" in *A Hard Day's Night.* "Fuck the Beatles, fuck the songs, fuck the cute direction and Marx Brothers comparisons," the late Lester Bangs once wrote, "it's BLATANTLY OBVIOUS that the most rock 'n' roll human being in the whole movie is the fucking grandfather!" So speaking softly, like a rabbi, Ginsberg spent a solid hour giving me hell for once calling Jack Kerouac a phony. Not because he knew him and I didn't, but because I hadn't read all there was to read, hadn't heard all there was to hear ("You don't know *Mexico City Blues,* do you? I didn't think so. I've just recorded it. I'll send you a copy."). Sitting there with Ginsberg, the America he had so often evoked so eloquently and so completely seemed small enough to see whole, and too hot to touch.

Rolling Stone, *May 29, 1997*

Tell-Tale Heart

In late May I was in England, trying to get people to read a book about Bob Dylan's 1967 Basement Tapes recordings, when the story that Dylan might be near death from a rare heart ailment hit the papers. The queer thing about the news was the seeming eagerness with which it was reported. You could almost hear a sigh of relief: "My liege, I bring great news! The '60s are over! Finally, we can close the book!"

You might figure if "the sixties" weren't over by 1997, they never would be. That didn't explain why what should have been straight news—diagnostic reports, information on the cancellation of Dylan's then-imminent U.K. and European tours—was freighted with preemptive obituaries. In paper after paper, lengthy career summaries were appended to the medical updates. Some dailies ran full-page essays probing the likely persistence or disappearance of the Voice of a Generation, if not the man, or the generation itself. It wasn't just the U.K. American papers, too, put out the call for obit writers. The network news shows wanted critics—not doctors—to draw deep breaths and wrap it all up. Showing its usual flair for matching the slick with the glib, *Newsweek* caught the mood with surpassing vulgarity, burning off the veil of solemnity adopted elsewhere: "The scary news blowin' in the wind last week was that Bob Dylan might be dying . . . Bob Dylan's *heart* in danger? It sounded like the death knell for the counterculture." You can almost hear them salivating, can't you? But why this breathless anticipation of a death that took place long ago?

Part of it is a fear that a singer who once seemed able to translate the vague and shifting threats and warnings of his time into a language that was instantly and overwhelmingly understood might be able to do it again. Part of it has to do with what Gerri Hirshey, in a recent *Rolling Stone* story on Dylan's son Jakob (in the top ten with his band, the Wallflowers, for all of the spring of this year), called "the foolish cultural myopia that has long plagued this country: We don't know what to make of artists who have the audacity to outlive their own revolutions." But there is something more. As Dylan hinted in the basement tune "This Wheel's On Fire"—theme song, rather frighteningly, for the culturally blasphemous '60s-in-the-'90s BBC series *Absolutely Fabulous,* and repeatedly keyed by Julie Driscoll's sly, certain reading of the line "If your mem'ry serves you well"—artists who stick around after their putative moment has passed are troublesome reminders of promises their audiences, perhaps more than the artists themselves, have failed to keep. So you can almost imagine the elegiac, funereal editorial cartoon, picturing a scattering of ashes and a caption: "Now Bob Dylan, too, is blowin' in the wind . . ."

Empowered media arrogance and arrant media stupidity bucked up against the perhaps little known but immovable fact that, as this near-celebration was taking place, Bob Dylan, no matter how ill—he did say, upon leaving the hospital, "I really thought I'd be seeing Elvis soon"—remained not merely a real person, but an artist at the very top of his game. Throughout the '90s he has been reshaping his music, honing a tight, cool little band, clearing his long-blocked throat with two dank, vitriolic, surreptiously ambitious albums of traditional songs, and reinventing himself onstage, not as a prophet or a careerist or a ruined reminder of better times, but as a lead guitarist. His shows began to jump: when I last saw him, two years ago, the long shout that kicked off his first number was like a flag unfurling.

The man so hopefully buried, dead or alive, as a creature of the past, as a prisoner of the counterculture he left behind long before it disappeared on its own, has spent the better part of seven years ("Seven years of this and eight years of that," he once said biblically of the true imperatives of folk music) biding his time. Earlier this year he recorded a new album, his first collection of original songs since 1990—unlikely to be released, I'd imagine, until Jakob Dylan makes room for it on the charts. If it does come out, it should be the first Bob Dylan album in well over twenty years to get whoever might hear it wondering what in the world it is.

The record is not like any other Dylan has issued, though the music isn't unlike some he's made: it has a dirt-floor feeling, the prosaic driving out the artful, with loose ends and fraying edges in the songs, songs that sound both unfinished and final. It all comes to a head with "Highlands," a flat, unorchestrated, undramatized monologue, wistful and broken, bitter and amused, that describes both a day and a life. The song, as I heard it one afternoon in a Sony Records office in Los Angeles, is about an older man who lives in one of Ed Kienholz's awful furnished rooms in the rotting downtown of some fading city—Cincinnati, Hollywood, the timeless, all-American downtown Nowheresville of David Lynch's *Blue Velvet*—getting up and going for a walk, maybe for the first time in weeks. In the course of the song he recounts his thoughts and adventures, recalls the people he met and those he avoided. In a certain sense nothing happens; from another perspective, a life is resolved.

"How long was that?" I asked the man who'd left me with a tape. "Seven minutes? Eight?" "Seventeen," he said. This from the man so many were ready to bury: a singer who, at the age of fifty-six, no longer a factor in the pop equation, can still beat the clock.

Interview, *August 1997*

August 16, 1997: The Drifter

Elvis Presley remains a singer. Just below the surface of the popular imagination, he remains a traveler.

This is not the story as it is currently reported. Elvis Presley, one will read everywhere on August 16, 1997, the twentieth anniversary of his death at the sad age of forty-two, is an icon. He is a hero to some and a joke to others. But more than anything he is a symbol of—

And of what it hardly matters. With Elvis Presley, it's as if it's the primacy of symbolism that's being celebrated.

The discourse of this symbology—the notion that an individual, a nation, or a whole borderless society of pop culture can be represented, or replaced, by a single Elvis-image, is barely interesting, if it is interesting at all. Perhaps more than ever before, the words "Elvis Presley" sell false memories, be they incarnated in dolls, key chains, T-shirts, books, statuettes, television shows, or news reports of thousands of fans from all over the world gathering at Graceland to walk in the footsteps of a man who, all these things exist to make it seem, lived mostly to be recalled as a martyr or a saint.

As interviewed by TV reporters from dozens of countries, women and men will step before the cameras and testify that, yes, it was in 1972, or 1975, in Baton Rouge, or Cincinnati, that they attended the first or last or twenty-third Elvis concert of their lives, "And I just got chills. It was as if he was singing just to me." But aside from a few obligatory film clips from 1956 or 1957, there will be no hint of what brought Elvis Presley, if not those who are now speaking, to such places.

It's in this sense that the memories are false. They contain no sense of the remarkable journey of a young man who took himself from the oblivion of poverty and scorn to the oblivion of unconscionable renown, all by means of the way he sang and looked and moved. Rather the memories reduce that journey to a fragment of speech as automatically replicable and transferable as any of the Elvis souvenirs meant to make the memory real, concrete: something one can touch. It's strange: if Elvis Presley sang, looked, and moved like nobody else, which he did, why are all the memories the same? But it is not strange. The reduction of memory to a few infinitely repeatable and exchangeable words is nothing more or less than the result that obtains when people are caught in a loop of pure capitalism—where, within a certain society, a certain market, a certain frame of reference, everything on sale sells everything else. And this process can proceed only if history and fantasy are both excluded.

In the case of Elvis Presley today, history means not the thousandth or even the first telling of Elvis Presley's rise and fall. It means an untold story: the still emerging fragments of his music as he made it, abandoned it, or forgot it, his testimony as he gave it, and then, with its echoes still reverberating everywhere, ceased to understand it. History means the barely contained teenage delight and lasciviousness of a 1955 Texas demo of Joe Turner's "Shake, Rattle and Roll," little noticed when it appeared thirty-seven years after the fact on *Elvis: The King of Rock 'n' Roll—The Complete 50's Masters;* or the fifteen amazing 1954–56 live performances recently collected on *Louisiana Hayride Archives, Volume 1;* or the 1968 backstage rehearsals on Ray Charles's "I Got a Woman" and

Rufus Thomas's "Tiger Man"—the sound of a jailbreak—only just issued on *Elvis Presley Platinum: A Life in Music;* or anyone's choice of their like. Here, with the sound the singer makes unmediated by his own adulation, either because in 1955 he does not yet believe in it or because for a single day in 1968, warming up for his first live audience in more than seven years, he cannot trust it, you can hear the making of music as the making of history. In a story that now seems preordained, you can hear incidents in that story that did not have to turn out as they did, incidents that sum up what the story is about and what it was for: the transformation of one man's personal culture into a world culture.

As for fantasy, that no longer means Elvis Presley as his fans, myself included, have so long presented him: as dreamer or hero. If not preordained, that story long ago reached the limits of its ability to tell anyone anything; as Isidore Isou, a Left Bank café prophet, put it in about 1950, "Truths no longer interesting turn into lies." For Elvis Presley today, real fantasy, fantasy that contains the engine of its own imaginings, means Elvis Presley as a bad conscience.

In death, Elvis Presley has become, for some, its angel. That means the emergence in fiction of unbelievably charismatic, sexually irresistible, mass-murdering demons in the guise of Jesse Garon Presley, Elvis's stillborn twin, as he appears as one Dewey in Sarah Shankman's 1992 Tupelo detective novel *The King Is Dead.* Impersonator or the real thing, emerging after more than fifty years of waiting his turn? You be the judge, Shankman says:

"Don't know what?" croaked Buddy at Slaughter, his little black face an angry fist beneath his fedora, which didn't make much of a rain hat.

"Don't know jack about the Presleys, I'll tell you that, you think Jesse Garon was born dead," said Slaughter.

"Who says he wasn't?" Harry wheeled.

"Momma. Momma says *her* momma, Granny, who delivered those twins said both of them were just as fine as wine. Two boys looked like they were gonna be identical."

"Boy's crazy," said Buddy. "Both of y'all's crazy. Him up there and you."

Dewey clutched the microphone with both hands. "All these years. Oh yes, *years* of darkness and pain. But the sunlight is here!"

It means passages such as these, from Kinky Friedman's 1993 New York City detective novel *Elvis, Jesus & Coca-Cola:*

I thought about a story McGovern had covered several years before, about a fourteen-year-old girl, a leukemia victim, who'd died somewhere in Kentucky. Her family at the hospital were at her side when she died. They were dumbfounded by her last words: "Here comes Elvis."

Tom Baker died as he was in the process of finishing a film on Elvis impersonators. Had he wrapped the film before his death? I couldn't ask him. Legs had worked on the film with him as his assistant. Couldn't ask Legs either.

It was well known that the Bakerman had been casual friends with Uptown Judy. His female admirers were legion. Could Tom and Judy have been dancing a good bit closer than anyone suspected? Couldn't ask Tom. Couldn't ask Judy.

Did Judy ever meet Legs? Couldn't ask Judy. Couldn't ask Legs.

There was no evidence of foul play in Baker's death, but then no one was looking for foul play. He was making an Elvis film and had mentioned to Ratso that he was afraid he'd end up meeting Elvis, and he did. Legs was helping Baker with the documentary. He ended up meeting Elvis, too. Could either of them have shown the film or talked about the film with Uptown Judy? Even assuming they had, what then? What was it about Elvis or a flock of pathetic impersonators that could set in motion the deaths of three people? Maybe it was far-fetched. Maybe it strained logic. But it was all I had.

I sat down and laid the cigar gently in the ashtray. I poured a strong portion of Jameson into the bull's horn and poured the bull's horn down my neck. I looked at the cat across the darkening, desperate afternoon.

"Here comes Elvis," I said.

The angel of death—but also its emissary, a rootless wanderer cut off from place and time, an angel of death not merely for this or that unlucky individual, but for the society he left behind. In the corners of the popular imagination to which the commercial media does not have ready access, Elvis Presley emerges as a brooding, wronged, unsatisfied, malevolent drifter, carrying with him memories of Charles Starkweather in Nebraska and Wyoming, Clutter family killers Perry Smith and Richard Hickock in Kansas, Richard Speck in Chicago, traveling under different names, with different faces, on a highway that in any case no longer recognizes him. This is the real-life Elvis Presley who former governor of Alabama George Wallace today says offered to have Arthur Bremer, the would-be assassin who left Wallace crippled for life, killed ("Of course I told him not to," Wallace says)—and it is the spectral Elvis captured most powerfully and most ambiguously in an art project by Ned Rohr of Arizona: an untitled 1997 Elvis calendar.

Here, month to month, in obsessively detailed photo collages and text, is the drifter's travelogue through an American wasteland. For each month's picture, Elvis Presley in a famous photo—a young Elvis reclining in bed, crawling facedown across a stage, or greeting fans backstage, an older Elvis emoting or just wearing a lei—is surrounded by members of indigenous tribes from all across the world: Ainu, Pygmies, Amerindians from the Amazon rain forest, Balinese. They are mostly silent, looking straight at the camera, which is to say at whoever is paging through the calendar. The tableaux can be very complex, as in April, where a young Elvis dances in front of a small '50s amplifier. Behind him is his original bassist, Bill Black, but also an old, bearded man dressed in the desert rags of a Bedouin, playing a rectangular stringed box. Behind the three men is a well-dressed crowd of curious African-Americans; only Elvis looks away.

He moves on through the year, mostly in the Southwest, but also in Missouri, Maine, Las Vegas, and somewhere off the fabled Highway 61, which runs from the top of Minnesota to the Gulf of Mexico. "Motel-6," he says in January. "Battle Creek, Michigan . . . Desperation drives me to another one of these places. The shoddiest I have ever seen. Shod being rare in any quantity, at the 6er's, I am spellbound. 6er's almost mythically sterile, antiseptic . . . This 6 crumbles at the edges. From the rusted steel and corroded cement of the big outdoor stairwells to the toilet that rocks a bit when mounted, wets the floor slightly with each flushing."

This is luxury on his road. Everything is breaking down. The people he meets are consumed by powerlessness and a lust for vengeance on enemies they cannot even name. "Slot machines to the horizon, well oiled and warm," he reports in November. "They sound like a Cadillac when you lose, like a beaten Chevy with the horn stuck when you win." In July he uses the soap dispenser in a McDonald's bathroom in Nogales, Arizona, as a microphone:

Very dimly lit by the conduction of daylight down a long yellow corridor. Closer inspection reveals that the fluoresecent tubes inside are barely glowing. Every twenty seconds or so they flash like an arc welder. The child in the stall next to me cries out at each burst of light. Mournful yelp fading in vibrato. Sometimes followed with a whimper. He was still in there when I left.

The tone of resignation and bemusement is steady, anger flaring up only when he remembers who he used to be, remembers a show he once gave, a song he once sang, the look in the eye of a girl he once met, but he won't name himself, only pretend he was someone else: "The music of Mister Brennan . . . THAT MULE, OLD RIVERS, AND ME . . . The women rush the stage. Tear at him, drool, convulse and buck. 'IIIIII am the nnnew, naked road man,' he sings, 'sssearching for the tiny blue lizards with thick legs.'" He is in an America where everyone hears the sound of the Cadillac, where everyone has already lost, where there is almost no one worth killing. As he could be remembering from a time before anyone knew the name Elvis Presley, from 1949, say, when the Presleys moved into Lauderdale Courts, the Memphis public housing project on Highway 61, he is in "the hostile, often pesky world of the uninsured," and only a fool can page through this 1997 and not feel judged.

Closing Ned Rohr's work, I imagined it being dropped from an airplane by the thousands over Memphis on August 16, while some unseen sound system pumped out that 1955 "Shake, Rattle and Roll," that 1968 "I Got a Woman," and I wondered what would happen—how those gathered at Graceland would respond, what they would say. I imagined people smiling and dancing, and throwing the calendars away. After all, who starts a new calendar in August?

Die Zeit *(Hamburg), August 15, 1997*

August 16, 1997: The Farmer

In a bank in Barcelona last fall there was an exhibition of photography under the title *Postwar Europe, 1945–1965, Art After the Deluge,* and a video to go with it, by M. Dolors Genovès. All she did was orchestrate stock footage from the postwar period—or rather she orchestrated the social war that followed the shooting war, using pop culture to undercut the authority and pomposity of official culture. On the Ed Sullivan show, Elvis Presley is performing "Hound Dog," smiling through the tinny kinescope sound. Dolors Genovès cuts simultaneously into the hard fullness of the studio recording of "Hound Dog" and to footage of Soviet commissars filling a steep auditorium, wildly pounding their fists as if in a mad attempt to keep time. The line "You said that you was high class, well, that was just a lie" comes up; it's matched to shots of Eisenhower, the Pope, de Gaulle. And then back to Elvis, who, mission accomplished, takes a bow.

That's the world-historical Presley, master of space and time. Someone very different could be found in a corner of the touring exhibition *Elvis + Marilyn: 2 × Immortal,* which recently closed in Honolulu after touching down in Boston, Houston, Charlotte, Cleveland, New York, Tulsa, Columbus, Nashville, and San Jose: the Presley in Joanne Stephens's 1991 *Homage to Elvis.*

It's a vision of where the Barcelona Samson came from; first, though, comes a vision of where he ended up. On top of a gilded, full-sized television set, Stephens has built a Byzantine altar, all in gold and studded with jewels. Dressed in the raiment of an Arabian caliph, a Young-Elvis doll holds a guitar and a microphone; cherubim surround him. Doves perch over praying hands reaching toward the diety; a halo of gold 45s is topped by a star. The assemblage is beautiful, absurd, gross, entrancing, its detail obsessive, its received, thirdhand, automatic conception undeniable. In other words, the work is too obsessive to be fake and too received to be real; it is absolutely contradictory and makes no sense. That's what draws you in: why would anyone work so long and hard, so lovingly and so carefully, on a parody of such an obvious idea?

Because, the piece as a whole answers, this is not a parody, this is a setting—or a setup. It's the TV set on which the altar rests that holds the drama.

Inside the screen, surrounded by wisps of white gossamer floss, is a diorama, in black and white, but mostly dulled brown. At its center is an image so small and colorless you can barely make it out: a cardboard cut-out of a famous photo of Elvis in 1955, dressed in the zoot-suit drapes of Memphis's Beale Street, his body loose, his head thrown back in ecstasy and abandon. His stage is dirt, his proscenium arch the gaping door of a barn, and his audience— gathered at a respectful distance—is a rapt crowd of cows, pigs, and chickens. The scene is uncanny in its stillness, without a hint of coyness or condescension; you get the feeling that something extraordinary is taking place in this silent concert. You lean forward, as if you could go through the screen, to take part.

There is the sense that this impossible concert actually happened—but only once. Or, like Abraham Lincoln giving his speeches to birds while standing on stumps, perhaps day after day, in Elvis's imagination, before he could allow himself to imagine a real audience, made up of human beings who might judge him. Still, as you look at the little cardboard figure, you can almost see it lifting off the ground and taking flight. You look at the altar first, look at it carefully, caught by its heedless elaboration, its visual noise, its shameless luxuria; after attending the concert taking place below the altar, you can't return to the altar without a sense of revulsion. The problem is, both the barnyard singer and the singing potentate are equally real; you cannot gainsay one with the other. Today, you can't have one without the other.

Turn on your own television on August 16: facsimiles of the altar Elvis will be all over it, as tapes from Memphis showing crowds of caped and jumpsuited Vegas-era Elvises unwind across the globe. Watching, you might hear yourself saying, "My God! Those lucky cows! What wouldn't I give to have been there!" But as Stephens imagined it and made it, the barnyard is a real aesthetic place, and you can get there listening to the rehearsal version of "That's All Right" collected on *Elvis Presley Platinum,* the four-CD set RCA has put out to mark the twentieth anniversary of the death of the barnyard singer, to mark the twentieth year of the reign of the angelic king.

Here you are on July 5, 1954, in Memphis, Tennessee, listening to a first, hesitant version of what would become Elvis's first single for Sun Records. You are listening to music that, had things turned out as they could have, might never have led to a finished record, might never have been released in any form, might never have been heard. You are listening to the first chapter of a story that might never have been told. Here you are in the barnyard, a cow, a pig, a chicken as you choose, and your reaction, now, even as you live in a world changed by the story as it was told, might be the same as that of any barnyard creature watching the skinny boy with the cool clothes dancing in the dirt: "Who is this guy? What in the world does he think he's doing?"

Salon, *August 12, 1997, with material from* Artforum, *January 1997*

A Map You Can Throw Away

The challenge of Bob Dylan's *Time Out of Mind* is to take it at face value. This is as bleak and blasted as any work a major artist in any field—and by major artist I mean an artist with something, a reputation, an audience, to lose—has offered in ages.

At first the music is shocking in its bitterness, in its refusal of comfort or kindness. Then it settles into something like a conventional set of songs, and then a curve in one of them—the finality of a life left behind in the way Dylan gets rid of the seemingly traditional lines "I been to Sugartown I shook the sugar down" in "Tryin' to Get to Heaven," perhaps, or the long, quiet drift of "Highlands," a number so unassumingly mysterious you feel it could unwind its ball of string over the entire length of the record without exhausting itself—upends any casual listening and throws every bit of wordplay or quiet testimony into harsh relief, revealing a tale that is finished and whole.

The story opens with the singer walking dead streets and ends with him walking the streets of an almost deserted city: "Must be a holiday," he mutters to himself, as if he couldn't care less if it is or not. Images of homelessness and pointless wandering drive song after song. Sometimes that motif suggests a man who doesn't want a home ("I know plenty of people," he tells you in a way that says he knows you won't believe him, "put me up for a day or two"); sometimes it calls up the tramp armies of the Great Depression, or the film director in Preston Sturges's 1941 *Sullivan's Travels*, disguising himself as a hobo and riding the boxcars like a real railroad bum so he can meet the masses, finding instead that the rags of poverty and anonymity are easier to put on than take off.

As in that old movie, made as the Depression was about to disappear into the maw of the Second World War, when *Time Out of Mind* plays another country comes into view. This is a land as still as the plains, its flatness broken only by a violence of tone or the violence of syncopation, of hard truths or a band's rhythms rushing up on each other like people running out of a burning house. "I thought some of 'em were friends of mine, I was wrong about 'em all," Dylan sings in "Cold Irons Bound," a number that harks back to Jack Kelly's 1933 Memphis blues "Cold Iron Bed," which is about a deathbed. Kelly's first record was "Highway No. 61 Blues," and now "Cold Irons Bound" moves like it's on it, Dylan letting the whiplashed rhythm carry his words around their turn. The line isn't stressed but swung—"*Wrrrrrong* about 'em *alllll*"—with the first word tipped up, the last tipped down, an organ sweeping up the song like wind. For a moment the landscape—which from song to song takes names, "Missouri," "Chicago," "New Orleans," "Baltimore," "Bostontown"—is erased by the movement taking place upon it, and the singer moves out of earshot; when he returns nothing has changed.

The country that emerges is very old, and yet fresh and in sharp focus, apparently capable of endless renewal. At the same time the place is very new, and all but worn out. "I got new eyes," Dylan sings coolly, in one of the deadliest lines of his writing life. "Everything looks far away." Verbal, melodic, and rhythmic signatures from old American music, from ballads, blues, and gospel, fit into the songs on *Time Out of Mind* as naturally, seemingly as inevitably as breaths—say, in the way a betrayed Dock Boggs, standing on the railroad platform of his "Danville Girl" in 1927, passes the song's cheap cigar to the betrayed singer now "Standing in a Doorway," trying to live his life "on the square." That the reappearance of the forgotten past in an empty present is a talisman of *Time Out of Mind* is sealed by the artwork imprinted directly onto the disc: Columbia's "Viva-tonal Electrical Process" label from the late 1920s, a label that ran one series for "Race" or Negro recordings, another for "Old Time" or country. Dylan's record spins on that label in the way certain of its choruses and verses seem to write themselves, tossed off with a throwaway gruffness that says Dylan trusts that after hearing half of a line the listener will automatically complete it even before he, Dylan, has sung it: "That's all right, mama, you / Do what you gotta do," as he drawls in "Million Miles." But the label also spins in reverse, until nothing on it can be read. For all the occasions where the music draws on some collective, illiterate American memory, as many incidents in the music seem to come out of nowhere, the nowhere that is both the present and the future of the country where the story Dylan is telling takes place: "Maybe in the next life," Dylan sings elsewhere in "Million Miles," "I'll be able to hear myself think." From song to song, with resignation and a sly, twisting humor, with the flair of a Georgia fiddle band or the dead eyes of a gravedigger, the singer poses the same question, sometimes almost grinning, as when he asks "if everything is as hollow as it seems."

Listening to *Time Out of Mind* is like watching people pass through a revolving door: the ambiance is that abstract, vague, and untouchable. You have as much right to expect someone to reappear as quickly as she vanished as to expect never to see her again. That's how it is with the central incident in "Highlands," where a man walks into a restaurant, empty except for a waitress. They banter, as if it's expected of them, almost flirt, but unpleasantly, neither willing to translate the sexual tension between them into a smile, and in an instant—an instant of fatigue, boredom, or his or her memory of too many instants just like it, any of that or just a single word given an edge it shouldn't carry—the mood dies. The room, the city surrounding it, the nation surrounding the city, its entire history and all of the pieces of music and dramatic scenes that so quietly enter and depart from this one—"One Meat Ball," Skip James's 1931 "Hard Time Killing Floor Blues," Jack Nicholson's diner routine in *Five Easy Pieces*, Dylan's own "Desolation Row" filtered back through Robert Burns's half-original folk song "Farewell to the Highlands"—all of that, from song to scene to nation, turns hostile and cold. For a moment the waitress turns her back, and the air in the restaurant is now so mean you're as relieved as the singer when he silently slips out of his chair. You can feel yourself tensing your muscles as he tenses his. Yet the singer barely has to go out the door, or the song down its Boston street, for you to imagine that this might have been the last conversation the singer ever had, that it's years and years in the past—or for you to imagine that, in Boston, on the ground where the nation began, it's the last conversation that could even begin to suggest the possibility of a story that hasn't been told here before.

That is what is new in *Time Out of Mind*, and in the country it traces, as if the disc were a map you can read once and then throw away. Though crafted out of fragments and phrases and riffs older than anyone living, bits of folk languages that joke and snarl as if for the first time, this is a map of a country that has used itself up, and the peculiar thrill of *Time Out of Mind* is in its completeness, its absolute refusal to doubt itself.

This new story does not come out of nowhere, or at the least it is not quite a solitary voice in the wilderness—it's a doubled voice in the wilderness. The same cynical, damaged, sardonic, utterly certain acceptance of one's own nihilism has been all over Bill Pullman's face in the last few years, in *Malice, The Last Seduction, Lost Highway*, and especially in the recent *The End of Violence*—for just as *Time Out of Mind* is an end-of-the-American-century record, closing with a fantasy of a retreat to the Scottish highlands, to the border country where some of the oldest American ballads first came to life, Bill Pullman, in this last film, is the ultimate end-of-the-American-century man. His face has the cast of entitlement, an expectation of triumph and adventure, as the movie begins; like the narrator in *Time Out of Mind,* he knows soon enough that in some essential way the story he has to tell ended before he even took the stage, and that knowledge only increases his wariness.

In *The End of Violence,* Pullman is a movie producer whose life, like that of Preston Sturges's director John L. Sullivan—played by all-American boy Joel McCrea, a match for Pullman in his romantic or heroic roles—is turned inside out. We first see him in his aerie looking down over all of Los Angeles, surrounded by computers and cell phones; soon he is dressed in rotting clothes, part of a crew of Spanish-speaking gardeners, hefting his leaf blower, moving through the perfectly groomed estates where, days before, he looked past his own gardeners as a lord. With an old baseball cap on his head, unnoticed by everyone else, a white incarnation of Ralph Ellison's invisible man, a drifter, unshaven and penniless, he misses nothing, but the more he understands, the less need he has to say anything to anyone. Who would listen?

Blowing his harmonica through passages in "Tryin' to Get to Heaven" until the song builds on itself like a folk version of the Ronettes' "Be My Baby," it's not a question Bob Dylan has to ask himself. Though most often spoken of today as a figure from the past, someone now marginalized along the dimmer borders of the pop world, Dylan might well answer that when the music is as uncompromised as it is on *Time Out of Mind,* it's the old songs and the people in them that listen; the dead streets of his new songs, as depopulated, somehow, as the streets of his 1963 "Talkin' World War III Blues," will have to take care of themselves. And Dylan may be far less marginalized than he seems; he may be less of a crank, or a pop outsider, than an embodiment of the sort of cultural memory he plays with on *Time Out of Mind*.

Last May, in the college town of Iowa City, on the Dubuque Mall, a soul band set up its amplifiers, and soon a woman was belting out Chaka Khan imitations, driving the afternoon street singers into corners, where their acoustic-guitar-and-harmonica renditions of Prince's "Purple Rain" and the Replacements' "I Will Dare" could barely be heard. As night came on the crowds got younger, the basement bars noisier, the street singers more numerous—by ten, there was one every twenty feet or so, each looking bereft and ignored, each with a girlfriend in idolizing attendance—and the repertoire more ambitious: "These Foolish Things," "You Belong to Me," the old folk song "Railroad Bill," something that must have been by Phil Ochs, the Rolling Stones' "Singer Not the Song." Every singer seemed to want nothing more than to sound like Bob Dylan, and in his own way every one did.

Die Zeit *(Hamburg), October 10, 1997 /*
San Francisco Examiner Magazine, *November 2, 1997*

The Story Untold

The end of the year is supposed to be a season of adding up accomplishments, separating winners from losers, and declaring, in a smug, vaguely bored tone of voice, that the year wasn't a complete waste of time. But a given year is more than anything else time that has passed, an occasion that will never return—and in 1997 most of what could have been done wasn't. Think about it that way and you might find yourself drawn not to ten-bests but to the cut-off, the broken-down, the used-up, the morbid. Never mind what Bill Clinton did or didn't do in the last twelve months; from this seat on the train, it's far more interesting to imagine what he'll be doing when it's all over. He'll be fifty-four when he leaves office, facing a future as blank as that of any pop star five years after her last hit. He'll spend the next twenty years as—U.S. Senator from Arkansas? California? Editor of *Newsweek*? Fixer for the Greater East Asian Co-Prosperity Sphere? Stuffed party animal for William Styron, Carly Simon, and the rest of the Martha's Vineyard crowd?

Bill Clinton may or may not have a future (who would have thought that Strom Thurmond, who in 1948 led the South out of the Democratic convention to protest the party's first civil rights plank, would still be poisoning our national life almost half a century later?), but it's taken for granted that pop figures don't have one, unless they're willing to perform the same songs in the same way forever. Thus while it's no fun at all to imagine what Mick Jagger might be doing in ten years, it's a game with Polly Harvey, but only if you leave the world of pop behind. With termite artists like Harvey—blind creators, boundary eaters, as Manny Farber defined them in 1962, right about the time the Rolling Stones were forming—it's impossible to imagine their work into the future, as impossible for the artist as for the fan.

Merely by showing up and doing it all over again, the Rolling Stones leave a blank spot in the pop atmosphere of 1997, a blank no one else is big enough to fill. In the same way, a real creator's absence can be more powerfully felt than most anyone else's presence. In ten years Harvey might be Annie Lennox, an ex-punk video nightclub singer with an occasional surprise in her; she might be a bar owner, a cultist, or dead. But the bye she took in 1997— no PJ Harvey records, no shows—casts a longer shadow than Sleater-Kinney's *Dig Me Out*, Van Morrison's *The Healing Game*, the studied hijinks of Oasis, or even the Spice Girls—right now the most politically potent act on the planet, given that the cultural reaction they embody seems to be the principal right-wing check on Tony Blair, who can read pop signs more clearly than Bill Clinton. Polly Harvey is unreadable, but you can't help trying—that's what she's all about. As a presence she's a black hole. No energy on the boards in 1997 was as alluring as her gone missing.

You can decipher almost any pop music these days as a marketing strategy before you hear it; that's never been true with Harvey. She appeared naked on the cover of her first album, but as record followed record, it was as if a layer of flesh—flesh as a kind of clothing, a body mask that gave the illusion of nakedness—was being removed with every new year, until finally, with *To Bring You My Love*, her last full project, she appeared on the cover in a glamorous red dress and in sound was exposed down to her bones. As in Josef Škvorecký's disturbing novella *Emöke*, or Shirley Jackson's story "The Lottery," the music had the feeling of a lost-and-found pagan ritual, as if the audience it was aimed at was either long gone or yet to come.

Touring at the time, in 1995, Harvey came onstage and left behind the one show I've ever seen that was so willed and yet so unstable only the word "profound" seemed up to it. Dressed in about eight layers of blouses, skirts, underwear, and scarves, she grimaced and whirled with the exaggerated movements and irresistible conviction of a silent-movie actress. She was Valentino's beautiful wife Natacha Rambova; she was Rambova's mentor Alla Nazimova, heroine of her own production of *Salome,* mistress in Hollywood of the Garden of Allah. For a moment you wondered if Harvey could possibly keep all the promises she was making, and then you flinched, certain that she could—including the promise that she could turn you into Lot's wife, or that to gaze upon her for another instant would be to turn to stone. There's an old album by the bluesman Johnny Shines, *Last Night's Dream,* with a cover that shows a woman waking to find that her hair has turned into a nest of snakes; this night, Harvey could have played that role, not cracking a smile until she was on her way to the wings. Time passes, occasions that will never return depart as if they had never been, and 1997 may be most memorable because as Harvey stayed off the stage, no one came close to holding her place.

If you read the papers, a sense of absence can overwhelm any presence, waste completely replacing the piling up of wealth and reputation. In the obituaries in 1997, certain generations began to disappear en masse. There was the first wave of the civil rights generation, mostly southern blacks and northern whites who in the '40s and '50s risked their lives and their names—their fortunes and their sacred honor, as their precursors put it—for a battle that at the time few believed would ever be really joined, let alone won. There was the generation that fought Nazis, or escaped them. "I was not there to witness the worst, only the beginning," wrote Mary

Jayne Gold, who died on October 5 at the age of eighty-eight, near Saint-Tropez. In 1940, as a young American heiress in Marseilles, a fancy tourist, she helped hundreds of Jews, among them Marc Chagall, Jacques Lipchitz, and Hannah Arendt, escape from France. "Even then," she remembered in her memoirs, "I was sometimes embarrassed into a sort of racialism—like being ashamed of belonging to the human race." She herself fled France in 1941; on the occasion of her death, a friend told the Associated Press that Gold "felt that only one year in her life really mattered." Again it is absence that is the greatest presence: ten, twenty, fifty years from now, who in the United States, who anywhere in the West, will say the same of 1997 for any form of public life?

Pop is a form of public life; maybe that's why I felt this absence most listening to *Meadville*, a live album recorded around Europe (Rennes, Amsterdam, Ljubljana, Hilversum) in 1996 by David Thomas with Keith Moliné and Andy Diagram, a.k.a. Two Pale Boys, on apparatus "generating two or three instrument voices at any one point," whatever that means. *Meadville* is stirring, worrisome, a joke, a joke with a constant, spooky undertow, and it's not even a real album you can go into a store and buy for $14 or so— it's attached as a bonus CD to a box set of the solo albums Thomas released between 1981 and 1987, when his band, Pere Ubu, was more or less on hiatus, a set sort of pompously called *David Thomas, Monster*. Meadville is a town in Pennsylvania; I don't know why the disc is named for it, but I think the reason I've played it more than any other music released in 1997 is that when Thomas's joke is at its best, the performance is all about uncertainty, about dread, a dread that spins the present into the future. Standing on his foreign stages as a backwoods, unwashed, uncivilized, un-shutupable American, testifying to The Way the World Looks Now, telling long, tangled shaggy-dog stories about the end of the Enlightenment and mishearing Tammy Wynette's greatest hit, Thomas is possessed by dread, possessed by the future, by whatever's coming next, because like a reader rushing to the end of Raymond Chandler's *The Big Sleep* but reading the best pages twice, he can neither wait to discover how it all turns out nor abandon the pleasure of not knowing, not yet. Listening to Thomas, you don't hear a career, though he has a long one—that is, you don't hear a marketing strategy, even though Thomas's place in the pop market is one of his constant subjects. You hear time passing, you hear time that has passed, you hear an odd commitment to the art of talking out loud, and a bet that someone might be listening, and might talk back, one of these days.

"Because I'm David Thomas, *legend*," he says from the stage, explaining why, at a party filled with rock stars, everyone wants to talk only to him. Assume the party never took place—Thomas carries the moment off. He's been around long enough. He appeared as a legend even as his career began, in the early 1970s, in a tiny Cleveland milieu that was all paradox, a milieu that was at once proto-dada and postpunk. Announcing himself then as Crocus Behemoth, he fronted an experimental, assaultive, abstract, Seeds-influenced band called Pere Ubu because, I've always believed, he looked just like Alfred Jarry's Ubu woodcuts—and sounded like Ubu at Colonnus. It was pure modernism: a performance of the end of the world as the best joke of all. "Maybe I'm nothing but a shadow on the wall," Thomas sang in 1975 on "Heart of Darkness," the band's first, do-it-yourself single; the reference seemed to be to images of men and women left on walls in Hiroshima.

Thomas bellowed, he whispered, he moaned, he squawked, he came up with the strangest cracker-barrel philosopher-king drawl; against the band's punk clatter and difficult-music cacaphonies he took his words and splayed melodies from old folk songs and the inside moves of the most degraded pop hits. If at first he gave off feral hints of Fatty Arbuckle, as the years went on his Ubu shaded off into characters harder to read: Ignatius J. Reilly from John Kennedy Toole's novel *A Confederacy of Dunces,* Jack Nance's

Henry Spencer in David Lynch's *Eraserhead*. By the time Thomas reached his European stages in 1996 he had become a creature of wonder, so alive to the possibilities of motion and chance in a word or a phrase that any given song he might choose to sing would be less a song than a road, a road out or a road back.

He's a free man; Pere Ubu never had any hits, so he doesn't have to sing them. Solo, he sings songs from the band's recent albums *Story of My Life* and *Ray Gun Suitcase*, but they aren't referents to anything; they're performed not as selling points but as routes from here to there, from love to death, hit to miss. "I found my thrill / In Nowhereville" might be the dullest, most obvious, most market-tested moment on the record (Fats Domino ran it through the focus group in 1956)—the only moment that explains itself.

Thomas's argument is that nothing worth understanding explains itself—he can't explain why he's singing or why you're listening; his bet is that you can't either—and that this lack of clarity, though fatal in the market, nevertheless keeps the conversation going, so long as the clues are as good as Raymond Chandler's, who never worried if a clue, like the dead chauffeur in *The Big Sleep*, led nowhere. Thomas may find a clue in, say, the suburban developer's slogan "If You Lived Here You Would Be Home By Now," locking into its impenetrable weirdness, excavating its mathematical absolutes and its epistemological slipknot, and doing so with a love of repetition for its own sake that only rock 'n' roll can justify. "Marching on the home of the blues marching on the home of the blues marching on the home of the blues," he chants, until you can see a whole army behind him, pitchforks waving, torches held high—for weeks I heard the phrase clearly not as "home" but as "House of the Blues," and thought Thomas was summoning true believers to the destruction of the nightclub chain, city by city, block by block, folk art collection by folk art collection, and now, just as Thomas can only hear "Stand By Your Man" as "Stand by,

Earthman" (the story of how and why is endless), I can't hear his blues chant any other way. You're a free listener, *Meadville* says— you write the songs. But it also says, there are no songs, no hits. What you love most you have misheard. If you lived there you would be here by now. As a matter of fact, you are. But no one else is.

"There goes old man Thomas," Thomas announces, describing the figure he cuts in his neighborhood, the kids on the street pointing and snickering: "There goes old *wheezer*." He breaks into a fit of coughing that's funny until it goes on too long. He's placed himself in the audience, pointing and snickering at himself as, a quarter century after he first stepped out of anonymity, he continues to mimic a pop star, describing from the stage, in indeciperable tones, how Pere Ubu once opened for Kool and the Gang, who could "talk to the *ladies*"—which, as avant-garde legends, Pere Ubu could never convincingly do. Time breaks up; the subject matter of *Meadville* is the last twenty-five years as an irrelevance that has prepared the singer for the next year, should there be one. In other words, on my favorite record of 1997, the year barely exists. It is all absence, a waste of passed time, and it performs a queer trick on time: to imagine Thomas in ten or twenty years into the future takes no more and no less effort than it does to imagine him just over the line into 1998.

"We did the first record not as a beginning, but as an ending," Thomas wrote of *The Modern Dance*, Pere Ubu's 1978 debut album, in the most moving words I've ever read in a press release— it was for the 1993 *Story of My Life,* which ends with "Last Will and Testament" and begins with "Wasted." (A sea shanty accordion behind him, Thomas declaims a firm, stately rhythm. "The sum of the years, the story untold," he says to a hearty male chorus, and together they plunge into the void: "We were *throwing time* away / Breathlessly *throwing time* away / Oh Oh Oh Oh *throwing time* away / Recklessly *throwing time away.*") "We wanted to leave an artifact that someone would discover. We were done—we were about to move on to real life." But it didn't work out that way, Thomas went on: "We had the misfortune to have a dream and vision at an early age that was too powerful to shake in older life. If you're young enough and if the vision is strong enough, you will never lose it—like people who became Communists in the '30s. They had no alternative but to continue. With us, it's a similar thing. We saw what rock music should be and could be and nothing less than that would ever do for us." The true vision always recedes before the visionary; if you lived there already, Thomas says over and over in 1997, you wouldn't be home by then, but don't worry about it. Worry about something else.

Artforum, *December 1997*

Part Three

. . . .

THE LAST
LAUGH

★ *1998–2000* ★

Andy Warhol and Bob Dylan at the Factory, 1965

J. T. Walsh

I like Oliver Stone movies, but I stayed away from his *Nixon* when it was in the theaters in 1995, and never rented it on video. As the child of good California Democrats, I grew up hating Nixon. When I was in my twenties and he was president, he gave me more reason to hate him than I ever wanted. When he died I didn't want to think about him anymore.

One night, though, flipping channels after the late news, I happened onto *Nixon* running on HBO, and I didn't turn it off. I was pulled in, played like a fish through all the fictions and flashbacks, dreaming the movie's dream: waiting for Watergate.

It came into focus with a strategy session in the Oval Office. Anthony Hopkins's Nixon is hunching his shoulders and looking for help. James Woods's impossibly reptilian H. R. Haldeman is stamping his feet like Rumpelstiltskin and fulminating about "Jew York City." Others raise their voices here and there—and off to the side is J. T. Walsh, the canniest and most invisible actor of the 1990s, doodling.

As almost always, Walsh was playing a sleaze, a masked thug, here a corrupt government official, White House advisor and Watergate conspirator John Erlichman—as elsewhere he played a slick Hollywood producer, a college-basketball fixer, the head of a crew of aluminum siding salesmen, a porn king who makes home sex videos with his own daughter, a slew of cops (Internal Affairs bureaucrat on the take in Chicago, leader of a secret society of white fascists in the LAPD), and a whole gallery of con artists, confidence men who seem to live less to take your money than for the satisfaction of getting you to trust them first.

Walsh in the Oval Office is physically indistinct; he usually was. At fifty-two in 1995 he looked younger, just as he looked older than his age when, after eight years as a stage actor—most notably as the frothing sales boss in David Mamet's *Glengarry Glen Ross*—he began getting movie roles in 1986. Except near the end of his life, when his weight went badly out of control, his characters would have been hard to pick out of a lineup. Like Bill Clinton he was fleshy, vaguely overweight, with an open, florid, unlined face, a manner of surpassing reasonableness, blond in a way that on a beige couch would all but let him fade into the cushions. He had nothing in common with even the cooler, more sarcastic heavies of the forties or the fifties—Victor Buono's police chief in *To Have and Have Not,* or the coroner in *Kiss Me Deadly,* their words dripping from their mouths like syrup with flies in it. He had nothing to say to the heavies appearing along side of him in the multiplexes—Dennis Hopper's psychokillers, Robert Davi's scumsuckers, Mickey Rourke with slime oozing through his pores, the undead Christopher Walken, his soul cannibalized long ago, nothing left but a waxy shell.

Walsh's characters are extreme only on the inside, if he allows you to believe they are extreme at all; as he moves through a film, regardless of how much or how little formal authority his character might wield, Walsh is ordinary. You've seen this guy a million times. You'll see him for the rest of your life. "What I enjoy most as an actor," he said in December 1997, two months before his death from a heart attack, "is just disappearing. Most bad people I've known in my life have been transparent. Not gaunt expressions—they're

Milquetoasts. It's Jeffrey Dahmer arguing with cops in the street about a kid he's about to eat—and he convinces them to let him keep him. And takes him back up and eats him. What is the nature of evil that we get so fascinated by it? It's buried in charm, it's not buried in horror."

Walsh's charm—what made you believe him, whether you were another character standing next to him in a two-shot, or watching in the audience—was a disarming, everyday realism, usually contrived in small, edge-of-the-plot roles, his work with a single expression or a line staying with you long after any memory of the plot crumbled. As a lawyer happily tossing Linda Fiorentino criminal advice while an American flag waves in the breeze outside his window, Walsh taps into a profane quickness that for the few moments he's on screen dissolves the all-atmosphere-all-the-time film noir gloom of *The Last Seduction*. In *The Grifters*, as Cole Langley, master of the long con, he radiates an all-American salesman's glee ("Laws will be broken!" he promises a mark) that makes the hustlers holding the screen in the film—Anjelica Huston, John Cusack, Annette Bening—seem like literary conceits. Yet it all comes through a haze of blandness, as it does even when Walsh plays a sex killer, a crime boss, a rapist, a racist murderer, as if at any moment any terrible impression can be smoothed away: *How could you imagine that's what I meant?*

In the Oval Office his Erlichman, whom America would encounter as the snarling pit bull lashing back at Senator Sam Ervin's Watergate investigations committee, retains only the blandness, occasionally offering no more than "I don't know if that's such a good idea" before returning to his doodles. It was this blandness that allowed Walsh to flit through history, in *Nixon* playing White House fixer Erlichman, in *Hoffa* Teamster president Frank Fitzsimmons, locked into power by a deal Erlichman helped broker, in *Wired* reporter Bob Woodward, who helped bring Erlichman down—but as Walsh sits with Nixon and Haldeman and the rest you can imagine

him absenting himself from the action as it happens, instead con-
templating all the roles in all the movies that have brought him to
the point where he can take part in a plot to con an entire
nation.

What makes Walsh such an uncanny presence on screen—to the
degree that, as the trucker in the first scenes of *Breakdown,* or
Fitzsimmons as a drunken Teamster yes-man early in *Hoffa,* he
seems to fade off the screen and out of the movie, back into everyday life—is while the blandness of his characters may be a disguise,
it can be far more believable than whatever evil it is apparently
meant to hide. Even as it is committed, the evil act of a Walsh character can seem unreal, a trick to be taken back at the last moment,
even long after that moment has passed—and that is because his
characters, the real people he is playing, can appear to have no true
identity at all. You can't pick them out of the lineups of their own
lives.

At the very beginning of his film career, in 1987, in David
Mamet's *House of Games,* Walsh is the dumb businessman victim
of a gang of con men running a bait-and-switch, then a cop setting
them up for a bust, then a dead cop, then one of the con men himself, alive and complaining, "Why do I always have to play the
straight man?" *The straight man?* you ask him back. In *Breakdown,*
in a rare role in which he dominates a film from beginning to end,
he first appears as a gruffly helpful trucker giving a woman a ride
into town while her husband waits with their broken-down car. She
disappears, and when the husband, with a cop at his side, finally
confronts the trucker, Walsh's irritated denial that he's ever seen
this man in his life seems perfectly justifiable—even if, as Walsh
saw it, that scene "had a residual effect on the audience. 'Don't
catch me acting'—when I lied, deadpan, on the road, you hear people in the audience: 'He's *lying!*'" The moment came loose from
the plot, as if, Walsh said, "I'm not just acting"—and that, he said,
was where all the cheers in the theaters came from when in the fi-

nal scene he dies. He had fooled the audience as much as the other characters in the movie; that's why the audience wanted him dead.

Walsh's richest role came in John Dahl's *Red Rock West*. The mistaken-identity plot—with good guy Nicolas Cage mistaken for hit man Dennis Hopper—centers on Walsh's Wayne Brown, a Wyoming bar owner who's hired one Lyle from Texas to murder his wife. As Brown, Walsh is also the Red Rock sheriff—and he is also Kevin McCord, a former steelworks bookkeeper from Illinois who along with his wife stole $1.9 million and was last seen on the Ten Most Wanted list. Walsh plays every role—or every self—with a kind of terrorized assurance that breaks out as calm, certain reason or calm, reasoned rage. He's cool, efficient, panicky, dazed, quick, confused. You realize his character no longer has any idea who he is, and that he doesn't care—and that it's in the fact that they don't care that the real terror of Walsh's characters resides. You realize, too, watching this movie, that in all of his best roles Walsh is a center of nervous gravity. His acting, its subject, is all about absolute certainty in the face of utter doubt. Yes, you're fooled, and the characters around Walsh's might be; you can't tell if Walsh's character is fooled or not.

At the final facedown in *Red Rock West*, all the characters are assembled and Dennis Hopper's Lyle is holding the gun. "Hey, Wayne, let me ask you something," he says. "How'd you ever get to be sheriff?" "I was elected," Walsh says with pride. "Yeah, he bought every voter in the county a drink," his wife sneers—but so what? Isn't that the American way? Get Walsh out of this fix and it wouldn't have been the last election he won.

Watching this odd, deadly scene in 1998, I thought of Bill Clinton again, as of course one never would have in 1992, when *Red Rock West* was released and Clinton was someone the country had yet to really meet. In the moment, looking back, seeing a face and a demeanor coming together out of bits and pieces of films made over the last dozen years, it was as if—in the blandness, the disarming charm, the inscrutability, the menace, the blondness, moving with big, careful gestures inside a haze of sincerity—Walsh had been playing Clinton all along. He wasn't, but the spirit of the times finds its own vessels, and, really, the feeling was far more queer: it was as if, all along, Bill Clinton had been playing J. T. Walsh.

adapted from "One Step Back,"
New York Times, *January 5, 1998,*
for O.K. You Mugs: Writers on
Movie Actors, *1999*

Heaven's Gate

In 1997, Jakob Dylan's band, the Wallflowers, sold four million copies of its second album, *Bringing Down the Horse.* Led by the single "One Headlight," it stayed in the top ten for most of the year. Sustained by the single "Three Marlenas," the album is still on the radio.

Thirty-five years after the release of his first album, Bob Dylan, Jakob Dylan's father, was all over the news. Death-scare headlines circled the globe in May when he was hospitalized with a heart infection. In September, he performed for the Pope in Bologna ("You ask me, how many roads must a man go down?" the Pope as music critic responded. "One road: the road of Jesus Christ!"). In October, he released *Time Out of Mind,* his first album of original songs in seven years, to universal acclaim; that same month, he received the Dorothy and Lillian Gish Prize for Achievement in the Arts. In December he was honored at the Kennedy Center in Washington.

This confluence of circumstances prompted a major metropolitan daily to send out calls to various they-should-knows asking if in thirty-five years Jakob Dylan would loom as large as his father does today.

Why should he? Its a dumb question; it's also irrelevant. Because so much money is at stake, pop music seems to be about careers.

But beneath the surface, perhaps on the level where the money is made, pop music is really about a social fact. At any moment, anyone might have something to say that the whole country, even the whole world, might want to hear, and maybe only one such thing. The ruling values of pop music might seem to be situated in the accumulation of fame and riches. They might be found in the way a song can turn your day around and disappear.

A singer reaches you with a song. He or she has no responsibility to reach you with another one, and you have no responsibility to respond if he or she tries. Heard or overheard, a song—on the radio, in a bar, hummed by someone standing next to you in line—diverts you from the path your day has taken. For an instant, it changes you, makes you want something, or fear something, that a moment before was the last thing on your mind. But you can forget about the song as surely as you may feel shadowed until you hear it again.

Or, rather, you may try to forget about it. You may not be allowed to. A hit song you don't like is an oppressive mystery: Why are people listening to this? Why won't it go away? Granted that almost every female person of my acquaintance considers Jakob Dylan the cutest thing walking on two legs, what was he doing dully offering "One Headlight" until spring turned into fall? It was like watching someone do a jigsaw puzzle with four pieces, over and over again.

As omnipresent hit singles go, "One Headlight" was too flat to be more than a mild headache, and of course you could always change the station. It takes a great single, like Hanson's "MMM Bop," the most ubiquitous record of last year, to produce a migraine. You need a piece of music so deliriously catchy, so insidiously marvelous, that you can't change the station, a song you can't stop hearing even if you turn the radio off.

That was the story in a skit built around Hanson's recent appearance on *Saturday Night Live*. The three teenage Hanson

brothers enter an elevator. Suddenly two terrorists—guest host
Helen Hunt and cast member Will Ferrell—rush in, shut the door,
and hold the boys at gunpoint. "MMMBop" has driven them insane, and they want nothing less for Hanson. Earplugs in place, the
terrorists stop the elevator between floors, put "MMMBop" on a
CD player set to "repeat," and wait. It takes only an hour or so for
the first Hanson to crack; his mouth jerks up in a horrible grin. A
few hours later a second Hanson succumbs. The third just keeps on
happily tapping his feet. Ferrell pulls out his earplugs; a smile
spreads over this face, and he too begins to move. Realizing he's
gone over to the other side, Hunt has no choice but to execute him
on the spot.

That's one way to settle the mystery of a hit single. But some singles, like the Wallflowers' "Three Marlenas," are mysteries that in-
tensify until they finally float off the airwaves and disappear into the
air.

The song walks in and out of the struggles of people who have
no money and expect none. Jakob Dylan plays the simplest cadence
on his guitar, never varying it. A piping organ makes the people
you're hearing about seem bigger than their circumscribed lives,
even heroic. Then all the orchestration falls away, and only the guitar is left, counting off the time. The whole piece pauses, and the
singer says the hell with it. He's going to get a car and drive it, with
the top down and the radio on. The eavesdropping tone of his de-
scriptions of other people is replaced by a bitterly casual James
Dean vehemence. "I'm going right out of state," he says. "Now, I
ain't looking back until I'm going / Right through heaven's gate."
He stretches the word "heaven" as far as it will reach. He bets all
he has on that word and the next, but without tipping his hand.
Though his face remains impassive, the phrase "heaven's gate"
works as a magnet, pulling in metaphors from every direction, filling up the hole that has opened in the music.

That hole is filled with the bodies of thirty-nine members of

Heaven's Gate, the seekers who last March left the earth for a comet, well after "Three Marlenas" was recorded, but before it reached the radio and stuck there. It is filled with Genesis 28:17, where Jacob, in terror, dreams his way up his ladder to "the gate of heaven," and with "Hark! hark! the lark at heaven's gate sings," from the seduction song in Shakespeare's *Cymbeline*. The song fills itself with the slowly building disaster of the 1980 Michael Cimino movie about the Johnson County War, where "Heaven's Gate" were words painted on a tented roller rink in Sweetwater, Wyoming, in 1892—a roller rink in which, for what it's worth, T-Bone Burnett, the onetime Bob Dylan accompanist who produced the Wallflowers' hit album, was the leader of the Heaven's Gate band.

Merely by working in culture, with all questions of intent moot, Jakob Dylan has called up these metaphors. With his song thus weighted by events he could never have foreseen and analogues he may never have known, he creates the sense that wherever the singer in his song is going, he isn't coming back. It's as if he expects to find heaven's gate closed and even hopes it will be, so he can drive right through it and break it down. Listening, you can almost see it happen, but the picture won't come into focus. So you listen harder every time you come across the song, wanting nothing more than to go all the way into the mystery it has presented, until finally you just get tired of trying. The day comes when you notice the song playing and you hear nothing at all. Like so many singles, the record has gone back where it came from, wherever that is.

"One Step Back," New York Times,
January 19, 1998

America at the Beginning of
the Twentieth Century

A mericanitis," trumpeted the advertisement for a 1903 patent
medicine made by the Rexall company. Was Americanitis the
disease or the cure? There was no way to tell from a first glance at
the brightly colored sign, a complex tableau of landscape, people,
and magic symbols; there was no way to tell after ten minutes of
staring.

It was the most amazing piece of promotion I'd ever seen, not
that it was obvious what was actually being sold. The ad was gorgeous, ambitious, a labyrinth of seductions and catchphrases, a
symphony of pushed buttons, all for a brown bottle promising an
unspoiled land, a loving community, and eternal life. It was the
proclamation of a would-be national icon, something that as a product the nation has long since forgotten, but that as an idea the nation has never left behind.

The thing was off in a relatively dim corner in the sort of nostalgia shop one might find in any quaint American tourist town. In
this case, it was Gail's Oldies and Goodies Old-Fashioned Cafe and
Ice Cream Parlour on Main Street in St. Helena, California, in the
heart of the Napa Valley wine country. The place was filled with a
collection of metal soft-drink signs from the '30s and '40s. In
thrilling reds and blues, the room glowed with smiles for Hires

Root Beer, Donald Duck Orange Juice, and, everywhere, Coca-Cola. From wall to wall, Coke Santa Clauses roared with laughter, Coke bathing beauties held up the perfect green bottle while languidly stretching their impossibly long legs, legs that on the all-purpose, all-American beach of the ads seemed to reach from Minnesota to New Orleans.

"Don't Grow Old," the Americanitis ad commanded in thick black letters. "We Guarantee Rexall Americanitis Elixir Will Make You Feel Younger."

"This has got to be a joke," I said to the person next to me. "Some snotty modern parody of all the stuff people used to believe."

"It's not a joke," said a woman eating lunch under the sign. "I have a bottle of it at home. A friend who collects antiques gave it to me."

"Does it work?" I asked.

It's hard to know where the America depicted in the big, broad Americanitis poster begins. At the top, in the background, there's a spectacular mountain range, the Rockies crowned with a steeple-like peak and covered with snow down to their lowest foothills, which suddenly turn green and smooth, a sylvan glade. Emerging from a line of great oaks at the base of the hills is a long parade of men, women, boys, and girls, all crossing a huge meadow and gathering at "The Fountain of Perpetual Youth." The fountain is made by an enormous bottle of Americanitis Elixir: "One of the Rexall Remedies of Which There Is One for Each Ailment," and this one "Especially Recommended for Nervous Disorders, Exhaustion, and All Troubles Arising from Americanitis." Emitting a white spray that forms a canopy of medicine and fills the fountain's pool, the bottle is as ugly as it is imposing; three winged fairies drape themselves around its side. On the ground, led by a boy or a midget dressed as a bellboy, throngs of excited children and calm, satisfied adults raise cups high, less to drink than to toast.

The picture all but screams with self-confidence, optimism, and joy, with a celebration of the American small-town utopia generalized into its natural setting. Here people gather to be cured of some vague malaise, some not-quite-diagnosable condition, but it's plain that the setting is itself a cure. In fact, as you look, the setting, the cure, is so blessed—with its marriage of benign nature and kindred spirits—that the disease it purports to cure is itself a kind of blessing. Without the disease, you couldn't have the cure, and the cure, patently, is what life is all about.

Still, any picture so full of detail as this one turns up oddities. The bellboy doesn't look human. It's a small-town utopia but there's no town. On one side of the fountain, where there are no adults, the children mingle, pressing their bodies together; on the other side everyone, old and young, stands apart. They don't look at one another; they don't seem to know each other. They seem peculiarly lifeless, residents not of Anytown, U.S.A., but of a sanitarium. Winding down from the beautiful mountains, a line of solitaries has come from all over to discover—Americanitis? Or America? As if it weren't there already? As if they've just heard about it? America or Americanitis? What is the cure, and what is the disease?

There's an odd, powerful displacement in the image. It takes you into the distant past as you stand in the present, as you stand in the unimaginable future of the advertisement—unless in fact nothing has really changed. We've disremembered Americanitis Elixir, and its weird question of whether it named the remedy or the affliction, but we still drink Coca-Cola. Coke, too, like Hires Root Beer or Dr. Pepper, began its life as a nineteenth-century patent medicine, a "nerve tonic" you took to banish fatigue and depression. At the beginning of the century, fatigue and depression seemed to be everyone's fate, at least if you read the new ads, and the ads were everywhere. In his breezily definitive 1993 study *For God, Country and Coca-Cola,* business writer Mark Pendergrast recalls a *New York Tribune* writer describing an "undulating country, breathing spring from every meadow and grove and orchard," not that one could "see a single furlong of it without the suggestion of disease." It was 1886; there were advertisements for cures painted everywhere, on barns, on trees, on rocks. "Americanitis" may have been a trademark, but the malady would have been recognized by all. As far back as 1881, Pendergrast notes, the writer George Beard, in *American Nervousness,* traced its causes to industrialization, an unstable economy, "too much freedom of thought," "repression of turbulent emotions," overspecialization, and above all the pressure of time.

Americanitis Elixir went on the market at a time when, to many, America itself was becoming unrecognizable. Between 1880 and 1910 the population of the country almost doubled, mostly because of immigration. Everywhere you went, there were people who didn't look like you, who didn't speak the same language: people who thought that they, too, were Americans. Before too long, assimilation had its effect, and the problem got worse. Just as you couldn't tell the disease from the cure, you couldn't always distinguish those who belonged from those who didn't.

You might argue that such a disease has always made the country what it is, but that would mean giving up a lot. It would mean that, despite the pull of all that makes the Americanitis sign what it is, there is no cure.

"One Step Back," New York Times,
January 26, 1998

Pennsylvania at the End
of the Twentieth Century

When David Thomas and a few other anti-hippie rock 'n' roll bohemians formed Pere Ubu in Cleveland in 1975, "in the ruins of the industrial Midwest," the original idea, Thomas later wrote of his ambitions for the band, "was to record an artifact" that "would gain him entry into the Brotherhood of the Unknown that was gathering in used record bins everywhere." The idea was to act and then disappear, to be forgotten, and then, sometime in the future, perhaps even after one was dead, to be discovered, and only then begin to shape the world.

Twenty-odd years later Pere Ubu remains as questing as it ever was, and the stance Thomas, the band's last remaining founding member, defined in the beginning has become a voice that can at times tell the whole story in a single phrase. On *Pennsylvania,* the most recent Pere Ubu album, the voice is that of a man talking in a crowd; you think he's talking to himself until you realize he's talking to you. All across the record, people turn off the main roads and find themselves in towns whose names they can't remember. "But I do remember the frozen quality of the hours we stayed there," Thomas says in "Perfume"; he might be guiding you back, by means of a '40s film noir voiceover, through the wreckage of what seemed like a good idea at the time. That's the feeling: a loser who's come to grips with the fact that he'll never win, but describing a glimpse of paradise. "I remember the waitress and what time we had to eat," the singer says to you, jostling you on the street to get your attention; the calm in his voice, the certainty that right here is where it all went wrong, makes you keep listening instead of shrugging the guy off. "I remember the faces of the other customers like they were my own family."

The song, and the others that share its bereft wanderings on *Pennsylvania*, have their source in Thomas's notion that today all towns are becoming ghost towns. "Geography has a sound," Thomas says, speaking from his home in Hove, England, a town near Brighton. "Music of the steppes, the Arctic Circle, the industrial Midwest; there's a reason people feel an attachment to a place, and a lot of it has to do with sound."

Pere Ubu, in the beginning, thought of itself as an avant-garde garage punk-folk band, Thomas once wrote. "The whole scene in 1974," he wrote of Cleveland—one of the places where rock 'n' roll began, in 1951, with Alan Freed's "Moondog Show" on WJW, by Thomas's time a city celebrated in song for the Cuyahoga River, so polluted, Randy Newman sang in "Burn On," it had set itself on fire—"amounted to not much more than fifty people. It was a small, isolated society living in a space as isolated as any pioneer outpost on the plains of Kansas. And they identified with the land, passionately. Except that the land wasn't rural." That tiny society had somehow found its way to a forgotten part of the city, and into a bar where a band was playing: "They had simply stumbled into a lost world where the sun would set, the inhabitants flee and the stones of the bridges, buildings and monuments whisper in the timeless dark, speaking in a dead language." That was the sound Pere Ubu tried to alchemize with synthesizer and electric guitars. But the sound of a place, Thomas argues now, depends on the place holding its shape, as a culturally distinct republic making its way through the politics of its age and in some essential way not changing, not changing its voice.

"Woolie Bullie," the first song on *Pennsylvania,* is about the effect such a place can have on a visitor. It begins with a rough, harsh scratch down the neck of a guitar, a hard beat establishing a relentless momentum, and then Thomas stepping up to the podium: "There's a diner out on Route 232, in western Pennsylvania. I spent my life there one afternoon."

It's a nice reversal of the nightclub comedian's joke about his last gig in a nowhere town, the sort of town that in that sort of comedian's act gets called "Cleveland": "I spent a week there the other day." But now, with the music rushing past him like a back-projection of *Thunder Road,* like footage of Robert Mitchum's bootlegger speeding on mountain roads in the dead of night with his lights out, Thomas is saying he will never get the sound of this place on Route 232 out of his head. And why should he? "I hear it when takin' a shower, readin' the paper," he says in a drawl he probably first affected in the diner. "I look up an' see it 'cross the valley. They tore down the Starlight down at the end of the road and put up a big Days Inn that blocks the view." He shifts into big, rounded, elegiac tones: "But I know that road's still there. I can feel it wherever I go, whatever I'm doin', and it knows that I'm still here."

"The places we live tend to separate, to come apart," Thomas said. "America is no longer America. When I'm in Germany, I say to people, Germany is no longer Germany, and they all nod their heads, as if they know exactly what I mean. I wish," he laughed over the telephone, "*I* knew exactly what I mean."

"Cleveland is all gone," he said. "They've taken everything I loved. They took away our Nike missile base, they tore down the Aeronautical Shot Peening Company. They put in puke palaces all down the river, places for teenagers to get drunk on cheap beer: nobody asked *me* about this. I began to notice that they were taking things away from me without asking me," he said like a madman, only to continue as a citizen: "The people in control didn't know what was stunning about Cleveland." With a fierce vehemence overwhelming all mere nostalgia, on the telephone Thomas matched the rant that ends "Woollie Bullie," that guy on the street now pulling on your coat and you pulling away and ready to run: "History is being rewritten faster than it can happen; culture's a weapon that's used against us. Culture's a *swamp,* of superstition, ignorance, and abuse . . . the land, and what we add to it, cannot lie."

Part of what is added, Thomas said, is a band's sound. "That works into the musician's intentions, and works into 'The Great Un'—the unexpected, the uncontrollable. It introduces the real world into art. It has to do with Elvis, it all goes back to Elvis—abstract thought was his *big* thing. Elvis introduced abstract thought into hillbilly music and rural blues: he was going for the *sound* of the thing. He didn't even have to write his own words!"

The fact that Elvis didn't write his own songs is usually held against him. Thomas was headed in another direction, reaching for the source of Elvis's appeal, and for the engine of the musical and social transformations that followed in Elvis's wake—among them Pere Ubu, and Thomas's own life's work. The sound of a place is fundamentally an abstraction, which is not to say that it isn't absolutely real: that was what Thomas was getting at. "This business of sexuality and adolescent rebellion has been *bolted on* to the history of rock 'n' roll ex post facto," Thomas said with indignation. "It's been grossly exaggerated! It's abstraction! That's why people are attracted to Elvis. People are attracted to the inarticulate voice.

"It's about sound emerging as a poetic force in its own right," Thomas said. "Rock music was the force that liberated sound from being merely a handmaiden to musical activity. Rock music is about that which is beyond words. Elvis was the singer as narrative voice.

Sinatra was a kind of avatar, but it was with Elvis that the singer becomes the priest, the mediator between the secret Masonic cult and the public."

"The singer is the priest?" I asked. "The secret Masonic cult is the band?" I was sure Thomas had gone completely off the map, but he knew precisely where he was. "Culture happens in secret, all art is secret," he explained patiently. "Ordinary people only see the ashes of art, or the failures, or frozen moments. Only rarely on-stage do bands achieve reality; mostly it's in rehearsals, in lost moments. Nobody ever sees that, or knows anything about it"—but, he said, referring to the great running back for the Cleveland Browns in the 1960s, later the star of *The Dirty Dozen* and king of blaxploitation movies, "Jim Brown would understand. I think baseball players and football players would understand the same thing."

Thomas's gnostic argument—that art exists to at once reveal secrets and to preserve them—makes sense of a particularly American, or modern, form of storytelling. In a big, multifaceted democracy, you're supposed to be able to communicate directly with everyone, yet many despair of being understood by anyone at all. Pere Ubu's orginal recordings, made nearly a quarter-century ago, Thomas has written, were the result of an "inward turning, defiant stance of a beleaguered few who felt themselves to be outside music, beneath media attention, and without hope of an audience." Many Europeans have felt a similar estrangement, of course, but in Europe elitism is always an answer: one has the privilege of considering oneself above media attention, not beneath it. In America, in the modern world, to feel yourself beneath media attention is to doubt that what you have to say is worth anyone's attention.

Out of this comes an American language that means to tell a story no one can turn away from. But this language—identified by D. H. Lawrence in 1923, in *Studies in Classic American Literature,* as the true modernist voice, the voice of Hawthorne, Poe, Melville—is cryptic before it is anything else. It's all hints and warnings, and the warnings are disguised as non sequiturs. The secret is told, but nonetheless hidden, in the musings, babblings, or tall tales of people who seem to be too odd to be like you or me, like *us*—like the author who puts his or her name to the story, insisting that he made it all up, that she just did it for the money.

For those people—people like David Thomas, whose history, as tracked by the progress of his voice over the decades, is the history of a wild, expansive, all-accepting, yammering private joke—no one can be at home in a place where everyone is presumed to understand everyone else. The whole existence of such people is premised on their attempt to tell a secret, perhaps to discover the secret in the telling, or in the stunned, shocked response the telling provokes—and their idea of democracy is premised on the conviction that no one can be at home in a place where it is presumed that there are no secrets, that all reality is transparent, that all people are the same. Thus those who tell this story, who want desperately to be heard, will likely mistrust even an imaginary audience. If they are like Thomas on *Pennsylvania,* they'll create an aura of portent and unease, but mostly, as it were, *sinistramente,* with the left hand, by means of unfinished sentences, dead-end monologues, floating images, outmoded phrases, archaic pronunciations, a tone of voice that is blank and addled by turn.

The tenor of all the wistful, vaguely paranoid tales of displacement on *Pennsylvania*—tales of abandoning the Interstate, getting lost, and finding the perfect town when it's too late to change your life and live in it—is caught in the weirdly menacing way Thomas pronounces "Los Angeles" in the tune "Highwaterville." It's the old flophouse, grifter's way, with a hard *g* and a long *e* at the end, *"Los Ayng-geleese,"* so that the place sounds like a disease. The same sense of the strange, the unacceptable in the familiar, is there in the song "Mr Wheeler," which sounds like an old tape of a very old telephone call, a tape that turned up in a box in a room in a house where no one has lived for twenty years. "Uh, Mr. Wheeler?" somebody says; as with every bit of talk in the number, it's followed by a long instrumental passage, as if some great drama is taking shape around fragments of a story that will never be put back together. "I have an old lightbulb," the man on the phone is saying, almost embarrassed. "One that you made yourself?" asks Mr. Wheeler, just like an FBI agent; when the first man claims this lightbulb he's trying to sell has been in his family for seventy-five years, it feels like he's trying to sell you an old atomic bomb.

What comes into view is a secret country: barely recognizable and undeniable. "It knows I'm still here," as Thomas says of the diner in "Woolie Bullie"; from England, he might be speaking of the U.S.A. or simply Cleveland, which for him will do for the U.S.A. Wherever they may live, all the present members of Pere Ubu are Clevelanders; they come together in Cleveland to rehearse, and record in the same studio where Pere Ubu has always recorded. "Cleveland is all gone," Thomas said again over the telephone, "but I'm like Saddam Hussein. I only trust people from my own village."

adapted from "One Step Back," New York Times,
February 23 and March 2, 1998

The Last Laugh

Keynote address at the conference
"Elvis: the state of his art,"
University of Memphis, August 14, 1998

I'm going to talk today about a joke America has yet to stop telling itself: the Elvis joke.

Today, almost twenty-one years after his death, Elvis Presley is something less than a joke, even an old, tired joke. Nobody laughs anymore at tabloid stories about a sixty-three-year-old wrinkled, white-haired Elvis spotted working at Burger King. The tabloids don't even run those stories anymore. Last year, the *Weekly World News* had Janet Reno on the cover, trumpeting the news that, according to one poll, 78 percent of Japanese men would rather be marooned on a desert island with our own attorney general than "any other lady on the face of the earth." Leaving aside the likelihood that 78 percent of Japanese men probably have no idea who Janet Reno is, her spokesman told the *Washington Post* that making the front page of the *Weekly World News* was nothing to sneeze at: she "beat out a four-page spread of Elvis climbing out of his coffin." There you have it: Janet Reno is the new Elvis.

Elvis is a punch line without a joke. My favorite example is an Elvis fetish object: a gracefully made ceramic hand, a woman's hand encased in a white buttoned glove, and in its palm a pink, heart-shaped box, with "I Love Elvis" printed on it in black and red, the "Love" being its own little heart.

A friend showed up at my door one day, offering it—un-wrapped—as a gift. "I saw this and immediately thought of you," she said. "Thanks a lot," I said. "This is absolutely disgusting." The heart-shaped box was a pillbox, obviously, but the hand itself, neatly cut off at the wrist, was a severed hand from a horror movie: *The Hand That Wouldn't Die*. They think they've killed her, cut her up into pieces and buried them, but then, in the middle of the night, they hear it—*knock . . . knock . . . knock*. They open the door, and there's this *thing*, slithering across the floor, dripping blood . . .

Just a punch line: there was the incident at a 1996 congressional hearing on Whitewater—another joke, really, that supposed financial scandal reporters and Republicans have been trying to pin on Bill Clinton from before he was elected to the presidency. Whitewater: a word that now stands for every sort of crime and malfeasance imaginable, or, more accurately, for an entire industry of smear and villification. A Republican senator says he's heard that conversations on the president's plane are taped; he wants them all subpoenaed. The Democrats aren't buying it. "Everything on Air Force One is taped?" says one. "Where'd you hear that?" "*Elvis*," says a second Democrat, while the Republican fumes. Then there was the banter running back and forth when, at the beginning of this month, the House assured passage of a bill to reform campaign financing. "You're more likely to see Elvis again than to see this bill pass the Senate," said Mitch McConnell, the Republican senator from Kentucky; "Better be on the lookout," said the only Kentucky congressman to vote for the bill. Days later, Geoffrey Fieger, Dr. Jack Kervorkian's attorney and the just-nominated Democratic candidate for governor of Michigan (and also, for those who remember "My Sharona," the brother of the lead singer for the Knack), came under attack for his views on religion: the *New York Times* reported that Fieger was on record as comparing "the belief that Jesus is divine to the cult of Elvis Presley. 'In 2,000 years we've probably made somebody who is the equivalent of Elvis into God, so I see no reason not to believe that in 2,000 years Elvis will be God,'" Fieger said. These stories aren't funny, they're just floating punch lines—but what's the joke?

Another item from 1996, a truly weird item: President Fidel Ramos of the Philippines—recently replaced by a charismatic actor described by some papers as a Filipino Elvis—and President Jiang Zemin of China are cruising around Manila Bay, dueting on "Love Me Tender." "That's the favorite song of Bill Clinton," says Ramos to Jiang. "You have to prepare. When he visits you, you will surprise him." This isn't funny at all, what with Clinton, at the White House later in the year, receiving the general who ordered the massacre of democracy demonstrators at Tiananmen Square, and then blandly accepting the general's lies that no massacre ever took place—but for the daily papers, almost anything with the word "Elvis" in it is a punch line.

Most meaninglessly, it seemed, the punch line without the joke came in the biggest movie of that same year, 1996: *Independence Day*. Evil aliens have all but conquered the planet—but finally the brave pilot played by Will Smith has disabled the alien mothership and zoomed off without a split-second to spare. "Elvis," he says smugly, harking back to the announcement that closed Elvis shows as long ago as 1956, "has left the building." The line seems automatic, just a verbal high-five, a stupid movie catchphrase like "YESSSSSSS!" or "I'm outta here" with somebody's name on it— but the punch line is there for a reason, just as all the other punch lines are there for a reason.

With the horrible severed hand, the ceramic pillbox, there's the promise, or the threat, or the curse, that Elvis Presley, a malevolent creature more like the thing in a horror movie than a dead human being, will never go away. He will never leave our culture. He will remain in the back of our minds. He will haunt the world forever-more. Not because his own country destroyed him—"How could

we have ever felt estranged from Elvis?" the late Charles Kuralt
said on CBS when Elvis died. "He was a native son"—but because
Elvis Presley, the real person, who lived in a body, not in the media, always knew how estranged the country was from him, how
from the day he first made himself known he was to most of the
country no more than a freak, an embarrassment. His own country,
his own people, always thought he was a joke—"One of the century's great jokes," *Boston Globe* columnist James Carroll wrote in
1997, "a figure of the American absurd, a vivid parody of the peculiar and, let's face it, banal sensibility that the U.S. has stamped
upon the globe"—and now he gets to be the punch line.

With the Whitewater hearing, the back-and-forth on campaign
reform, and the Michigan governor's race, as with the coy strate-
gizing of the Philippine and Chinese presidents, there is a lost
echo of the 1992 American presidential campaign, when the identification of Elvis Presley and candidate Bill Clinton was ever-
present. Something similar is going on in *Independence Day*, with
its pointedly Clinton-like president, played by Bill Pullman. Pullman soon enough found himself in the White House—the real
White House, not the one that's blown up by aliens in the
movie—watching his own film with the real president sitting by
his side. Right there you can see the broken Elvis joke trying to
put itself back together: to reappear, for however brief a moment,
as something like real life—as a version of the history the joke actually made.

Elvis Presley won the 1992 election for Bill Clinton—presumably the Elvis that, just after the election, Ian Shoales called
"America's secret angel." Our best, secret self, Shoales might have
meant—unless he meant the unnamed, half-glimpsed Elvis who
appears as Christian Slater's guardian angel in the 1993 movie
True Romance, an Elvis played by an uncredited Val Kilmer. He
gives Slater the courage to take chances, to risk everything—his
usual advice being, "Shoot him in the face." Or it's the angel Joyce

Carol Oates brought down to earth in her poem "Waiting on Elvis, 1956"—an angel who appears and disappears like the Lone Ranger, leaving behind not a silver bullet but a moment of bliss. Oates's poem was written in 1987, but it suggests a more complete and convincing match than anything I know between Elvis Presley and Bill Clinton: one man who could, and one man who can, charm you almost to death. Oates put herself in "This place up in Charlotte":

This place up in Charlotte called Chuck's where I used to waitress and who came in one night but Elvis and some of his friends before his concert at the Arena. I was twenty-six married but still waiting tables and we got to joking around like you do, and he was fingering the lace edge of my slip where it showed beneath my hemline and I hadn't even seen it and I slapped at him a little saying, you sure are the one aren't you feeling my face burn but he was the kind of boy even mean-ness turned sweet in his mouth.

   Smiles at me and says, Yeah honey I guess I sure am.

   It's not likely that June Juanico, Elvis's girlfriend in 1956, knew this obscure poem, but in *Elvis: In the Twilight of Memory,* a mem-oir she published last year, she told an almost identical story—ex-cept that here she and Elvis and his pals in their two Lincoln Continentals are driving in Florida, not North Carolina, and the waitress has never heard of Elvis. He orders fried chicken, compli-ments the waitress on how good it is, but he can't resist trying to get her to recognize him, to see if he can ring her bell: "If you want some good fried chicken," he says, "you should come to Memphis, Tennessee. Nobody does chicken as good as my mama." "That's not all she did good," the waitress said.

   It was Elvis as angel that in 1992—with Bill Clinton assured of the Democratic nomination for president but supposedly already out of the race with George Bush and Ross Perot—sent Clinton onto the Arsenio Hall show with his saxophone, to try his luck with "Heartbreak Hotel." It was this angel that sent Clinton out to show the country someone who, as he sought the presidency, the country had perhaps never seen before: a man willing to cut himself down to size, and at the same time try to take off and fly. A man willing, for a moment, to pretend he could be Elvis. *Yeah,* the country seemed to say in reply. *I remember that guy. Yeah,* said Clinton right back. *I do, too.*

With the new year, the Post Office put its new Elvis stamp on sale, Bill Clinton took the oath of office—and then, as a presence in culture, never mind politics, Elvis Presley all but disappeared. He had, in a certain way, once again changed history, as he had first done in the 1950s—but this time as a ghost. He had put his stamp on the nation, just as the nation was now putting his stamp on its mail. In an oddly doubled manner, Elvis Presley had finally become official—and as soon as that happened, all the stories of shoppers sighting Elvis in supermarkets, of Elvis statues on Mars, of Elvis himself working in Boca Raton as his own Elvis impersonator, came to an end.

As Clinton began his presidency in a flurry of confusion, as the national media immediately turned on him, as if to make sure he understood that as they made him they could break him, as tabloid Clinton stories replaced tabloid Elvis stories, the Clinton-Elvis identification dissolved. The good joke turned sour—and, at least as the White House came to see it, the joke turned on the man who won with it.

In the spring of 1996, I was talking to one of Clinton's speechwriters. I reminded him of Clinton's appearance on the Arsenio Hall show, his hair up high like an Elvis pompadour, hipster shades over his eyes, and I said lightly, but seriously, that it was just that spirit—of playfulness, of convincingly appearing not to care what people thought, of acting at once casually and boldly—that Clinton had lost. It was a spirit he needed to find again, I said.

The speechwriter wasn't impressed. "That night on the Arsenio Hall show might have won him the election," he said, "but it also ruined his presidency."

It made Bill Clinton seem like a real person; it also made him seem, as a real person, as the person behind the mask the president might be wearing on any given occasion, unpresidential. "Unpresidential," the speechwriter said, muttering the horrible, deadly word: unserious, immature, a southerner, a party boy, a fool. In a word, a joke. In a phrase, just another Elvis. Bill Clinton had told the country a serious joke; the country got the joke, the speechwriter was saying, but the joke was on the man who told it. And you could hear it all come whiplashing back this spring and summer, with Clinton battered daily with Monica Lewinsky tapes from Linda Tripp in *Newsweek*, with rumors of long-ago Arkansas rape floated by Paula Jones's lawyers, with Independent Counsel Kenneth Starr attempting to embarrass Clinton out of office with a virtual Mississippi of leaks while affirming that the only issues were probity and the rule of law, with Washington's opinion-makers bringing it all back home, defining what was truly at stake: "Having vulgarians like the Clintons conspicuous in government," George Will wrote in the *Washington Post*, "must further coarsen American life . . . Something precious has been vandalized. The question is, who should come next, to scrub from a revered institution the stain of the vulgarians?"

"The stain of the vulgarians"—where had you heard that before? "He gave an exhibition that was suggestive and vulgar," said the *New York Daily News* of Elvis's appearance on the Milton Berle show in 1956, "with the kind of animalism that should be confined to dives and bordellos." That was the Elvis joke Clinton had become, summed up in February of this year by a cartoon depicting the Carter, Reagan, and Bush presidential libraries, all gleaming with masonry and towers, and then Clinton's: a country shack with the sign "Adult Books" on the roof and a pickup truck parked out back. "Send the Clintons back where they came from," one right-wing columnist or talk show host after another demanded, meaning, back out of *our* country, back to the South. Back to nowhere: as the magazine *America* said in 1956, summing up Elvis's performances, "If the agencies (TV and other) would stop handling such nauseating stuff, all the Presleys of our land would soon be swallowed up in the oblivion they deserve."

The story of Bill Clinton and Elvis that Clinton's speechwriter told me is a version of *Faust:* selling your soul to the devil. America's secret angel, Christian Slater's guardian angel, comes down, awards the prize to the deserving soul mate, to another boy even meanness turns sweet in his mouth, and then America's secret angel turns into America's secret demon, and demands payment.

Thus late in the 1990s Elvis began to creep back: as a sleazy talk show host, as a child rapist, as a serial killer, as a fascist, as a really bad joke. He was the "troll" in Darcey Steinke's 1997 novel *Jesus Saves,* as his young victim twists her taped wrists to read her mad kidnapper's "love letter":

Michael Jackson told me he never liked Lisa Marie, but he had to marry her because the King came to him in a dream and demanded that he be her second husband. If he has on white, then he's the real King, the Love Me Tender King and you should listen to him. But if he has on green sequin trousers and a silk shirt then it's the fake king and you should disregard everything he says. You may wonder why I took the girl, that's very secret and only for the King to know himself . . . . People don't know, but Jesus once had a girl he tied up.

He did many things to her, like sprinkle whiskey on her forehead and feed her plums. Even though she was heavy he carried this girl on his back like a baby and he'd test her to make sure she was real. The Last Girl is a white cat with a pink tongue. Anyone can fuck her anytime they want.

He was Jerry Springer, arriving at Temple University and finding the place full of police. "He peers through the darkened limo windows," one could read this year in *Rolling Stone,* "and says, 'Why all this security?' Steve Wilkos, who travels with Jerry on these trips," the reporter goes on, "says, 'You're speaking, man! You're like Elvis, man!' Jerry says, 'Christ, I'm not a fucking terrorist.' Wilkos says, 'You're Farrakhan, baby!' "—Louis Farrakhan, head of the Nation of Islam, in the calypso '50s himself a singer with a guitar, dreaming of replacing Elvis on the charts as "The Charmer."

He was Oliver North, running for the U.S. Senate in Virginia in 1996, as described in a *San Francisco Examiner* dispatch about *The Perfect Candidate,* a film on North's campaign:

Surrounded by an aggressive security detail, complete with earphones, North signed Bibles as throngs encircled his computer-equipped motor home, "Rolling Thunder," in the parking lots of 7-Elevens. "He is Elvis," the candidate's senior advisor, Mark Goodin, told the filmmakers.

In one scene, Goodin urges North's lieutenants to stir up white rural voters after advertisements for [incumbent Democratic Senator Charles] Robb skewered the Republican campaign for defending the Confederate flag. "He's played the race card, and it's going to work for him," Goodin said. "We play the race card, and it's going to work for us."

He was Andrew Cunanan, still at large in July of 1997, with his most-wanted face on the front page of every paper in the country

after the stunning broad daylight murder of fashion designer
Gianni Versace—for whom, just the year before, Lisa Marie Presley had posed in an ad for designer jeans. "Tales abound," the *San
Francisco Chronicle* reported, detailing Cunanan's life in San Francisco's gay subculture,

of close encounters with Cunanan in bars and discos and tony dinner
parties, and many gay men have expressed shock and distress at just
how widely known—and popular—the suspected killer appears to
have been.

"Cunanan is the 'Patient Zero' of serial killers," said San Francisco
writer David Israels [referring to the airline steward once named as
the man who spread the AIDS virus across the United States]. "Patient
Zero was supposedly everywhere and connected to everyone, and this
guy was also everywhere and connected to everyone. He's been seen
in more places than Elvis."

And he was Terry Nichols, convicted last December for his role
in the bombing of the Federal Building in Oklahoma City in
1995—he was Nichols or, as with Val Kilmer, looking over Nichols's
shoulder. The *New York Times* described prosecutor Beth Wilkinson's summation to the jury:

Turning on its head a phrase that [defense attorney Michael] Tigar had
used in his opening statement, she said Mr. Nichols was not building a
life, "he was building an alibi."

Ms. Wilkinson attacked the defense presentation of witnesses
who swore they saw others who might have helped in the bombing, including the suspect who was first identified as John Doe
No. 2, a man who was later found to have nothing to do with the
plot.

"As a result of the media frenzy, sightings of John Doe 2 were about
as common and credible as sightings of Elvis," she said.

But those Elvises were credible enough for the jury. With the evidence for political mass murder nearly up to the courtroom ceiling, the jury came back for voluntary manslaughter. The prosecutor told an Elvis joke; it came back and shot her in the face.

America's secret angel; America's secret demon. The first person to really see this double was Andy Warhol, in 1962 and over the next few years, as he made his giant silkscreen collages of a still from the 1960 Elvis movie *Flaming Star.* It's Elvis dressed as a cowboy, his legs spread in a gunfighter's stance, his gun pointed forward.

Warhol doubled the image or even tripled it, in grey, silver, red, purple—the latter color allowing the decoding of Warhol's Elvis as a gay icon. In whatever configuration Warhol's work may form the most productive Elvis image, the most generative. It's been copied again and again, as if it were Elvis, not just a picture of a picture. As far back as 1971, the Los Angeles artist Raymond Pettibone silkscreened a version of Warhol's silkscreen—as a punk artist, he would go on to make scabrous Elvis-in-hell cartoons. In 1990 Peter Halley made an abstract *Double Elvis,* taking Warhol's usual title, bending lines into squares, in color on one side, black and white on the other. In 1992 Deborah Kass produced her wonderful "My Elvis" series: any number of doubled and tripled *Red Yentls, Silver Yentls,* an image of Barbra Streisand from the 1983 film *Yentl,* where Streisand, as a young Jewish woman in Eastern Europe at the turn of the century, disguises herself as a boy, because that's the only way she can get an education. She holds herself to the side, not forward as Elvis does; still, the physical connection, the movie star connection, the connection between two people willing to reinvent themselves to become what they want to become, is close enough to stick.

The two most powerful uses of Warhol's *Elvis* don't just play with Warhol's image, or take it over like a fading singer covering an old Top 40 hit, hoping something recognizable will be a quick route back to the charts: they take up the duality that Warhol found. Louis Lussier's 1993 *Elvis Shadow* is a big, black-and-white superimposition, more than four feet by five feet. In the foreground, two disembodied hands brandish six-shooters at each other. They're about to fire. In the background is a figure so dark and dim you can barely make it out as a figure—Warhol's *Flaming Star* Elvis, holding his own gun, blessing the shootout that's about to take place. "Shoot him in the face," he's saying; he doesn't care who gets shot.

And there is Jerry Kearns's fearsome, unreadable *Earth Angel,* from 1989—a photo-collage the size of a small mural, more than six feet by eight feet. The title—it's that angel again, but maybe to throw you off. One of the sweetest rock 'n' roll records there is, "Earth Angel" was a 1954 hit by the Penguins, a black vocal group from Los Angeles; accompanying himself on piano, with doo-wops from his pals in the background, Elvis recorded a lovely version in the late '50s, in the Army in West Germany. Now Elvis, taken directly from Warhol, as Warhol took him from *Flaming Star,* stands doubled, one Elvis on each side of Kearns's big piece, each one with a gun in his hand. Warhol's Elvises always face directly forward; here, each Elvis is angled just to the right or the left, as if in readiness for some unseen enemy.

Kearns's Warhol Elvises are shown in black outline against a creamy, off-white background; across the picture, splattered all over the Elvises, is what looks like a wash of blood. As you look into the picture, you see that blood is exactly what it is. The splatter resolves itself into two familiar and violent images: a naked Vietnamese girl running down a road in terror, napalm burning her flesh off—and a young woman kneeling, crying, screaming, over the body of a young man, just shot dead by National Guardsmen at Kent State University in Ohio, shot dead for protesting the war in

Vietnam. And the picture makes you ask: What's Elvis doing here? Which side is he on?

What's going on in Andy Warhol's *Elvis,* in his *Double Elvis,* in his *Silver Triple Elvis*? Elvis's legs are spread, his gun is pointed— but he's no gunslinger. Your eyes are drawn to his, he's looking straight ahead, but his eyes are confused and full of panic. His eyes are ringed in black: the terror in his eyes squashes his face like a marshmallow. The terror in his eyes makes him ugly. You can't trust his aim.

Double Elvis, Triple Elvis: it only seems like some sort of com- ment on the American iconography of power—the movie cowboy, the six-gun, the fast draw, the showdown. But Warhol's work isn't about Elvis Presley symbolizing power—it's about Elvis Presley symbolizing powerlessness.

Here is a man who, as a nineteen-year-old, as a twenty-year-old, sparked a transformation of American culture, of culture world- wide—a transformation that we are still living out. We are living it out far more certainly than it would have seemed anyone was in 1962, when Warhol went to work on Elvis in the Factory—when Elvis Presley had disappeared into his own Hollywood movie fac- tory, disappeared far more definitively than he has since he actually died.

As an agent of transformation, Elvis did something new. No one is sure exactly what he did. If he said that all things were possible—"In an America that was wide open, when all things were possible," as Bob Dylan said of Peter Guralnick's *Last Train to Memphis: The Rise of Elvis Presley*—then today almost any characterization of what he did is possible. Whether it was the way he looked—part white and part black, to some; the sexiest thing that ever lived, to others—or the way this person sang, spoke, moved, and dressed, the way he smiled, shouted, whis- pered, or just looked over his shoulder—he gave voice to emotions that couldn't be contained. And then he was himself contained, in the oldest, stupidest, most obvious straitjackets of fame and success.

The Elvis Presley in Warhol's pictures holds a gun—but never has a man with a gun looked less armed. He points a phallic symbol because he's been neutered, and his eyes say that he knows it. "Here's a song that says you can do anything," Elvis said to the crowd at the Mississippi-Alabama Farm and Dairy Show in Tupelo in 1956, just before diving into "Blue Suede Shoes," but the man whose music said that anything was possible appears in Warhol's work—and in much of his own work, of course—as a eunuch. The Warhol who made the Warhol Elvises was not working as a eunuch, despite the fact that he liked to appear as one. His work says that he, Andy Warhol, as an artist, has the power to say what he means—a power that Elvis Presley, in the picture, no longer has, if he ever had it. I think the real intent of Warhol's *Elvis*es was to make you doubt that Elvis Presley ever did have that power, that he ever was an artist.

Warhol's *Elvis*es would not have proved so fascinating, so irresistible to other artists if there weren't more to them than that. By homing in on the instablility of Elvis's eyes in the *Flaming Star* still, Warhol got pictures that seem to vibrate. The eyes seem to dart from side to side, as if the whole figure, most powerfully in *Triple Elvis*, is itself ready to start firing blindly at any moment. *Blind Man with a Pistol*, in Chester Himes's perfect phrase—and that's the Elvis that turns up, all unready, in *Earth Angel*. There the figures stand, nervously looking off to one side and to the other at the same time, the black outlines of Elvis's bodies fading into the red covering the little Vietnamese girl and the dead student and the woman bending over him.

The whole complex of who Elvis is, where he came from, where he went, is in this picture. I can't begin to make it hold still, to make it talk. The Elvises in this picture can't talk, and they don't even try. Shoot first, ask questions later.

When I first saw Kearns's *Earth Angel*—as a reproduction in a catalogue—I thought it was fixing Elvis as the killer, the killer of the little girl, the killer of the student. This, I thought, was the Elvis who went dutifully into the Army, the Elvis who always did what he was told. "There was no telling which side Elvis was really on," the critic Howard Hampton wrote last year in *Film Comment,* imagining that upon his return from the Army Elvis was cast not in *G.I. Blues* in 1960 but, two years later, in

The Manchurian Candidate, a film that captures the secret, encrypted side of Presleyan myth: the shellshocked, brainwashed soldier as a version of the post-Army Elvis . . . his Manchurian Elvis would suggest the tangled double-agency of the real one, at once pawn and King, hero and dupe, emblem of liberty and of the all-American craving to just follow orders.

But when I saw the picture itself, in a museum, so big, overwhelming, really, Elvis looked like the defender. He seemed to stand between the victims and their murderers, like Alan Ladd in *Shane,* Gary Cooper in *High Noon,* Charles Bronson in *Once Upon a Time in the West,* with all of America's might and power now embodied not by Elvis Presley but by the sadistic villains in those movies, as played by Jack Palance, Lee Van Cleef, Henry Fonda, with the Elvises vanquishing that power with America's rightness and good. Or do Kearns's Elvises, standing with their guns drawn but not fired, their eyes still terrified under all that red paint, stand for helplessness, impotence, an America frozen in terror in the face of the might and power of another America, as, in fact, the antiwar movement froze up in terrror after the killings at Kent State? Maybe this was the first and final evil of Elvis Presley—when he was needed, he wasn't there. When the time came for him too to take a stand, he was silent.

Or, at least, this is Warhol's *Elvis,* an Elvis now diffused throughout our culture: an Elvis who, unlike Warhol, was never granted the power to approach an unseen audience as an artist. A fascinating cipher, but a cipher nevertheless. But of course there was payback.

Andy Warhol's *Elvis* is now worth millions in any form—single, double, triple, red, silver, purple, gray.° But in the world of signs and meanings, of symbols and epiphanies, Andy Warhol's *Elvis* did not come without a price any more than Bill Clinton's "Heartbreak Hotel" came without a price—at least not in the iconography of our culture, where Elvis, as an image, a sound, an idea, floats free.

In 1996, the ads for Mary Harron's movie *I Shot Andy Warhol* used a familiar image—an image no less swirling and unstable than Jerry Kearns's *Earth Angel.* There in the film was Lili Taylor as Valerie Solanas, the Factory hanger-on who in 1968 shot Andy Warhol and almost killed him. In the ads, she was shown looking down and to the left, in jeans and an open shirt, her legs spread, with a gunbelt around her waist and a pistol in her hand—in her tripled hands, because this was a tripled image, in gray and black, with a red band for the movie's title. As much as it was a portrait of a real person, *I Shot Andy Warhol* was a portrait of Valerie Solanas as an unstoppable cultural force: a person who, whatever her moral insanity, was working in culture, asking such cultural questions as,

---

°When Bob Dylan came to the Factory in 1965 for a screen test, Warhol gave him a *Double Elvis.* Dylan gave it to his manager, Albert Grossman. Dylan lost a fortune; unlike the others in the story, he's still alive.

Who am I? Who made me? Can I make myself? If I can't make myself, can I destroy whoever made me? If Andy Warhol made me, can I destroy him? The ads made it as clear as could be: part of Valerie Solanas was Warhol, and part of her was Elvis. Andy Warhol put a *Triple Elvis* on the Factory wall; in the film, there's a shot of Solanas standing in front of it. On the wall, Warhol's Elvis is pointing a gun; it could not have occurred to Warhol that the gun was pointed at him, but it occurred to Mary Harron. This was a real joke, not just a punch line; courtesy of Mary Harron, by way of Valerie Solanas and Lili Taylor, this was a joke Elvis got to tell.

Finally, then, the joke was on Andy Warhol—but with Bill Clinton it may be too soon to know. Once more, as with that thing that wouldn't die, that severed pillbox hand, slithering through time and space, the joke may be turning back toward the man who, so long ago, afraid to be too much like Elvis, put away his saxophone.

As always, you find it in the punch lines, in the throwaways, around the edges of news stories. The identification of Clinton and Elvis died, became its own ghost, when Clinton became president. Now, courtesy of Kenneth Starr—one of whose lead prosecutors, Hickman Ewing of Memphis, used to go out, before his spiritual awakening, get drunk, and sing Elvis songs until he'd used them up (his spiritual awakening, for what it's worth, took place the year Elvis died)—the ghost is creeping back.

Reuters, November 13, 1997:

Convicted Whitewater figure James McDougal said prosecutor Kenneth Starr will use a check to President Clinton from Madison Guaranty Savings & Loan to "hang" the president and his wife.

McDougal told the Washington Times in an interview that the 1982 cashier's check, recently discovered in the trunk of an abandoned car, was a loan from the failed savings and loan and that he and Clinton had agreed to conceal the transaction.

Clinton has testified that he never got a loan from Madison.

. . . Workers at a Little Rock junkyard found the check for $27,000, payable to Clinton, in the trunk of a car abandoned by a former Madison courier 10 years ago.

The check was not endorsed.

Clinton's lawyer, David Kendall, said the find "may have the authenticity and credibility of a newly discovered and freshly written Elvis autobiography."

But Henry Floyd, the former Madison employee who owned the abandoned car, said . . . "If that's so, then we'd better get investigators out there, because Elvis Presley's alive."

Creeping back, courtesy of Dolly Kyle Browning, author of *Purposes of the Heart,* a self-published novel about Browning's supposed thirty-year affair with Bill Clinton. Before taking over as the go-between—or cut-out—for the Linda Tripp tapes, literary agent Lucianne Goldberg had been trying to sell the book, but not even the famously right-wing publisher Alfred Regnery would take it. In the following passage, Clinton is Cameron Coulter, the young attorney general of Mississippi; Browning is Kelly McClain. They've just separated after having sex in her El Dorado:

Out on the highway where Cameron had accelerated to God-knows-what, Kelly floated along at the speed limit. She pushed the Elvis tape into the eight-track and reveled in the sunshine, imagining Cameron harmonizing with them as she and Elvis sang, *"Treat me right, Treat me good, Treat me like you really should, 'Cause I'm not made of wood, And I don't have a Wooden Heart."*

—Dolly Kyle Browning has some taste in Elvis songs—

Kelly dreamed as she drove through the beautiful Mississippi country-side. It seemed that each of Elvis' songs held its own memory with Cameron. When she finally ejected the tape and was reaching into the glove compartment for another one of her Elvis favorites, she heard the radio announcer mention his name.

"Yes, the King is dead in Memphis and all the world mourns."

Kelly was stunned. She knew that Cameron would be shocked and saddened by Elvis' death. She wanted to comfort him. She wanted to be with him, now, listening to Elvis. She wanted to be with him for-ever, listening to Elvis, but now Elvis was gone and forever was gone, too.

And still creeping back. Again last fall, Bill Clinton nominated Bill Ferris of the University of Mississippi to head the National En-dowment for the Humanities. At the university, Ferris had spon-sored Elvis conferences; the 1995 conference caused a scandal when Lee Crow, otherwise known as Elvis Herselvis, a lesbian Elvis impersonator, appeared onstage. Though he was confirmed by the Senate, thanks to home state Senator Trent Lott, the Re-publican majority leader, Ferris's appointment also drew scorn. This was not a joke everyone wanted to hear. The National En-dowment for the Humanities, said John M. Ellis of the Association of Literary Scholars and Critics, needed someone "who has strong feeling for what is central, not what is peripheral, and a person who sponsors conferences on Elvis, it would seem to me, does not have that sense."

But this was nothing compared to what has occurred in the past few months.

In February, not long after the story of Bill Clinton's affair with White House intern Monica Lewinsky burst into the news, Ken-neth Starr's office let it slip to the *Wall Street Journal* that Clinton's personal steward had observed Lewinsky alone with Clinton, and had found "stained" tissues in a wastebasket, which left the steward, the story said, "personally offended." (The leak, it later turned out, was accurate but misleading: while the implication was that the tissues in question were stained with semen, it was lipstick.) Starr called the steward before his Grand Jury; Bayani Nelvis took the stand. No one commented on "Elvis" hiding in the name of the steward, but the door was open. From the *New York Times,* just a few days later:

While the White House contended that Mr. Starr was leaking information to support his investigation, Republicans suggested that the White House was leaking the same information to destroy his inquiry . . .

Others speculated that someone in Mr. Starr's office was out to disrupt [Starr's] investigation by leaking, or that Ms. Lewinsky's lawyers were out to accomplish something by leaking, although no one seemed clear on precisely what.

"We're going through the 'Elvis lives' phase of all this," said one person involved in the controversy. Insisting on anonymity . . . he added in an accurate if vague description of himself: "You can use any of that as 'an administration official.'"

Not that it mattered, Jonathan Alter wrote in a *Newsweek* column dated the same day as the *Times* story: "The people have decided: Bill Clinton may be a hound dog, but he's *our* hound dog." But the hound dog has ranged so widely through our culture, the recent prediction that, if the increase in the number of Elvis impersonators over the last twenty years holds, eventually all Americans will be Elvis impersonators, is redundant: enough of the actors in this drama already are. Everyone knows that the entire Lewinsky explosion came out of depositions that Bill Clinton and Monica Lewinsky gave in Paula Jones's sexual harassment suit against Clinton—depositions illegally leaked to the press either by Jones's lawyers, or illegally passed by them to Kenneth Starr, and then leaked by his office in turn. It is not well known, though, that Paula Jones's husband, Steve Jones, was once an actor, and, following his calling, appeared in Jim Jarmusch's 1989 movie *Mystery Train,* playing the ghost of Elvis—probably the least convincing impersonation of Elvis Presley ever captured on film. That Jones's suit was dismissed deprived us of the spectacle of the trial, with one Elvis righteously defending the honor of his wife against the depredations of another Elvis—but for that we are all better off.

The Elvis stamp was launched twelve days before Bill Clinton became president. Two days from now people from all over the world will be here to mark the death of Elvis Presley; the day after that, Bill Clinton will testify to Kenneth Starr's Grand Jury, and that day, many people believe, may mark the death of Clinton's presidency. But coincidences make metaphors, and metaphors make culture.

"My problem with Clinton," Howard Hampton wrote me two weeks ago,

is that he's less Good Elvis or Bad Elvis than Arena Elvis—always milking the crowd, playing to the audience's most petit-maudlin impulses while wearing that big Memphis/Little-Rock-mafia grin as he winks at Sonny and Red in the wings. But all that shit about dignity and propriety misses the point—the Comeback Kid doesn't need to do a public "Crying in the Chapel" plea, he needs to pull a '68 Comeback Special on the bastards, and finally tell Kenny and the Kongress, "If you're lookin' for trouble / You've come to the right place."

"In my dreams," Hampton said—but it's not just dreams. Culture is a word that signifies how people explain themselves to each other, how they talk to each other: how they discover what it is they have in common. All of the people in the tale I've tried to follow have something to do with each other. In one way or another, Elvis is what they talk about, or what describes them. Elvis Presley is common ground, and, more than that, "Elvis Presley" has become a language we speak—and if this language takes the form of a joke, it's far from finding its real punch line. Or, as Priscilla Presley puts it on the label of the "First Vintage" of Graceland Napa Valley Chardonnay, available at better wine dealers for $22 a bottle, "We invite you to enjoy the alchemy now or savor the mystery for years."

University of Memphis,
August 14, 1998

Demand the Impossible

Never before, in all our history, have these forces been so united AGAINST one candidate, as they stand today. They are UNANIMOUS in their hate for me, and I WELCOME their hatred.

—Franklin D. Roosevelt, Madison Square
Garden Campaign Rally, 1936

Hillary Clinton was relentless. For a moment it was shocking: to see and hear someone speak so plainly, without cant, without bending words into euphemisms, putting it all on the line. That was how it seemed—if only for a moment. The country was up for grabs. So was its ability, or its will, to talk real talk, to talk to itself. Almost thirty years ago, at commencement ceremonies for Wellesley's class of '69, Republican Senator Edward Brooke of Massachusetts, the main speaker, had just concluded his remarks on student protest ("a perversion of democratic privilege") when Hillary Rodham, the first Wellesley student ever chosen to address her own class, stepped up in turn. She put aside her speech and talked back, calling up the May uprising in France the year before: "As the French student wrote on the wall of the Sorbonne, 'Demand the impossible.' We will settle for nothing less." For a moment, you could imagine you were picking up an echo.

It was one evening this fall, before anyone knew what would happen. It was a campaign event, a relatively low-rent fund-raiser for a liberal senator in trouble, an event both commonplace and extraordinary. Commonplace because it was the sort of event repeated endlessly that season, with partisan hopes raised ritually by buzzwords and slogans. Extraordinary because it was a night of fear—for a whole way of life, for lifetimes of beliefs that dark forces hovering in the air over the dull hotel ballroom were poised to devour. Those were the emotions, the too-familiar, unplumbed emotions everyone brought with them that night. Those dark forces—once, more than six decades ago, FDR stood before a madly cheering crowd and named them, one by one ("business and financial monopoly, speculation, reckless banking, class antagonism, sectionalism, war profiteering"), and then sucked them into his lungs as if they were no more than a satisfying deep breath at the end of a mountain climb: "And I WELCOME their hatred." Sitting at a table at the back of the ballroom, I wondered if anyone on my side could still speak that language, if anyone dared, if anyone could make an ordinary word like *stand* ring as FDR had rung it that night, like a bell.

As Hillary Clinton stepped up out of an elite, cordoned-off section in front of the stage, forty years of the century collapsed in an instant. She was a vision of 1958. With her famously changing hairstyles, you never know who she will appear to be, what role she will seem to be assuming, what costume will give her pleasure or nerve. Here, with her hair an unmoving bowl around the grin locked on her face, she looked exactly like a middle-class matron addressing a group one step down from the Junior League. That wasn't how she came off, though.

Not like the lawyer, political operative, surrogate, automaton, or Stepford First Lady some people present were expecting, she delivered a long, hard-edged speech as if it were one tiny step on a long road, one league in a journey that had begun long before she was born and would continue long after she was dead—or, if the forces of darkness were to triumph, might not continue at all. Her eyes flashing, she used no notes, and there wasn't a hint that anything was memorized. Rather, it was if the questions were so clear—*Who is to govern this land, and for whom?*—that any *decent* person, anyone with a commitment to justice, to fairness, to hope, to compassion, could speak the truth without notes, could summon nostrums about this policy or that with heart and soul.

The vapid unreality of what was actually being said—"Our children are our future," Hillary Clinton said, and she spoke of "the people" and of "how politics impacts on their lives"—dissolved, for the moment, in the face of the weird spectacle of a figment of the public imagination returning herself to flesh and blood. Just once, as she began, as she warmed up, she had referred to "the blizzard of *stuff* that's out there." *Stuff:* a code word for scandal, bloodlust, sorrow, betrayal, opportunism, impeachment. A code word for what, around that time, people from columnist Anthony Lewis to Representative Zoe Lofgren, a Democratic member of the House Judiciary Committee, were beginning to speak of as a coup d'état. But now, as Hillary Clinton plunged ahead, moving from "a woman's right to choose" to education, from job creation to patients' rights, it was hard to remember all that. This was an autonomous performance. You could forget who "the president," even the "Bill" she kept referring to, was, or who he was to her. Her face seemed her own, as did her voice. After all the years, the comforts of Chicago and Wellesley had been burnt out of it: "getting" was now "gitting," and it was no affectation, merely the leavings of a life lived elsewhere. She stepped up to the podium in the fog of lifelessness left by the Democratic motivational speakers who had preceded her: the liberal senator, the disappointingly minor actors reading from books by the senator and Hillary Clinton and Eleanor Roosevelt. (Sharon Stone was supposed to have been there.) They had cast a negative spell. The hard, cracking sounds coming out of Hillary Clinton's mouth broke it cleanly.

This wasn't armor, it was a force field. You could try to read all the serious or sniggering media commentary on the true nature of Hillary Clinton's marriage, her "arrangement," her "deal," with the evidentiary pillars of the Starr Report including a section quoting a friend of Monica Lewinsky quoting Lewinsky quoting Bill Clinton saying, *Well, kiddo, you never know—I might be alone in a few years,* back on her, but you couldn't do that any more than you could read his betrayal on her face. She was a pathetic dirty joke; the assumption was that she was naked in the public square and could be treated as such. "Predictions for the Year 2000," announced Conan O'Brien a few nights later: "Hillary Clinton will divorce Bill and re-marry—Charlie Sheen!" It was the most leaden joke imaginable, but as a violation absolutely nothing compared to the sober dis-course in publications advertising their guardianship of propriety and rectitude. "I think Hillary could be a powerful sexual partner," said one expert on contemporary mores in the *New York Times Magazine*, "but I don't think the president can see it. It's too much like being in bed with your law partner for him." Never mind how little even your best friend understands of your marriage, or you of his or hers; with this woman exposed to the crowd, anyone could feel empowered to see through her skin. But as Hillary Clinton spoke of the country's business and who might best pursue it, some-how her complete inhabitation of a public role was the most pow-erful affirmation of privacy: the most effective *fuck you*.

For all that the words of her speech rang hollowly. They seemed to trail a great future behind them. It was in fact a desperate night, with every possible vote counted in advance—with every vote counted against any word that might lose a single one of them. Hillary Clinton could not speak as Franklin Roosevelt had once spo-ken, with fearless musicality and delight. Speaking plainly, speaking the truth, she might have said what he said: "They are UNANI-MOUS in their hate for me, and I . . ." But if she had said that, she would have been dismissed as a self-important paranoid tending to her mad theories of right-wing conspiracy and anti-Arkansas con-tempt. She would truly have been back in the '50s: just another housewife ready for the barbiturate prescription and the straitjacket.

So, as Hillary Clinton spoke on this commonplace and extraordi-nary night, she said nothing with flair and elan. She revealed how impoverished our political speech has become, how scared it is of what it might say. The dark forces hovering over the hotel ballroom, over the bad food that everyone was happy to eat for the chance to

be on the side of good and right, could have been named, as
Franklin Roosevelt had named the dark forces of his time. The different country that those dark forces desire, a different home for all
of those present, could have been described. But because the fear
of that new country could not be talked about, the event was suspended in time. Fear was the subject of the speech that nobody
gave, the speech that those present silently addressed to themselves.

The uninvited guest was king; no speaker said what she meant.
Yes, this policy or that—but not, "For his own reasons, whatever
they were, the president opened a breach in his wall of defense
against those who mean to destroy him and everything in this country that we cherish, and now it is our choice to stand with an un-
worthy but irreplaceable man, or in disgust and tiredness turn and
walk away." But we didn't know what his reasons were. We couldn't
fathom them. It was a mystery—not "the mystery of democracy"
Bill Clinton spoke of on the night he was first elected, but not quite
separate from it, either, as the single citizen, for all of his or her secret crimes and hidden corruptions, is not separate from the republic, but one part of its body. In that body, private evil can be
transformed into public good, but this night emptiness held court.

I began thinking about where, when the real story might get told,
its language might be found. I could imagine Bill Clinton—in his exile, in Little Rock, a lawyer who can still cut a deal, or in Des Moines,
warming up the crowd for Tony Robbins—sitting down to pull out of
himself a true confession, to solve his own mystery. I could imagine
too that he never would—but that just as Robert Penn Warren found
Huey Long, dug out his heart, held it in hands, and then placed it in
a fictional body, someone as good might come along and knit Bill
Clinton's story to that of the republic, from which, now, it is almost
certainly pulling apart. I know that our present-day political speech
cannot ennoble, can't even really damn, what our politics are now
made of. I know that political speech cannot make our political body
speak. Only cultural speech can do that, and it will be a long time

coming, if it is not already gone. So in my head I replayed a Hank Williams record I'd bought that week, an odd little collection of performances, all of which I already had, a disc called *Alone and Forsaken*. Records are fetish objects; I bought this one because I wanted an album named after my favorite Hank Williams song.

"Alone and Forsaken," a solo recording with guitar released only after Williams's death, is Williams at his most bereft, his most broken, his most artless, his least protected by craft and style. Quietly, slowly, the peformance is all doom. There is a hollowness in the singing, but it's not the hollowness of speaking falsely; it's the hollowness that echoes when you open your mouth to speak and you know no one will hear you. In Williams's thin, reedy voice was the sound you make in a dream, faced with mortal danger, trying to scream and unable to raise a whisper.

The late news led with footage of Hillary Clinton's speech, people outside the hotel denouncing Bill Clinton with overwhelming conviction, and an update on the McGuire-Sosa race—a race that will likely be remembered more vividly than any other race of the year. As almost everybody knew, both men had this night hit their heretofore unimaginable sixty-sixth home runs. The sportscaster, a sharp man, came on to announce that Sammy Sosa of the Chicago Cubs had hit his forty-sixth home run, and that, exactly forty-six minutes later, Mark McGuire of the St. Louis Cardinals had followed with his own forty-sixth. It wasn't a mistake; it was an inexplicable moment of madness. The sportscaster smiled a hard smile, refusing to admit that anything was wrong; the anchors at his side looked on in utter confusion, dumbfounded, frozen, the true event of the night now suspended not in time but out of it.

—September 30, 1998

Contribution to City Pages
Artist of the Year Issue

Anthony Lewis is the *New York Times* columnist who has so doggedly stayed on the heels of the con artist of the year, prosecutor Kenneth Starr. It was in 1998 that Starr, abandoning all pretense of a true-crime story, proved himself master of the long con (as opposed to the mere "Hey, that was a twenty I gave you, mister, not a ten" short con). He produced an elaborate, carefully set up and sustained story that preyed upon the mark's need to believe, on his sense of entitlement, and most of all on his vanity. And in this case the mark was the most vain of all the nobles in the land: the Washington press corps.

Starr fed their fantasies that they too could be Woodward and Bernstein, that they too could bring down a president, that they too could save the country—as Meat Loaf says, two out of three ain't bad. The deal was simple: give Starr the coverage he wanted, and he'll give you stories. Write with distance, write with skepticism, and the pipe is cut off. Thus the fantastic spectacle, as the year went on, of reporters soberly chronicling the scandal of Starr's illegal leaking of Grand Jury material as if it were an insoluble mystery—as if they had somehow forgotten just who had leaked to them.

For years, Lewis has insisted on the disregard for civil liberties that has marked the Clinton administration: the instinct for censorship, the craven abandonments of habeas corpus and other citizens' protections for a few polling points. The problem, Lewis once wrote, is that Clinton has no bottom line: no position on the Constitution from which, finally, he won't retreat. But Lewis never gambled on anyone like Starr, a man prepared to destroy the Constitution in order to destroy a president he has plainly judged the embodiment of evil, of chaos, of that dread and floating idea, "the sixties"—a man Starr knows in his bones is the Antichrist and, what is worse, a man whose very existence Starr takes as a deeply personal affront. Thus Lewis has written carefully, like a good crime reporter, stripping away the euphemisms of the rest of the press, cutting through the bland and obfuscatory reportage of his own newspaper. And, like a linguist, like an epistemologist, he has turned the facts in the public record over and over until they fell into place and spoke a real language: he kept at it until he cracked the case.

He did on December 1, in a piece called "The Starr Trap." He boiled the case down to the "we-didn't-have-sex" affidavit that Monica Lewinsky had sworn out as a deposition in the Paula Jones case—but which, when Starr's men descended on Lewinsky as Linda Tripp set her up in Pentagon City, had yet to be filed. Swearing a false affidavit is not a crime; filing one is. Lewis: "This is why [Starr's] deputies worked so hard to keep Ms. Lewinsky from calling [her lawyer] Fred Carter. If he knew what was happening, they realized, he would not file it. And they wanted a crime." Thus Bill Clinton, another vain noble, went forward with testimony that, had he known what was happening, would never have been given. It was the first trap of many, and, as an article in Lewis's own paper would put if a few weeks before Lewis's column appeared, something that no longer mattered. All that mattered was the wonderful story the paper got to publish every day.

They will be forgotten, all the breathless dispatches from the

Washington bureaus, all the weighty, considered, serious, pompous *New York Times* editorials on decency and responsibility, on leadership and obligation, the thousands and thousands of heavy words overseen by editorial page director Howell Raines, like Bill Clinton a white southerner in his fifties, who every day must ask himself one question, one question on which his oversight of the republic rests: *How come that shmuck's president and I'm not?*

This does not seem to be a question that has occurred to Anthony Lewis, who, working with what was hiding in plain sight, rewrote the daily news as a detective story that may be read with gasps of shock long after he and everyone else mentioned above is dead.

City Pages (Minneapolis),
December 30, 1998

Center of the Universe

In a signal moment during the jam sessions that highlighted Elvis Presley's 1968 comeback TV special—the most explosive music of his life—he told a funny story. It was 1956, he remembered, in the midst of the national scandal over his celebration of his own body. "The police filmed a show one time in Florida, 'cause, uh, the PTA, the YMCA, or somebody thought I was . . . something. They said, 'Man, he's *gotta* be crazy.' So the police came out and filmed the show, so I couldn't move. I had to stand still. The only thing I moved was my little finger."

There's an awful match for this moment early on in Peter Guralnick's *Careless Love: The Unmaking of Elvis Presley*, the second and last volume in what is now a twelve-hundred-page Presley biography. The first, the acclaimed *Last Train to Memphis*: *The Rise of Elvis Presley,* took the story to the fall of 1958, closing with the death of Elvis's beloved mother. Now Elvis is in the Army in West Germany, surrounded by a payroll of pals from Memphis as one night, in mufti, he enters a seamy Munich strip club called the Moulin Rouge. "Almost from the moment he arrived," Guralnick writes, "the band started playing Elvis Presley songs and did their best to coax their famous guest up onstage." But the hand of Presley's canny manager, Colonel Tom Parker, who always knew the value of keeping his asset under wraps, reached even across the Atlantic. As Guralnick re-creates Presley's life, it seems there is no one living he hasn't spoken to, hasn't gotten to really tell the tale in the cadences of real talk, in language you can instantly distinguish from the stilted, self-serving memoir excerpts he sometimes has to use—thus, forty years after that night in Munich, the regret and revulsion felt by a German woman who was there haven't dimmed: "He began to sing, and one of his bodyguards said that he should stop—he should know that he is not allowed to sing; it is forbidden. Then he was singing at the table, and that wasn't allowed either. So then he beat the time, and that wasn't allowed either."

"Elvis Presley performed existential acts which helped to liberate an entire generation," Guralnick wrote in a 1968 review of the comeback special, but that is not the language of his biography. "I wanted to rescue Elvis Presley from the dreary bondage of myth, from the oppressive aftershock of cultural significance," Guralnick wrote in *Last Train to Memphis;* his first goal, he said, was "to allow the characters to breathe their own air." In both books, he has realized that remarkable ambition. But what if the air his characters breathe is itself oppressive, their everyday culture a form of bondage? That is the air the reader, like the characters, must breathe all through *Careless Love,* so perfectly named for an old folk song about how idly hearts are broken. Presley's artistic discoveries of the early Sun sessions in Memphis, his national and then world conquests—all are left behind. What remains is a chronicle, across nearly twenty years, of a king locked in his own prison. Here, every true, distinct event marking a day actually different from the one before it—a recording session in 1960 where passion leaped up; the first performances in Las Vegas in 1969, with Elvis madly, hilariously declaiming his life story from the stage; the strange meeting with President Richard Nixon in 1970—is felt as a jailbreak, with the prisoner soon captured or, worse, returning to prison of his own accord. That is the air one breathes as, in 1977, his last year, Presley is propped up and pushed out onstage night after night while those around him all but place bets on how long it will take him to die.

The story has been told before, but never so convincingly or with such an absence of glee or condescension—and never to such a point of stupefaction. In *The Count of Monte Cristo,* which in its unabridged form is even longer than the two volumes of Guralnick's biography, it is the length itself, the slow, steady accumulation of events, that hypnotizes the reader; bent on revenge, the Count comes to seem all-powerful, the center of the universe. Here, the same accumulation, but of meaningless repetitions— woman stacked upon woman, drug piled upon drug, humiliating movie after humiliating movie filed on the same shelf, one hired friend after another squeezed into the Edwardian phone booth that was Graceland—is equally hypnotizing. The difference is that the story doesn't build, it evaporates. At the center of his own universe, Elvis empties out, and so fully that as the pages turn the outside world all but ceases to exist. Guralnick so completely absents himself from this nihilist epic that the odd critical comment comes to seem as anomalous, and as momentarily liberating, as Elvis gone missing, the writer's escape from his own story as he has defined it: "In the closed world in which they lived, the same stories were passed back and forth until they became common property, taking on the status of a larger myth whose literal origins were no longer relevant."

Last fall in Nashville, Guralnick and I shared a literary forum. I've known Guralnick for thirty years, and I felt he sold himself short when he stated his credo: "My approach to writing is the same as my approach to coaching baseball. I tell the kids, 'Don't speculate. Stay inside the game.'" My approach is the opposite— speculate; get outside the game—and I think that to find a person who so completely entered the souls of others as Elvis Presley did, you have to do that. "The one sure thing in life is that you never know what's going on in someone's head—that's what the novel was invented for," the cinema verité filmmaker D. A. Pennebaker said recently. "You can't point a camera at someone and find out what's in their heads. But it does the next best thing: it lets you speculate." I think that is where Elvis lives, outside of the game as his golden, impoverished life defined it. As Pennebaker suggests, you can see it in our faces, as the Presley story continues outside the Graceland walls. I saw it not long ago, flipping channels, when I lucked into the familiar ending of John Dahl's *Red Rock West*.

Nicolas Cage, Lara Flynn Boyle, J. T. Walsh, and Dennis Hopper are jammed into a car, on their way to the graveyard to dig up the money, the only question is who's going to die, and they all look like Elvis. Walsh is carrying too much weight, barely in control of himself, the older, damned Elvis; terror is the only real emotion in his eyes, with every other feature forming a mask of puffy, sallow flesh. With her hooded eyes, short, jet black man's pompadour, and Eisenhower jacket, Boyle is somewhere between the '54 Beale Street zoot-suiter and the black-leather flash of the '68 comeback; take your eyes off her and you're dead. Whether in costume or not—as a hillbilly cat in *Wild at Heart*, the '70s clown in *Honeymoon in Vegas*, a drunk chasing death in his own clothes in *Leaving Las Vegas*—Cage is always Elvis; here he's at the wheel as if onstage, sweat pouring, hair askew, ready for anything. Hopper has his own pompadour, gray but higher than Boyle's. He's a '50s rockabilly stud carrying his own fifties as easily as the gun he holds on the rest of them. He's also as much an impersonator as Cage is the real deal; the gun makes Hopper a big shot, but you can hear the whine of the small-time in his mouth. "You think you're better than me, don't you, Mike?" he says to Cage, sticking the pistol into Cage's temple. It's a line Cage will use as payback when Hopper finally falls down dead: "You know, Lyle, you're right. I am better than you." Naturally, he's the only one who gets away.

Do they look like Elvis because they want to, or because, in the alchemy of culture, this oddball from Memphis had something almost everybody wants? It takes all four of them to even come close to what you could read in Elvis Presley's face: all those things that, like blessings and curses from the Pandora's box he opened, he set loose upon the land. Those things were always present, but not with such glamour, with such a spark of perfect rhythm: desire, madness, mastery, waste; bravery, cowardice, generosity, malevolence; beauty, ugliness, humility, vanity. Elvis remains a haunting; it's more comforting to see those supposedly contradictory aspects of a common identity in a cast of faces than in one. Is that why we still turn away, embarrassed by the stirrings of Presley's arrival, or disgusted by the way he left? As the last verses of "Careless Love" have it:

> Once I wore my apron low
> I couldn't scarcely keep you from my door
>
> Now my apron strings don't pin
> You pass my door and you don't come in

Esquire, *February 1999*

Pleasantville

History speaks as it is made: *Invasion of the Body Snatchers*—
that fable of alien seedpods devouring their human hosts and
replacing them with an entire society of soulless replicants—is a
tale we will not escape any time soon. First taking shape on film in
1956, the persistence of the story implies that the fifties remain the
haunted house of the American century. A diabolical experiment
was performed then, the movies say: maybe something to do with
atomic radiation, as Kevin McCarthy's small-town doctor speculated as the saga began, or, as critics have speculated ever since,
maybe something to do with politics, with Communist brainwash-
ing or government witch-hunts. The latest version of *Invasion of
the Body Snatchers*—certainly the most imaginative version—is
Pleasantville.

Released last fall, it was a cute picture with no big ad campaign
and no big stars. It left behind a collection of reviews focusing
mostly on its gimmick: two nineties teenagers fall through their TV
set and into the world of a family sitcom from the fifties called
"Pleasantville," and under their influence everything and everybody goes from black and white to color. With all of the uplift and
release of the good guys winning in a Frank Capra movie, the film
means to prove that America always contains a secret country, a

zombie second self—and that that zombie America can be overthrown, in this case with sex and art. It's a fairy tale, but it's not as if it isn't a fairy tale that has already been lived.

The story was never modest. In Don Siegel's original film, *Invasion of the Body Snatchers* was an exploitation metaphor for J. Edgar Hoover's Enemy Within. In claustrophobic black and white, the movie is unrelievedly creepy and nerve-wracking; after half an hour any given movement can startle you out of your seat, and you can forget that any real world exists outside the film's frame of reference. Meeting in secret, passing out the seedpods to be left in the basements and gardens of those yet to be transformed, the new pod people really do seem like members of Communist cells, spreading the propaganda that, in the fifties, it was somehow assumed Americans could never resist. But by the end, with the whole of a town changed and in mad pursuit of the two humans left, the pod people have turned into a traditional American lynch mob and the humans into the demonized Commies—in the fifties, liberal schoolteachers far more commonly than Red screenwriters—who must be stamped out.

In Philip Kaufman's still-terrifying 1978 remake, the pod people were New Age revolutionaries. "What happens?" a human asks Leonard Nimoy's turtlenecked pod psychiatrist as he prepares to inject a sedative so that she might receive her new body. (All versions of *Invasion of the Body Snatchers* agree they get you when you sleep.) "You'll be born again into an untroubled world," he says. Soon, the few stray remaining humans are exposed by pointing fingers and screams so awful they can make you feel dead. Abel Ferrara's 1994 *Body Snatchers* was about the collapse of the family—unless it was about the chance to see Gabrielle Anwar naked in a bathtub, hundreds of pod tendrils growing around her body and into her nostrils, sucking out her soul as she nods off.

In writer-director Gary Ross's *Pleasantville,* the old story is hidden inside a reversal of its premises. The town the two present-day teenagers discover is America after the pod people have triumphed. It's their achievement, their utopia: the zombies are happy in their black-and-white world. But this utopia is also an old media dream of the American '50s, a common dream the country has been dreaming through official representations—TV shows like *Ozzie and Harriet* and *Leave it to Beaver,* full-page *Life* magazine ads for new vacuum cleaners and the housewives to run them, new cars and the prosperous men to drive them—ever since that insoluble little era of good feeling and atomic bombs got under way. The '50s are a dream the country has never been able to wake from, as blessing or curse: once upon a time everything was boring, every day was the same (as Thomas Pynchon once wrote, "One of the most pernicious effects of the '50s was to convince the people growing up during them that it would last forever"), and everything was OK.

When Reese Witherspoon's slutty Jen and Tobey Maguire's curious David, her twin brother—now "Mary Sue" and "Bud" in Pleasantville's George and Betty Parker family—find themselves in the pod nirvana, you're as amused as they are to learn that here it never rains and nothing burns, that the bathrooms have no toilets and going all the way means holding hands, that all books are blank and the outside world does not exist. (An aerial view of Pleasantville shows it hidden in a peaceful valley between high mountains: James Hilton's, or Frank Capra's, Shangri-La.) Everyone is chirpy, white, and content. "Is that what TV in the fifties was really like?" the twenty-six-year-old in the seat next to me asked, in other words asking if this was really the self-portrait America had once presented to itself. I wasn't sure; it seemed too weird. "Yes," said a voice one seat over, and suddenly it wasn't weird at all. The Great Depression and the Second World War had left an entire society shell-shocked; no one knew anymore what normal was, but everyone wanted to know. The diabolical experiment that was performed in the fifties, that was at once celebrated and concealed within the everyday culture of the time, was an exchange of real life for an idea of normal life.

In *Pleasantville*, though, it's the pod people who change. The aliens, the transported kids, come to make the pod people human; change means shedding, not assuming, one's pod skin. At the soda shop where David has an after-school job, it's the cook who cannot function once David breaks the routine they've always followed, but who soon enough will begin to cover the town with outrageous murals of falling buildings and naked women. It's the high school basketball star who Jen fucks silly. (Dazed after he drives her home, he sees the first bit of color in Pleasantville, a red rose wet with dew on the bush, just like the little pods glistening on rose bushes at the beginning of the 1978 *Invasion of the Body Snatchers*.) Most hauntingly, though, it's Jen's new mother, Joan Allen's Betty Parker: a precise replica not only of all the starched and ironed housewives of fifties TV, but also of the shriveling Pat Nixon she played in Oliver Stone's *Nixon*. "What goes on at Lovers' Lane?" she asks Jen. It's a place where couples once sat apart looking at the stars; Jen has turned it into a field of rocking cars. "Is it holding hands and that kind of thing?" "That, and . . . well, sex," says Jen. There's a long pause; you expect Betty to be shocked that the change she's sensed all around her has gone so far, but that's not it. "Oh," Betty finally says. "What's sex?"

Now, it's rare to see an actor's character actually think as you watch, but with Reese Witherspoon that's her whole performance. She's a hundred pounds of doubt and querulousness. She's got the fastest mind on the screen today, and so an entire universe of choices, an infinite array of words and deeds, opens up on her face in a close-up; anything is possible and everything is at stake. How does a human daughter explain sex to her pod mother? She goes back to her high school sex ed movies, left over from the seventies; she bridges the gap. "You see, Mom," Jen says, "when two people love each other very much, and they want to share that . . ." The movie has sucked the whole of the postwar neurosis into itself and given it back as one great, terrified joke.

Soon Betty wakes up horrified by the new color on her face. A race war breaks out—beween the black-and-white people and the "coloreds," with the remaining pod people attacking colored people like the pod people hunting down humans in the earlier films— and, in footage that looks like old newsreels, inescapably like white people pointing and screaming at black students as, for the first time, they entered Central High School in Little Rock, Arkansas. Then a cultural war breaks out, and then there is a happy ending, offering you the sort of smile you can only get at the movies. On the soundtrack, Randy Newman's music takes your hand and guides you out of the theater and into the street.

But there you find that you and those around you still carry traces of that old experiment; that the haunted house is not the theater but where you live; and that the wars left behind in the film are still going on. You leave the theater feeling more alive; it's as if the wars have just started.

Esquire, *March 1999*

A Look Back

If you look back over the last ten years, you can, if the notion appeals to you, choose an artist who most shadows these times: the Coen brothers, Oliver Stone, David Lynch, Bill Pullman, or Jim Carrey in the movies, Mike Judge on TV, Tupac Shakur as an icon in the life-proves-art game, Dr. Dre, Puff Daddy, or Master P as entrepreneurs and empire builders, Bill Clinton as fast-talking, slow-walking, good-looking Mohair Sam. You can regret those who had a chance to speak in a new voice and lost it, or simply let it go: the Geto Boys, Snoop Doggy Dogg, Sinéad O'Connor. I could make a better case for the music of PJ Harvey, the Pet Shop Boys, Corin Tucker in Heavens to Betsy and Sleater-Kinney, Bob Dylan, or David Thomas—but if Kurt Cobain, speaking through Nirvana, had done nothing but write and record "Smells Like Teen Spirit" and make it hit, he might still be a step ahead, even though he left the decade to its own devices before it was half over.

In the time he took, Cobain used the decade up—and in a sense "Smells Like Teen Spirit" used his music up even as it announced it. You can hear every other song Nirvana made in what this one song asked for, in what this one song was convinced it would never get. From the first time they heard it, for every time afterward—in the two-and-a-half years between the tune's entry into the charts, in the fall of 1991, and Cobain's suicide, in the spring of 1994, and in the five years since—more people than myself or maybe you have felt the chill of the slow, transparent, chiming notes that are the repeated signature of "Smells Like Teen Spirit." You hear all that is lucid, simple, and unrushed—a between-past-and-future suspension of time lovely enough to convince you that the world itself has paused to listen—pulling against the desperation and hurry of everything else in the performance, the everything else that finally sucks up those brief prophecies of clarity and wipes them out.

Still, those silken notes hang in the air, a mourning for the failures of the past, the suggestion of a future to be made or lost, a sense of starting over stopped in its tracks, remaining as an echo that rebukes you for your own failures. The song is big, loud, ambitious, definitively unsettling and a definitive release, with the singer as sure of what he means as he is that it's a waste of time to explain it to anyone who might hear him.

In the world called up in "Smells Like Teen Spirit," there was room for small, quiet, perfect Nirvana tunes like "Something in the Way," and huge, rolling screams like "Tourette's," for sterile manifestos like "Serve the Servants" and fabulous shaggy-dog stories like the band's bootlegged cover of the Doors' "The End" (the Oedipal tragedy here reduced from eleven minutes to two and set entirely in a Belgian waffle house)—room, in other words, for anyone who felt the song stake its claim to a moment it insisted couldn't last. "A denial! A denial! A denial!" Cobain said as he ended the song, in a voice that tested the body more than the soul, over and over, again and again: "A denial! A denial!" Of what? Of what you want most, of what you know you can't have. But as its sound pulls against its words, the song says something else: if you can have something as good as this, why can't you have what you want most?

There is a great, whole drama taking place in Nirvana's music, a drama that holds its shape, a drama that is also small and odd, a drama made with costumes but not masks. Kurt Cobain plays all the roles here; band mates Krist Novoselic and Dave Grohl are the chorus, standing off to the side, free to comment on the action but not implicated—positioned, as the drama hits its notes and runs its course, neither to reap the glory for the deeds performed nor pay for the crimes enacted.

You can see it in the opening and closing footage of Kevin Kerslake's 1994 video documentary *Live! Tonight! Sold Out!!* with Cobain appearing onstage in chopped reddish hair, a scruff of beard on his chin, a cigarette in his mouth, wearing nothing but a grossly overstuffed Frederick's of Hollywood–style black slip. Behind the drum kit, Grohl is stripped to the waist, typical metal-drummer attire except for Grohl's black bra; Novoselic is literally the straight man, a telephone pole with short hair and a Kmart cotton shirt hanging out of his pants. This is true grunge: not some music-business catchphrase, but dirt. The self-portrait Cobain presents is vaguely repulsive before it's anything else; before it's silly, the ultimate fulfillment of the Beavis and Butt-head dream Nirvana acted out better than any other band; before it's disturbing, before it's confirming, before you dimiss it with a laugh or scratch at it under your skin.

Grohl and Novoselic look funny here, as if they're having a good time, amused with the show. On Cobain's face, and in the way he holds his body—if it's even his anymore—is an unreadable, unstable smear of sarcasm and self-contempt, a cheap joke on the audience's presumed gender politics and an absolute refusal of things as they are. Cobain offers male as female, rapist as rape victim, prom queen as the ugliest girl in school ("People just left me alone," Cobain told critic Jon Savage in 1993. "They were afraid. I always felt they would vote me Most Likely to Kill Everyone at a High School Dance"), guitar hero as cultural terrorist, pop star as star of the bad dream you'd be ashamed to have, let alone imagine the star himself of having, the THIS WAY OUT of the band's biggest hit always available, really the end of every song: *Oh well, whatever, never mind*. At the end of this particular concert, at the end of the film, Cobain, his slip now more like a film of grime on his skin than a garment, his eyes dark and seeing something you're not seeing, crawls off the stage on his hands and knees like an animal.

The drama played out in Cobain's performance was a drama of abjection and abasement, of worthlessness and redundancy, a drama of surplus population, be it that of a solitary nobody who nobody liked or a generation the economy didn't need and the culture didn't want. "Raised in a home with six baby boomers, all I ever set out to do was find out why I felt so different," Gael Fashingbauer Cooper wrote in Minneapolis's *City Pages*, in a readers' forum published just after Cobain's death. "I celebrated their past through every trivia game and hundreds of history books, and one day it occurred to me that, however short it is, I might have a past of my own. Nirvana spoke to that, even if they had lives that were way more messed up than your own, even if you never liked them."

This drama, an acting out of the truth that you can make your own history, that you have to, was taken to extremes—in the screams out of Cobain's throat you couldn't gainsay as effects, in the band's punk war against its own success. More commercially successful than any other punk band, Nirvana was also the band most infected by the folk virus: the suspicion that if what you do is accepted by a mass audience, then your work must be either devoid of content or a sellout, and you yourself the enemy you set out to destroy. And yet the band made great drama even out of something as puerile as this—a doctrine inherited less from Johnny Rotten than Pete Seeger. There is a sequence in *Sold Out!!* when, through the milky, indistinct tones of what seems to be a tenth-generation bootleg video dub of "Love Buzz" as performed somewhere in South America, you see Cobain dive off a low stage into the crowd, which is pressing up against the stage as if it's bellying up to a bar. A guard roughly pulls Cobain back, then smashes him in the head and knocks him down. As Cobain pulls his arms and legs into his chest, the guard stomps him. This wasn't staged, it was real—and yet there was a way in which this event was staged, because it was always present in the music. The glimpse you are given of the man inside the publicity, a defenseless loser named Kurt Cobain inside a star who happens to have the same name—something the thug in the guard has suddenly glimpsed, and just as suddenly acted upon—is shocking.

But it's not as shocking as a *Sold Out!!* clip from *The Jonathan Ross Show*, apparently a U.K. TV variety program. A smiling Ross introduces Nirvana and "Lithium," musically a relatively moderate number in the group's repertoire; the band appears and, on this pleasant, orderly show, on a small, neat set, plays a harrowing version of "Territorial Pissings" instead. The band utterly explodes the context—which means that as you watch, nothing fits. More than that, what you're seeing is in some inarguable way not right. Every sound, every gesture, is wild, rough, and scraping: scraping the paint right off the walls, scraping your knowledge that in a setting such as this everything is ritualized right out of your head. Even as you watch, you can't imagine this was ever on TV. It's too strong, the song too far outside of itself, the musicians too far outside of themselves, the performance too far outside of any rules for it to be brought back into the strictures of expectation and result, for it to be returned to the frame of reference within which entertainment rests—and because this is a play, staged inside the little theater of the TV show, its reality is paradoxically far more complete than the real-time event of the guard attacking the performer. The shock is total: a denial, and as a denial a violation, someone killing everyone at the high school dance, yourself included, no matter how much you say you always liked the song.

"Nirvana was about our distrust and dependence on popular culture," wrote Darin Smith of St. Paul, another contributor to the *City Pages* forum. "We hate it because it's shallow, sentimental and dishonest. There are more points of similarity between Mariah Carey and Eddie Vedder than there are differences. I wear the same dumb stare when I put my Walkman on . . . Kurt didn't offer any solutions, he just railed against the ugliness and made it his home. We got a cheap thrill from celebrating our wretchedness with him. He wasn't brilliant or even all that articulate, but I liked to scream along. He didn't want to be my voice, and I know there was nothing healthy about singing 'Rape Me' every day on the way to work, so maybe it's best he's gone. Or maybe 'Rape Me' will feel even more compelling now." It does: so many of Cobain's last songs were draped in a curtain of noise, but today that curtain hides nothing. All the demands in the music—the demand to be heard, to be left alone, to come as you are and leave when you choose—stand out clearly, and all of those demands remain unsatisfied.

Rolling Stone,
May 13, 1999

The Man from Nowhere

One supposes that if Bill Clinton roamed the corridors of the
White House shooting everyone in sight and then, soaked in
blood, seized the airwaves to declare that he is the living
Antichrist, his public approval rating would continue to soar.
                    —John Carman, *San Francisco Chronicle*,
                                              February 4, 1998

O
n November 2, 1998—the day before the midterm congressional elections that, contrary to predictions of substantial
Democratic losses, were to result in the loss of five Republican
seats in the House of Representatives—staff writer Sally Quinn
published a story called "Not in Their Backyard" in the *Washington Post*. The piece was about the response of official—which is to
say unofficial, but real—Washington to the year-long scandal over
President Bill Clinton's affair with White House intern Monica
Lewinsky: about how offended, shocked, and disgusted the people
who run Washington were, and their offense, shock, and disgust
that the rest of the country apparently did not share their judgment.

To set the scene, Quinn cast back to Clinton's first Inaugural Address. His presidency was only a few minutes old, he had arrived
from Arkansas just days before, and he spoke of the capital as "a
place of intrigue and calculation," where those struggling for power
often forgot the people who sent them to Washington, and why
they had been sent. "With that," Quinn wrote, "the new president
sent a clear challenge to an already suspicious Washington establishment." She went on to contrast that event with one taking place

five years later—an event she clearly found more significant. Clinton advisor Rahm Emanuel—who, Quinn noted, "unlike the president, had become part of the Washington Establishment"—was speaking at a fund-raiser to combat a disease afflicting the son of two well-known members of the Washington press corps. Emanuel spoke of the gathering as an "extraordinary moment" when Republicans and Democrats, journalists and politicians, generals and diplomats, lawyers and loybbists (that night including Secretary of State Madeline Albright, Senator John McCain of Arizona, Representative Bob Livingston of Louisiana, Federal Reserve Board chairman Alan Greenspan, Jim Lehrer of PBS, and Maureen Dowd of the *New York Times,* "all behaving," Quinn said, "like the pals that they are") "came together as a community."

Actually, Quinn went on, it wasn't extraordinary at all. The capital is a place where "Washington insiders"—such as, to take Quinn's most pointed example, Washington attorney and Independent Counsel Kenneth Starr—have "many friends in both parties. Their wives are friendly with each other and their children go to the same schools." Partisanship dissolves among those whose fundamental interests are the same: "When Establishment Washingtonians of all persuasions gather to support their own, they are not unlike any other small community in the country." Because they had a "proprietary interest in Washington and identify with it," just like the citizens of, say, Smithville, Tennessee, or Kill Devil Hills, North Carolina, Establishment Washingtonians "call the capital city their 'town.'" "And," Quinn continued in a portentous one-sentence paragraph, "their town has been turned upside down."

The reason was the sleaze emanating from the White House: the sickening stories of extramarital sex, oral sex "not to completion" and "to completion," in the language of the Starr Report, semen stains, and lies about all of it. "People are outraged," Quinn wrote. "This is their home. . . . They feel Washington has been brought into disrepute by the actions of the president."

"He came in here and he trashed the place," Quinn quoted *Washington Post* columnist David Broder, "and it's not his place."

You can take that two ways: it's not Clinton's town, and, more to the point, he doesn't know his place. Both meanings make up the subtext of Quinn's piece; they also underlie the main lines of attack emanating from the Washington press corps almost from the time Clinton assumed the presidency. This attack greatly deepened in intensity after the public emergence of the Clinton-Lewinsky scandal—after months of concerted work by former White House employee Linda Tripp, her putative literary agent Lucianne Goldberg, their beard Michael Isikoff of *Newsweek,* the Internet gossip columnist Matt Drudge, such self-described "elves" as the right-wing cable TV pundit and lawyer Ann Coulter, the attorneys carrying Paula Jones's sexual harassment suit against Clinton, their funders at the Rutherford Institute, and the office of the independent counsel—but it did not really change in tenor or purpose. The purpose was profound: the attempt by much of the press, traveling along with the Republican congressional minorities and, from 1995, majorities, to deny Clinton's legitimacy as president, which is to say as titular head of any "Washington Establishment."

It's a matter of who and how. Sally Quinn was a writer for the *Washington Post* when she began an affair with the married editor. She married him, and assumed the position of influence she now holds. This is no secret; everyone in her "town" knows all about it. (As *Esquire* put it in its January 1999 issue without fear of reprisal, including Quinn's "Not in Their Backyard" in the "White House in Crisis" subsection of its "Dubious Achievements of 1998": "Fucked the boss, broke up his marriage, became the toast of Washington. Twenty years later, decides to get self-righteous with Clinton.") The difference between herself and Clinton, Quinn goes on to explain in her piece, through other people's words ("God knows, most people in Washington have led robust sexual lives," says history professor Roger Wilkins, coyly smiling over both adultery and le droit du seigneur), is that she didn't lie about it.

At least, as Quinn might paragraph it, not under oath.

So far as one knows.

This old D.C. gossip—the back story of "Not in Their Backyard," as it were—is meaningful only as a way of underlining the argument Quinn, speaking for all those who make up her chorus in the piece (such figures as presidential historian Doris Kearns Goodwin, presidential consultant David Gergen, reporters Elizabeth Drew and Cokie Roberts), is really making: some people belong, and some people don't.

That is the true meaning of the seemingly innocuous description of Washington as "like any other small community, where people come together to support their own"—and shun those who are not their own, who are not like them, who do not belong. In the America of the Washington that is "their 'town'"—which does not include, of course, most of the people who merely live in Washington, D.C.—the rest of America is of no account. The Clinton sex scandal, Quinn quotes presidential historian Michael Beschloss, "affects our psyche more than someone who might be farming in Wyoming."

The real audience for Clinton's first Inaugural Address, Quinn says—the audience to which the address was truly directed—was not the country at large, but "an already suspicious Washington Establishment." Why "already suspicious"? Is this an after-the-fact judgment meant to make the Establishment Washingtonians seem perspicacious and far-seeing? Or is it an acknowledgment that an outsider president, from a foreign place, must rightfully be seen as a threat before he is seen as anything else? Clinton's audience, Quinn was saying, was there before he got there and will be there when he's gone. Before they can accept such a person from elsewhere, he must prove that he knows what their rules are and that he will play by them. He cannot assume he can govern without their consent.

One might recall, from early 1999, First Lady Hillary Clinton speaking about how she thought a bias against Arkansas played a part in the contempt in which she thought the national media and the Washington establishment held both Bill Clinton and herself. She might have been saying that they were being punished because neither of them had ever learned the language. When Hillary Clinton speaks, the hard words left by the dropped g's and the flinty, resentful, I-Know-You-Think-We're-Dirt consonants she picked up during her years in Arkansas make up a good part of the momentum her voice carries; when Bill Clinton speaks in any unscripted situation, the ease in his speech—the way elisions between words become near-words in themselves, the sense communicated that no human problems are that terrible compared to the weather, and the sense that, like the weather, a righteous, defensive, all-consuming anger can break out at any time—is a good part of why, were he to take to the airwaves to declare himself the living Antichrist, his public approval ratings might indeed rise. The press immediately and unanimously mocked Hillary Clinton's assertion as paranoid, if not demented—just as it had her earlier, perfectly factual assertion that a right-wing conspiracy was behind the attempt to force Bill Clinton from office.

Hillary Clinton surely spoke for much of Arkansas. Certainly the now eight-year pursuit of legal wrongdoing by Bill and Hillary Clinton is commonly seen in Arkansas as an attempt by the national media to punish the state for having the temerity to send to Washington not a John Doe, but a greased Razorback hog. It is an old story; Arkansas has long held a special place in the iconography of the American nowhere ("Bill Clinton's hair," John Updike wrote in the *New Yorker,* is "closely modelled on the opossum fur of his beloved Arkansas . . . in any case composed of an unidentifiable salt-and-pepper substance, like spill-proof carpeting"—like, he is saying, the carpets people use in trailer camps), and especially in the negative iconography of the South itself. "Texans say," Alan Lomax writes in *The Folk Songs of North America,* "that in the early days one fork of the big road going west led to Arkansas, the other to Texas. On the latter road there was a sign reading, 'This road to Texas.' According to Texans, all who could read pressed on to the Lone Star State, while the rest settled in Arkansas." There is no equivalent Arkansas joke about Texas. From the media construction of Clinton as "Bubba" (imagine a Jewish president being commonly referred to by commentators as "Bubeleh") to the ranting segregationist governor Orville Faubus in the 1950s to Al Capp's creation of Li'l Abner in the 1940s and far back from there, the place has been a national joke for more than a hundred and fifty years—which is the approximate age of "The State of Arkansas," a song best heard in a 1927 recording by Virginian Kelly Harrell, collected as "My Name Is John Johanna" on Harry Smith's 1952 *Anthology of American Folk Music.*

Under a painfully swaybacked melody played on his fiddle, Harrell tells his tale:

> My name is John Johanner
> I came from Buffalo town
> For nine long years I've traveled
> This wide world around
> Through up and down and miseries
> And some good days I saw
> But I never knew what misery was
> Till I went to Arkansas

There follows a hilariously gruesome tale of the best hotel in Arkansas as the worst hotel in America, "walking skeletons" with "pity and starvation in their faces," and a labor boss seven feet tall, whose filthy hair hangs "down in rattails / Below his underjaw," who promises his men fifty cents a day but pays them in rock-hard corn dodgers and rotten meat.

That's the Arkansas that lies latent in the national imagination, and with which, for the last eight years, the national imagination has been so relentlessly teased: the worst place in the country, hell on earth. Anyone who stumbles into the place has only himself to blame if he can't get out. Kelly Harrell gets out alive, but just barely: if he ever sees the place again, he says, "I'll be looking through a telescope / From here to Arkansas."

This was precisely the tone of "Race to the Bottom," a March 9, 1998, *Newsweek* story by Howard Fineman and Daniel Klaidman, with Mark Hosenball and Michael Isikoff, on the obstacles facing Kenneth Starr, who is made of sterner stuff than Kelly Harrell. "Even the shrewdest prosecutor would have had a tough time with the Clinton crew," the *Newsweek* crew wrote. "They have a shared history and intense combat training." This is war, the reporters were saying, and must be fought as one, as against aliens, people who are not like you or me: "Starr was a stranger in the strange land of Arkansas, operating in a cousinly place where everyone knew everyone else's business and where politicians were used to dealing with—and attacking—elected prosecutors."

Now, this is bizarre: what is this "used to attacking," let alone "attacking elected prosecutors," as if Starr were elected? It is the projection of Arkansas as no less a closed society than Quinn's Washington—but cast here entirely in the negative, with the familiar replaced with the scary, the reassuring with the threatening, probity with deception, and a natural confluence of interests and perspectives ("Their wives are friendly with one another and their childen go to the same schools") with conspiracy. But change the tone from the ominous to the humorous and the message remains the same. On April 10, 1999, the *New York Times* carried a dispatch on Starr's continuing prosecution, in Little Rock, of Susan

McDougal, a former partner of the Clintons in the Whitewater development: "Whereas a Studious Juror Nearly Causes a Mistrial for
McDougal." The report concerned a controversy involving John T.
Purtle, a former justice of the Arkansas Supreme Court: a signed
copy of a law book Purtle once owned had been brought into court
by a juror while deliberations were under way. There were vague
suggestions of tampering. The story was entirely meaningless, save
for the smirking tone of its headline (imagine: a studious hillbilly!)
and, save for maintaining the story within the story, offered a completely gratuitous conclusion. Though it turned out the justice had
nothing to do with the juror obtaining the book, the *Times* reported
(the juror lived in a house in which Purtle once lived, where Purtle
had left behind a number of books), "Mr. Purtle's background
starkly demonstrates the intertwining of issues and personalities in
Arkansas. He was originally named to the State Supreme Court by
Mr. Clinton when Mr. Clinton was governor. While on the court,
Justice Purtle ruled in favor of Ms. McDougal and her husband at
the time, James B. McDougal, in a matter involving a savings bank
they owned which is at the heart of the current trial."

This is Arkansas: a "strange land," where everyone is in bed with
everyone else. And it is not hard to see how such behavior might
seem when transferred to the White House: "the holiest," as Sally
Quinn quotes Roger Wilkins, "of America's secular shrines." Two
who should know are Muffie Cabot, social secretary to Nancy Reagan, and Tish Baldrige, social secretary to Jacqueline Kennedy—
women whom, it would seem, were predestined for their jobs by
their names. "Watergate was pretty scary," Cabot tells Quinn, "but
it wasn't quite as sordid as this." "We want there to be standards,"
Baldrige says. "We're used to standards. When you think back to
other presidents, they all had a lot of class."

"A lot of class"—the phrase slipped into our language in the
1960s, but it is always worth paying attention to who uses it, and
whom it is used against. A lot of class, like Ronald Reagan, who

though he conducted a coup against his own government by devising the private financing of a foreign policy Congress had refused to fund, always "put on a coat and tie" when he went into the Oval Office, "even on weekends." A lot of class, like John F. Kennedy, bringing prostitutes and Mafia party girls into the White House for drugs and orgies.

The whole sickening, antidemocratic discourse—of "class," of "standards," of hair like possum fur or spill-proof carpeting—is brought into perfect relief in a few breathtakingly condescending lines from Richard Goodwin, a speechwriter for Kennedy (and after that for President Lyndon B. Johnson, though that is not part of the résumé in which Goodwin generally dresses). With the sense of having just barely escaped sullying himself by contact with Arkansas rubes and their relaxing of standards, Goodwin was speaking to *Boston Globe* columnist Mike Barnicle, in a piece carried in the *San Francisco Chronicle* on March 3, 1997. Stories about the 1996 Clinton reelection campaign opening the Lincoln Bedroom to major contributors had hit the papers, and the White House had released a list of all those, identified by profession, who had spent the night there during Clinton's terms. "Mr. Goodwin and his wife, Doris Kearns Goodwin, belong to a distinct minority," Barnicle wrote. "In 1994 they slept in the White House for the donut because the two of them are smart, famous and insightful while both their hosts remain star-struck social climbers from Arkansas." "Using the White House like this is obscene," Goodwin told Barnicle (and it is, especially if you believe that campaign contributors of the past have never been treated similarly, or that the presence in the Clinton White House of someone like Goodwin, who has lived off his Kennedy connections for decades, speaks better for Clinton's judgment than that of Steven Spielberg or David Geffen). "We've gone from presidents saying 'Let the word go forth,'" Goodwin said, in case anyone missed his claim to Camelot, "to 'let the overnights begin.' And Massachusetts, which used to send great political leaders such as Adams and Kennedy to the White House, now sends Leventhal and Solomont, developers. At least," Goodwin said, "we were listed as writers." And not writers with Jewish names.

The ease with which northerners especially speak of Clinton with contempt is part of the contempt with which much of America has greeted white male southerners (perhaps the last group in our society that can be comfortably denigrated as such by the sort of liberals who would never say a public word against blacks, women, Asians, or Hispanics) from Elvis Presley to LBJ: unlike Jimmy Carter, southerners without apology. Many people reacted with a can-you-believe-this-guy-is-president amazement when Clinton, talking about growing up in Arkansas, referred to a pickup truck he once had with Astroturf in the bed as "a real southern deal"—a few reacting with delight, more with horror. Certainly the political opposition understood from the first that if Clinton could be denied personal legitimacy, he could be denied political legitimacy.

American political legitimacy has to be reestablished each time the presidency changes hands. It isn't simply because presidents write, produce, and perform plays about the meaning of national life, it being hard to start over with a new script when it feels as if one has been stranded in the middle of the old one. For all of the sophistication of a Constitution that is at once a machine and a nearly Cubist work of modern art, America remains in some ways a politically primitive country: a country less than fully convinced that, as a national polity, it even exists, or, if it does, that it should. America remains a young country: itself a strange land, with a before and an after. The country was invented. The country may or may not have existed as a society before it existed as a polity, but the fact of its invention overwhelms all that is social and, by so doing, deprives the political of the social bases of its legitimacy. Other societies can pull their social history, which in the case of, say,

Japan, China, Russia, France, Italy, Germany, Ethiopia, Mexico, or Great Britain, seems to extend back into the mists of time, into the unrecorded and the unknowable, into its political history, and the two are not completely separable. The Constitution does not countenance the social, or even the American specific. It makes certain fundamental assumptions about the base motives that govern all human beings and then attempts to design a censorious but self-renewing set of rules and procedures by which government might protect citizens from each other and citizens might be protected from government. The arrangement is neither ordered nor blessed by God; it presents itself as the product of reasoned suspicion and perhaps irrational hope. There is no State, in the European sense: an apparatus of power that carries its own principle of authority. The only authority given the national government of the United States of America is the consent of the governed. At any given moment, any given American can and likely will feel that his or her consent has not been given, or that it should be withdrawn.

It was in this spirit that, on Election Night 1992, Bob Dole, as Senate minority leader and presumptive Republican presidential candidate in waiting, declared that as Clinton, in a three-way race, had in defeating the incumbent Republican president been elected with less than half of the popular vote, he was not really president. (As a Republican congressman would say to a Democratic colleague on the floor of the House in the next year, Clinton was "your president," not his.) Thus, Dole promised, until the apparent accident of Clinton's election could be reversed, he would take it upon himself to represent those Americans who had not voted for Clinton—to represent, that is, the majority, as Clinton had no right to do. Though he himself had neither sought nor received a single vote, Dole promised to be, in essence, an other president. That night, Alan Ehrenhalt, editor of *Governing* magazine, wrote in the *New York Times* on December 20, 1998, Dole refused to acknowledge the "routine transfer of power" mandated in presidential elec-

tions by the Constitution, and "hinted at the way his party planned
to conduct itself in the months ahead: it would filibuster any significant legislation the new Democratic President proposed, forcing him to obtain 60 votes for Senate passage"—more than
Clinton's party could muster.

Ehrenhalt went on to describe minority Republican conduct in
the Senate as "an unreported constitutional usurpation. It should
have been reported at the time, but it wasn't. The punditocracy
chose not to notice." The strategy was enormously successful. Able
to paint Clinton as incompetent at anything other than raising
taxes, Republicans achieved majorities in the 1994 congressional
elections and, the next year, shut down the national government,
the legitimacy of which many of them had denied since the election of Ronald Reagan in 1980. "For all the millions of words that
have been written about this event before and since," Ehrenhalt
said, "the reality of it has rarely been portrayed in succinct terms.
This was not a political showdown—it was an attempted constitutional coup."

That Clinton won this fight only increased the conviction, on the
right and among much of the press, that he was a trickster, or a demon: that, were he to roam the corridors of the White House
shooting everyone in sight and then, soaked in blood, seize the airwaves to declare himself the living Antichrist, he could, were he
still eligible, be elected to the presidency all over again. And it was
for this reason that when, in early 1999, Clinton's acquittal in the
Senate of the bill of impeachment filed by the House became certain, both spokespersons of the American right and members of the
press began to question not only the moral decency of Bill Clinton,
but of the people as a whole.

The Republican rule that Clinton ended had one fundamental
public message. It was in a sense a secret message, because people
were able to convince themselves they weren't hearing it, at least
while it was delivered by Ronald Reagan, who as a seemingly genial

president so powerfully masked the fury and rancor he had displayed as governor of California. The secret message was that some people belong in the United States, and some people don't; that some are worthy, and some are worthless; that certain ideas and opinions are sanctified, and some are evil; and that with the blessing of God, God's messengers will separate the one from the other.

Whatever Clinton has been about, it isn't that. As a political man, he has never, by word or gesture, said to another citizen, "I am an American, and you are not." As an outsider who has never been accepted in the city to which the electorate twice brought him, and perhaps never wanted to be, Clinton has communicated the opposite of that sentiment from the beginning of his presidency through his impeachment. It might be that sentiment, and the way that he communicated it, that made it possible for him to be impeached; it was certainly the fact that he did communicate it that kept him from conviction.

In the summer of 1964, after my freshman year at the University of California at Berkeley, I went to Washington to work as an intern in the office of Representative Philip Burton, Democrat from San Francisco. After a year of being constantly reminded that "Berkeley isn't the real world"—and this was the year before the Free Speech Movement, with its months of student demonstrations, made Berkeley a watchword, or a warning, all over the world—of being told that Berkeley was smug, self-referential, an intellectually closed place that saw itself as, and for that matter was, a complete exception to the rest of the country, I learned something about Washington, D.C.: it wasn't the real world, either. It was even less so, despite its absolute conviction, its almost absolutely seductive conviction, that it was the world. Washington was far more insular than Berkeley, more petty, status-mad, and gossip-driven. Sucking up to professors, hinting at how "close" one was to this charismatic lecturer or that world-famous scientist, was one thing; sucking up to power was worse, and as opposed to Berkeley, in Washington no one was outside the game. Washington, I learned, was another country. I learned one thing more: in Washington, the country was another country.

That this is not the country Clinton has embodied as president has made a difference, one that will take many years to see clearly, or perhaps to see at all. Just as, in the mid-'50s, Elvis Presley revealed one America to another—revealed America to itself, and in so doing made the country a bigger place than it ever was before— I think many people feel at home in the United States, feel part of it, feel they have to make no argument to justify that feeling, who did not feel the same before Clinton was president. I assume that because Clinton will leave office people will not automatically surrender that feeling, or for that matter surrender it without a fight. Maybe that, finally, is what so many who call Washington "their 'town'" can't abide: that Bill Clinton, who for the months of his impeachment sat in the White House as a specter of shame and defiance, daring his fellow citizens to believe they were better than he was, really did come from the country.

Cultural Critique, *Fall 1999 (Spring 2000)*
San Francisco Examiner Magazine, *May 28, 2000*

Part Four

NOWHERE

A Backward Glance
October 14, 2000—A Look into Bill Clinton's Future

Version One

Everyone recognized President George W. Bush's pardon of ex-president Bill Clinton as a master stroke. Following Bush's surprisingly comfortable victory over Al Gore, Independent Counsel Robert W. Ray—who had replaced Kenneth Starr in 1999, and, though the law creating his office had lapsed, remained on the job, determined, as he said, to pursue all allegations against Clinton to their rightful conclusion—announced the indictment of the still-sitting president on eight counts of perjury and obstruction of justice. Most citizens had assumed that the legal questions arising out of Clinton's testimony in Paula Jones's dismissed sexual harassment suit against him, in regard to his affair with White House intern Monica Lewinsky, had been settled by Clinton's 1999 acquittal in the Senate on impeachment charges brought by a bare Republican majority in the House of Representatives; the public reaction to the Ray indictment was stupefaction. Ray went on the morning TV news programs to quietly affirm his courage in being the first prosecutor to secure the indictment of a president. Pundits assured the nation that there was no chance of conviction—while lawyers responded that, in a trial, there was always a chance of conviction. Clinton declared his intention to take his place before the court and defend himself, even though, in Arkansas, with Democratic

judges, many of whom owed their careers to him, recusing themselves, he had already been stripped of his law license.

Speaking to Barbara Walters, prosecutor Ray made it clear that
"of course, the president will be permitted to surrender himself."
Thus it was a surprise when, at the conclusion of President Bush's
inauguration on January 20, 2001—when the echo of Bush's para-
phrase of Lincoln's "With malice toward none, with charity for all"
("With charity, we say, lift yourself up by your own bootstraps; without malice we say, good luck and godspeed, you're an American,
you're on your own") had faded, when all the paraders had passed
by, when the former president and Senator Hillary Clinton of New
York, along with everyone else, followed the new president down
from the reviewing stand—that Ray himself should appear with a
team of FBI agents to arrest Mr. Clinton, for Ray to exercise his
discretion as a federal prosecutor to mandate and oversee the
shackling of his prisoner, not with cuffs but with chains, on both the
hands and legs, and then to lead him away.

Just as George W. Bush, when confronted with the coincidence
that as a young oil man he had sold his stock in his own company
just before his own company issued the report of poor quarterly
earnings that led to the immediate collapse of his own company's
stock, denied that he had benefited from any inside information,
the new president pronounced himself "shocked, shocked" at the
former president's arrest and, with TV crews following, went directly to the White House, where, as his first official act, he signed
the pardon that was waiting on his desk in the Oval Office.

Clinton was immediately released. He insisted he wanted his
day in court, but the pardon was not his to dispute. As president,
Bush had ended all legal proceedings against his predecessor; Clinton no longer had a case to make.

Bush did. The pardon instantly defused any Democratic hostil-
ity toward him and opened up a storied "Hundred Days" of leg-
islative upheaval not seen since the first months of Franklin D.

Roosevelt's New Deal. With Clinton and Gore banished to that special oblivion America reserves for losers—with the pardon magically transforming the giant figure of Clinton the Winner into a shriveled impostor, an embarrassment of bluster and shame—and with the Democrats thus without credible leaders and providing support reminiscent of that they had given Ronald Reagan's enormous first-term tax cuts, the small Republican majorities in the new Congress rewrote the New Deal in a manner so radical some whispered it brought a smile to Reagan's lips, even though it had been years since the old man had formed a single sentence anyone could understand.

Bush all but eliminated taxes on the rich. The privatization of Social Security, presented by Bush as a two-percent experiment during the campaign, was put into law with a clause making the entire program voluntary after ten years, effectively ending it. Medicare was turned over to private insurers, who, in exchange for a promise to cover part of the cost of prescription drugs to current Medicare recipients, were granted the right to determine who was and who was not eligible for the program as a whole.

With the political resignations of Chief Justice William Rehnquist, appointed by Richard Nixon and elevated by Reagan, Justice Sandra Day O'Connor, appointed by Reagan, and, for reasons of health, Justice Ruth Bader Ginsburg, appointed by Clinton, their respectable but hard-right replacements—most notably the new chief justice, Frank Easterbrook, only fifty-two, formerly a federal appeals court judge, appointed by Reagan in 1985, renowned for his brilliance, his energy, his contempt for those appearing before him, and his disregard for the Constitution—remade American jurisprudence. Within a year, *Roe* v. *Wade*, the 1973 Supreme Court decision recognizing a woman's right to terminate a pregnancy, was overturned—though, to the surprise of many, few states were able to enact anything like a full ban against the practice. Perhaps as important, the new Easterbrook court swiftly decided a whole series of cases concerning the purview of the federal government and the rights of property owners, effectively depriving even the concept of federal standards regarding environmental protection and market fraud of any legal basis.

With the income tax in wreckage, the national debt began to rise, and all talk of budget surpluses disappeared. Investment capital dried up. Unemployment rose. Panic buying produced inflation, which fed on itself. Bush and his party leaders announced what the country was beginning to feel as a collapse was nothing more than a correction after the "excesses" of the Clinton years, and in any case "a small price to pay for freedom."

Clinton appeared on *Saturday Night Live,* performing with house Clinton impersonator Darrell Hammond in the skit "Dueling Clintons"—a saxophone parody of the "Dueling Banjos" set piece from *Deliverance,* with Clinton, the southerner, now playing the incest-riddled moron with the flying fingers. At the end of the program, Linda Tripp appeared amid the traditional celebratory crowd of cast and guests. Clinton's face turned gray, and for the second time in the history of the show the word *fuck* went out over its air.

The pardon was a knife in the back that could not be removed. It had saved Clinton money he did not have and rescued him from the distant but real possibility of prison. But the pardon deprived Clinton of anything like a real life. All the years of cabal and conspiracy on the right, from the billionaire Richard Mellon Scaife and his "Arkansas Project" and Jerry Falwell and his Clinton Hit-List videos to the new Republican chairs of congressional investigative committees from 1995 on to the independent counsels and their bottomless investigations into every form of criminality imaginable—all of it had come to nothing. Aside from the Iran-Contra affair—Ronald Reagan's illegal sale of arms to Iran in order to generate funds for the Nicaraguan contras Congress had refused to provide—it was the greatest hoax in American political history. Starr requiring that Hillary Clinton make a public "perp walk" into his grand jury, forcing Clinton to say, to a smirking junior prosecutor, on video to be broadcast to the entire world, if he understood the meaning of the oath he had just taken—he had beaten it all. None of it was there. All his enemies had, finally, was, in Philip Roth's words from *The Human Stain*, his novel about the impeachment year, "a virile, youthful middle-aged president and a brash, smitten twenty-one-year-old employee carrying on in the Oval Office like two teenage kids in a parking lot"—that, and any jerk's desire to cover it up in front of his wife, his daughter, and everybody else. He had beaten it all and now it all stuck.

There was nowhere to go. His daughter was making her own life. His wife was in Washington. The house in New York was a base of operations but he had nothing to do. The library in Arkansas was too boring to think about. No one wanted a book unless he was willing to talk about what he was never going to talk about.

After the defeat of the Democratic congressional majorities in the fall of 1994, with the ascension of new House Speaker Newt Gingrich, who all but announced himself the new, real president, Clinton had fled from the light. The election had been a referendum on him: on the Democratic tax increases of 1993, which set the stage for the economic resurgence that was still exploding when Clinton left office, on the national health plan that no one understood and no one could explain, on the man who, in his first two years in office, had seemed more than anything confused, cowardly, a betrayer of his friends and a supplicant to his enemies. The Clinton whom the pardon had erased from national memory, the Confidence Man, the Riverboat Gambler who had beaten the Republicans with their own marked cards, had emerged only when the Republicans, in full glory that the country was theirs in fact and only the formality of the 1996 presidential election stood between them and title, shut down the national government in the fall of 1995. But in 1994 the country had spoken: it had voted by proxy against Bill Clinton, and it could not wait for him to leave.

So Clinton called upon various well-wishers and soothsayers for advice and comfort, among them the bizarrely prognathous, gargantuan avatar of American self-help seminars, part Ralph Waldo Emerson, part Amway, part Paul Bunyan, part Newt Gingrich himself: Tony Robbins. Robbins told the president that his strength was within himself, that even as a positive attitude could make millions, it could move millions.

In the years since, Robbins had continued to tour the country and fill the cable airwaves with hour-long infomercials. His huge Success Seminars featured not only himself, and not only winner-loser professional football quarterback Fran Tarkenton (who, having set countless passing records while failing ever to gain a championship, spoke with the dull cadences of the convert as Robbins towered over him like a statue), but also such victims of history as Mikhail Gorbachev and Margaret Thatcher. Once they had ruled. Now they were as bereft, as forgotten, as you or I, but they remained to spread the word of Tony Robbins's Personal Power System III, to proclaim that you too could Awaken the Giant Within, that It's Up to You, that No One Can Do It for You, that The Life You Save May Be Your Own—that, in a phrase, America's way is God's way, that you're on your own and there are no politics. Now, hard into the twenty-first century, those leaders of the Soviet Union and Great Britain, those who left a different world behind, one rejected by his own people, another by her own party, had to cede the spotlight.

Clinton joined the tour as the unquestioned star. He closed the show. He read the script. "I was the president of the United States," it began. "I think I was a pretty good president. Some people"—and here there was a pause in the script—"agree with me. But you know what? I don't know what's out there. I don't think I ever really did. Compared to what I've learned in the days and nights Tony and I have spent talking, really *talking*, compared to the fact that now I know *anything* is possible—well, being president, *it was a great first step."*

He started blowing his lines the second day out. He never pulled a stunt, never started ranting from the stage: *When I left office this country was flying into the future, and look at it now, it's a train wreck, it's not your country anymore, it's not mine anymore, the people who own it, who run it, don't want you here any more than they wanted me here, if they could do what they did to me, think what they could do to you*—he never said any of that, not on Tony Robbins's stage. He took the money and didn't show up for the second week.

He moved to California, with his eye on the seat of a retiring Democratic senator. There he was still larger than life. Especially in the Bay Area, in San Francisco, Berkeley, Oakland, Palo Alto, he was still the man they'd been waiting for—and his daughter was still there, in medical school. It was uncanny, this place: it was ages since 1992, 1996, and there were "Clinton-Gore" stickers on cars everywhere.

To make a living, he charged admission for his campaign speeches. The crowds were good at first; then bigger, when the word got out how much of the talk in the halls came from the audience. It took only a few moments to open the discourse people wanted to hear. "You've heard it said, 'If they could do what they did to me, think what they could do to you.' Well, they have. The difference is, they—the people who are now running the country in our name—did it all at once. The country you thought you lived in when the last election was held no longer exists. I want to go back to Washington and say this over and over until even I can't stand the sound of my own voice."

That was years ago. He's still there.

Version Two

Despite Al Gore's tight victory over George W. Bush, his election was greeted by a sigh of relief that was felt from Maine to California. No, there wasn't going to be a Bush dynasty. Yes, there would be real government. No, despite the tempting bribes Bush had offered the country, proffering dollar bills in his hand at campaign stops like John D. Rockefeller handing out his dimes to street urchins, the electorate would not have to see itself refected back from Bush's tight little preppy face. That story was finished.

Gore hit the ground running. His administration began on an even keel and stayed there. Republican congressional leaders, who had barely held their majorities, waited for Gore to stumble; he didn't. Soon enough they began to play ball. Three new appointments to the Supreme Court solidified a centrist Democratic approach to both personal rights and federal power. The hard right on the court—Justices Antonin Scalia and Clarence Thomas—found itself isolated as Reagan appointee Justice Anthony Kennedy more and more sided with the block led by newly elevated Chief Justice Stephen Breyer.

With an eye on reelection in 2004, Gore quietly raised vast amounts of unregulated party money while noisily pushing the McCain-Feingold fund-raising reform bill, which outlawed that precise practice; when Gore signed the bill, Republicans were caught flat-footed. The economy continued to expand at a rate even retiring Federal Reserve chairman Alan Greenspan admitted might be consistent with an absence of inflation; the unemployment rate dropped to within two and three percent. Carefully, Gore introduced a broad package of incentives and mandates that began to cut the number of citizens without health insurance; before long, the country was ready to consider a comprehensive health plan for the nation as a whole.

Having built this stage and left it, Bill Clinton was no longer needed—or wanted. As the press celebrated President Gore's Reagan-like domination of both the news and an opposition Congress, Clinton again and again pulled an old piece by *Los Angeles Times* columnist Robert Scheer out of his wallet. "What a gutless wonder Al Gore is turning out to be," Scheer had written in August of 2000. "Instead of rising to the defense of an administration that deserves to be celebrated, for his running mate he turns to Connecticut Sen. Joseph Lieberman, a carping Clinton critic."

He skipped down as he always did to the fourth paragraph: "The fact is, Clinton"—and here he read more slowly—"has . . . been . . . a . . . great . . . president, presiding over eight years of unprecedented prosperity and progress toward world peace. Under the Republicans, pundits were writing books about the need to learn Japanese. After Clinton, the Japanese are desperate to emulate the U.S. economy. Clinton has stopped the far right in its tracks, reduced Newt Gingrich to a fading memory and—"

This was where Clinton always stopped; now he, too, was a fading memory. The temporary buildings for his presidential library were in place, with visual displays by Industrial Light and Magic, but Clinton had soon tired of greeting the adults asking how it felt to be "Mr. Hillary Clinton" now that she was in Washington and he was not, the children hanging back as if they'd been warned by their parents that this very important man had once done a very bad thing—tired of his fellow citizens, not to mention the endless stream of would-be Monicas.

He played a lot of golf. He put on weight. He spent the summers, as he had for so long, up on Martha's Vineyard, with the crowd that had greeted him so warmly as First Houseguest. But one day, when he'd told host William Styron he was going out for a walk and forgot to go, he overheard the great novelist laughing on the porch with the rest of the usual crowd: Carly Simon, Paul

Simon, David Remnick of the *New Yorker*, Lewis Lapham of *Harper's*. "Gettin' *old*," Styron said, the Virginian trying on an Arkansas accent. "He be all *moochin'* and nothin' comin' *back*. And," Styron said, returning to normal speech, "it's not like *he* ever wrote anything!" It was true enough: Clinton's *My Hope for America* had been rejected by every New York publisher; Louisiana University Press couldn't offer enough to pay a ghostwriter.

Something snapped in Clinton after that day at Styron's. He found himself listening too often to "Lone Pilgrim," that weird, quiet song about a voice coming from a grave that ended Bob Dylan's 1993 album *World Gone Wrong*. When he was trying to think about something else, he thought of those funny stories about Elvis faking his death both to escape "the pressures of fame" and to "commune with his people," traveling the land incognito, living off odd jobs in, as one fantasist had had it, "the often pesky world of the uninsured."

He grew a beard, slipped his Secret Service detail, and went to Graceland; after that he visited Elvis's birthplace in Tupelo. He felt nothing. People sometimes looked at him funny, but if they recognized him they didn't give themselves away. It was as if, after every shred of privacy had been stripped from him during his presidency, people now respected his privacy—or simply didn't care.

He thought about the hilarious Carl Hiassen murder novel *Double Whammy*, the one with the story about the idealistic Florida governor who, discovering that the entire state was a racket for developers, one day upped and disappeared, turning himself into a swamp rat named Skink who lived off roadkill. God knows how many times during his presidency that sounded good. He thought of the old Preston Sturges movie *Sullivan's Travels*, where the rich Hollywood comedy director Sullivan—Joel McCrae, it was, they didn't look so different—went bumming on the road to find out what the People really cared about, jumping freights, getting into a fight with a railroad bull, ending up in prison.

From the Tupelo birthplace he made his way to the edge of town. He hitched a ride; then he started walking. After a few days on the road, sleeping out of doors, living off the money he'd been carrying, he looked like any old Irish drunk: red face, a gut hanging over his belt, gray and matted hair. In an alley in a town in northern Louisiana he shared a bottle with a crowd of white bums, pretending to chug while keeping his tongue against the mouth of the bottle. No one had ever believed that line about how he smoked marijuana and didn't inhale, but of course it was true; he was never going to lose control. This was an experiment.

Two men jumped him from behind and began pulling down his pants while a third man pulled down his own. He swung the bottle at the head of one man; he fell down dead. Everyone ran.

After that he was Judge Crater. He was the man who one night went out for a cigar and never came back. He was a joke; he was presumed dead. Hillary and Chelsea put on a convincing show of grief, though they always knew. They knew what state he was in, what little town hadn't had a lawyer until the gaunt, stooped man with a dubious law degree and a surprisingly high score on the state bar exam had shown up to prepare wills, negotiate disputes, write up deeds, refer suits over fraud and misrepresentation to people better able to handle them, and less likely to have to prove who they were. He made a living.

Gore had his suspicions, but he didn't ask. He figured the man would raise his head again someday; he wasn't looking forward to it. Clinton wondered about Gore, wondered what, if anything, he was owed, but mostly he read novels and watched movies. *Young Mr. Lincoln* was on all the time and he liked it, with Henry Fonda talking down the lynch mob, just as he'd done, when the lynch mob was supposed to be the country itself and the good citizens of the town, that fat fuck Starr and all the rest of them, kept their sober faces while their hearts were pounding with glee, and like Lincoln he'd waited them out, waited until the mob turned into a crowd and then a meeting and began to listen to him and think it over. He liked that, but not as much as *Point Break,* with Keanu Reeves's FBI agent infiltrating a bunch of surfers who turn out to be the un-stoppable Ex-Presidents, a gang of bank robbers with Nixon, Ford, Carter, and Reagan Halloween masks covering their faces, and Reagan, of course, running the show.

The novel he read most, and most loved, and liked least, was Fitzgerald's *Tender Is the Night.* To him it was all about disappear-ance, about giving everything and everyone taking as if it was their due, as if nothing was owed. Dick Diver knew it, but he never ad-mitted it to himself: that he was the fool of people who once they'd taken the blush of his personality, the light in his eyes, would pass him on the street and never know it. Clinton never admitted it ei-ther, but he knew it, too, and that was why, getting close to the end of the book, every year or so, he always stopped. Without letting the words into his head, he knew the ending. Dick Diver, no longer answering his wife's letters offering money, just letting her know he had a practice in a small town, that he needed nothing, and she thinking of him as General Ulysses S. Grant, out of the army and drinking in Illinois as the Union headed toward disaster and he waited for a call to return. But there was no disaster and no call ever came.

The Guardian (*London*), *October 14, 2000*
San Francisco Examiner Magazine, *November 5, 2000*

Works Cited

Atkins, Ace. *Crossroad Blues*. New York: St. Martin's Press, 1998. Where Elvis kills Robert Johnson—symbolically, anyway.

Babes in Toyland. *Spanking Machine* (TwinTone, 1990).

Beatles. "Real Love" (1979/1995), from *Anthology 2* (Capitol, 1996).

Booth, Stanley. *Rythm Oil: A Journey through the Music of the American South*. London: Jonathan Cape, 1991, and New York: Pantheon, 1992. The Pantheon edition omits a portfolio of William Eggleston color photographs.

Browning, Dolly Kyle. *Purposes of the Heart*. Dallas: Direct Outstanding Communications, 1997.

Clinton, Bill. *Bill Clinton Jam Session—The Prez Blows* (Pres, 1994).

Clinton, Roger, and Politics. *Nothing Good Comes Easy* (Pyramid, 1994).

DePaoli, Geri, ed. *Elvis + Marilyn: 2 × Immortal*. New York: Rizzoli, 1994. Exhibition catalog.

Donovan. "Bert's Blues," from *Sunshine Superman* (Epic, 1966).

———. *Troubador: The Definitive Collection 1964–1976* (Epic Legacy, 1992).

Double Trouble. Dir. Norman Taurog (MGM, 1967).

Dylan, Bob. *Good as I Been to You* (Columbia, 1992).

———. *MTV Unplugged* (Columbia, 1995).

———. *Time Out of Mind* (Columbia, 1997).

———. *World Gone Wrong* (Columbia, 1993).

Eleventh Dream Day. "Bomb the Mars Hotel," from *Beet* (Atlantic, 1989).

Erickson, Steve. *Leap Year*. New York: Poseidon Press, 1989.

Europa de postguerra, 1945–1965—Art després de diluvi. Dir. M. Dolors Genovès (Barcelona: Fundació "la Caxia," and Televisio de Cataluna, 1995).

Faithfull, Marianne. *Faithfull* (Island, 1994).

———. with David Dalton. *Faithfull: An Autobiography*. Boston: Little, Brown, 1994.

faith healers, th. "Hippy Hole," from *Lido* (Elektra/Too Pure, 1992).

Finkelstein Nat. *Andy Warhol: The Factory Years*. Edinburgh: Cannongate, 1999.

Includes a portfolio on Bob Dylan's Factory screen test: Finkelstein: "A Jewish potlatch commenced. Andy gave Bobby a great double image of Elvis. Bobby gave Andy short shrift."

Friedman, Kinky. *Elvis, Jesus & Coca-Cola*. New York: Simon & Schuster, 1993.

Geto Boys. "Mind Playing Tricks on Me," from *We Can't Be Stopped* (Rap-A-Lot, 1991).

Ginsberg, Allen. "A Western Ballad" (1948) and "America" (1956). Collected in *Selected Poems 1947–1995*. New York: HarperCollins, 1996. "America" is included on Ginsberg's box set *Holy Soul Jelly Roll: Poems and Songs 1949–1994* (Rhino Word Beat, 1994) in a 1956 live stand-up comedy version and, more somberly, on the box-set anthology *The Beat Generation* (Rhino Word Beat, 1992), in a recording made in 1959.

Guralnick, Peter. *Careless Love: The Unmaking of Elvis Presley*. Boston: Little, Brown, 1999.

———. *Last Train to Memphis: The Rise of Elvis Presley*. Boston: Little, Brown, 1994.

Halley, Peter. *Double Elvis* (1990). See DePaoli, 23.

Hanson. "MMMBop" (Mercury, 1997).

Harrell, Kelly. "My Name Is John Johanna" (Victor, 1927). Collected on *Anthology of American Folk Music* (1952), ed. Harry Smith (Smithsonian Folkways, 1997) and on *Kelly Harrell: Complete Recorded Works in Chronological Order, Volume 2 (1926–1929)* (Document, Austria). A cousin of this song, "Diamond Joe," is included on Bob Dylan's *Good as I Been to You*. In an April 24, 1994, *Hartford Courant* column, Colin McEnroe elaborated on the way the national media had excluded Arkansas from the Union: "Like the Clintons or hate 'em, everybody agreed that part of the problem was that Arkansas was . . . not our sort of place, dear. Once the snobbery started, it became a gusher. It is nothing to see Arkansas described as a crude Australopithecan social organization where persons who have more than two chromosomes together are regarded as geniuses." McEnroe went on to "The Grishamization of Whitewater": "Rose Law Firm has been transformed, in certain imaginations, into a place where they take you out for a nice lunch right before they kill you and shred your body, and poor Vincent Foster Jr.'s suicide has been turned into 'Weekend at Bernie's'-meets-Clue, with complex scenarios in which Foster's body is found here, brought there, posed briefly with Elvis in a supermarket frozen foods aisle, etc."

Harvey, PJ. *Dry* (Indigo/Too Pure, 1992).

———. *To Bring You My Love* (Island, 1995).

In the Name of the Father. Dir. Jim Sheridan (Universal, 1993).

I Shot Andy Warhol. Dir. Mary Harron (Orion, 1996).

Joplin, Janis. "Ball and Chain" (as part of Big Brother and the Holding Company), recorded June 17, 1967, at the Monterey Pop Festival, from the box-set retrospective *Janis* (Columbia Legacy, 1993) or *The Monterey International Pop Festival* (Rhino, 1992).

Kass, Deborah. *Double Double Yentl* (1992). See DePaoli, 40.

Kearns, Jerry. *Earth Angel* (1989). See DePaoli, 25.

Kingston Trio. *The Capitol Years,* 1957–64 retrospective box set (Capitol, 1995).

Landau, Jon. *"John Wesley Harding." Crawdaddy!* (May 1968). Collected in Craig McGregor, ed. *Bob Dylan—A Retrospective* (1972), reprinted as *Bob Dylan: The Early Years—A Retrospective.* New York: Da Capo, 1990.

Lussier, Louis. *Elvis Shadow* (1993). See DePaoli, 78.

Marat-Trech, Garat (Ed Baxter). Review of Margaret Thatcher, *Salute to Democracy. The Wire,* October 1992.

McBride, Martina. "Independence Day" (RCA, 1994).

Mudboy and the Neutrons. "Money Talks," from *Negro Streets at Dawn* (New Rose, 1993).

Mystery Train. Dir. Jim Jarmusch (Orion, 1989).

Nadja. Dir. Michael Almereyda (October, 1994).

Nirvana. *Live! Tonight! Sold Out!!* Dir. Kevin Kerslake (Geffen Music Video, 1994).

———. *Nevermind* (DGC, 1991.

———. "Smells Like Teen Spirit" (DGC Video, dir. Samuel Bayer, 1991).

———. *Unplugged in New York* (DGC, 1993).

Oates, Joyce Carol. "Waiting on Elvis, 1956" (1987), in Jim Elledge, ed. *Sweet Nothings: An Anthology of Rock and Roll in American Poetry.* Bloomington, Indiana: University of Indiana Press, 1994. Oates takes off from an incident described by Kays Gary in "Elvis Defends Low Down Style," *Charlotte Observer,* June 27, 1956: "The waitress brought his coffee. Elvis reached down and fingered the lace on her slip. 'Aren't you the one?' 'I'm the one, baby!'" (see Guralnick, 1994, 288–89).

O'Brien, Glenn. "Culture" (1992). In *Soapbox: Essays, Diatribes, Homilies and Screeds, 1980–1997.* Gent, Belgium: Imschoot, 1997.

Pendergrast, Mark. *For God, Country and Coca-Cola.* London: Weidenfeld and Nicholson, 1993.

Pere Ubu. *Datapanik in the Year Zero,* retrospective box set, 1975–82 (DGC, 1996). See especially, in the liner notes, Thomas's unsigned manifestos and excerpts from Charlotte Pressler's "Those Were Different Times."

———. *Pennsylvania* (Tim/Kerr, 1998).

Perkins, Carl. "Blue Suede Shoes" (Sun, 1956).

Pettibone, Raymond. *Andy Warhol, Elvis, 1964* (1971). See DePaoli, 24.

Pleasantville. Dir. Gary Ross (New Line, 1998).

Poison. "Every Rose Has Its Thorn" (Capitol video, 1988).

Presley, Elvis. "Earth Angel" (c. 1958–60), from *Elvis: A Golden Celebration* (RCA, 1984, 1998).

———. *Elvis Presley Platinum: A Life in Music* (RCA, 1997).

———. *Elvis: The King of Rock 'n' Roll The Complete '50s Masters* (RCA, 1992).

———. *Louisiana Hayride Archives, Volume 1* (Brandon Gold, 1954–56, 1996).

———. "Papa Oo Mau Mau." Untitled 1968 fragment, preceding "Going Home" on *Collectors Gold* (RCA, 1991).

———. "That's Someone You Never Forget" (1961). See *Elvis: From Nashville to Memphis—The Essential 60's Masters I* (RCA, 1993).

Red Rock West. Dir. John Dahl (Columbia, 1993)

Reed, Lou. Letter to Delmore Schwartz, 1965. Courtesy Gary Takata.

Rivard, David. "Cures" (1988). In Jim Elledge, ed. *Sweet Nothings: An Anthology of Rock and Roll in American Poetry.* Bloomington, Indiana: University of Indiana Press, 1994.

Rohr, Ned. *1997.* Self-published Elvis calendar.

———. *1998.*

———. *1999.*

Roosevelt, Franklin Delano. Campaign Address, Madison Square Garden, October 31, 1936. Recording collected on the Library of Congress anthology *Historic Presidential Speeches (1908–1993)* (Rhino Word Beat, 1995), though without the astonishingly here-spontaneous, there-manipulated crowd response that makes up a good part of the drama; for that, see *F.D.R. Speaks* (Washington Records, 1960).

Rush, Otis. "Double Trouble" (Cobra, 1958). See Rush, *Groaning the Blues: Original Cobra Recordings 1956–58* (Flywright, UK).

Savio, Mario. The complete text of Savio's December 2, 1964, speech can be found in *The Berkeley Student Revolt: Facts and Interpretations,* ed. Seymour Martin Lipset and Sheldon Wolin (Garden City, New York: Anchor, 1965). Excerpts can be heard on *Is Freedom Academic? A Documentary of the Free Speech Movement at the University of California, Berkeley, 1964* (KPFA-Pacifica Radio LP, 1964). For Savio's talk on the occasion of the Thirtieth Anniversary Reunion of the Free Speech Movement, see "Two Anniversary Speeches," *Threepenny Review* 62 (Summer 1995).

Shankman, Sarah. *The King Is Dead.* New York: Pocket Books, 1992.

Sonic Youth. "Shaking Hell," from *Confusion Is Sex* (1983, reissued as *Confusion Is Sex/Kill Yr. Idols,* DGC).

———. "Youth Against Fascism," from *Dirty* (DGC, 1992).

Steinke, Darcey. *Jesus Saves.* Boston: Atlantic Monthly Press, 1997.

Stephens, Joanne. *Homage to Elvis* (1991). See DePaoli, 147.

Thomas, David, and Two Pale Boys. *Meadville* (recorded 1996), from *David Thomas, Monster* (Cooking Vinyl, 1997). Includes "Can't Help Falling in Love."

Velvet Underground. "Heroin," from *The Velvet Underground and Nico* (Verve, 1967).

———. *Live MCMXCIII* (recorded in Paris, Sire, 1993).

Wallflowers. "Three Marlenas," from *Bringing Down the Horse* (Interscope, 1997).

Warhol, Andy. *Elvis I and II* (1964). See DePaoli, 22.

Williams, Hank. *Alone and Forsaken* (Mercury, 1995).

Williams, William Carlos. "Abraham Lincoln," from *In the American Grain* (1925). New York: New Directions, 1956.

Zevon, Warren. "Porcelain Monkey," from *Life'll Kill Ya* (Artemis, 2000).

Acknowledgments

Though most of the pieces collected here have to a greater or lesser degree been rewritten or reedited—to restore material originally cut for space, correct factual errors, and omit redundancies—while most have been retitled, and while in some cases I have combined material from different sources into a single piece, my primary thanks go to the editors and publishers who first saw this work into print. Most of all, over eight years, I relied on the flinty encouragement and responsiveness of Graham Fuller and Ingrid Sischy at *Interview*. Paul Wilner at *Image*, which later became the *San Francisco Examiner Magazine*, has been an unfailing source of ideas. I can alway count on *Rolling Stone* to call when someone dies, and sometimes even when someone doesn't; working with Joe Levy, Anthony DeCurtis, Robert Love, and Nathan Brackett has always been a pleasure, though I still think Jann Wenner should have written the Mario Savio obituary himself. *City Pages'* annual Artists of the Year issue has been a constant source of surprise because of Steve Perry, Will Hermes, Terri Sutton, Jim Walsh, and Michael Tortorello. At *Esquire* in 1992 I worked with my old *Rolling Stone* colleague Terry McDonell, along with Michael Hirschorn and Bill Tonelli; in 1998 and 1999 I took cues from David Granger and Peter Griffin. *Artforum,* probably more than any other place I've written in the last twenty years, was a free space for me, and as I have before and hope to again, I acknowledge a debt to David Frankel, Jack Bankowsky, Sydney Pokorny, and Anthony Korner. I thank as well David Shipley, John Darnton, Martin Arnold, and especially Olive Evans at *The New York Times*; Kit Rachlis at *LA Weekly*; Evelyn McDonnell and Bill Wyman at *SF Weekly*; Mark Sinker at *The Wire*; Gary Kamiya at *Salon*; Roger Trilling at *Details*; Moritz von Uslar at *Süddeutsche Zeitung Magazin*; Isabelle Graw at *Text zur Kunst*; the staff of *Die Zeit*; Julie Burchill and Matt ffytche of *Modern Review*; and Jochen Schulte-Sasse and Cecily Marcus of *Cultural Critique*.

Other people left their mark on these pages in countless ways, passing on news items, proffering strange gifts, making connections, inspiring by example, teaching me how to use a computer, letting me try out ideas in front of audiences, or ratcheting up the day's scale of incredulity, which by the end took some doing: Paul Alexander, the staff of Amoeba Records in Berkeley, Gina Arnold, John Bakke of the University of Memphis, Rabbi Alan Berg of Temple Beth El in San Mateo, California, Adam Block and Adam Block (you know which is which), Betsy Bowden, Robert Cantwell, Charlie Conrad, Madelyn Crawford of the San Jose Museum of Art, Sue D'Alonzo, Erika Doss, the staff of Down Home Music, Steve Erickson, Helen Gustafson, Howard Hampton, Niko Hansen, Clinton Heylin, Mary Hancock Hinds, Jim Jarmusch, Michele Jordan, Scott Kempner, Doris Knecht of *Falter* in Vienna, Jon Langford and Carlton B. Morgan (as Chuck Death and Colin B. Morton of Great Pop Things), Emily Marcus, Karal Ann Marling, Dave Marsh, Jim Miller, Sheila Muto and Lisa Weber of the University of California at Berkeley, Lynda Myles, Ramona Naddoff of Zone Books, Jeffrey Perl and Robert Nelsen of *Common Knowledge* and the University of Texas at Dallas, Melissa Pierson, Ann Powers, Robert Ray, Ger Rijff, John Rockwell, Gil Rodman, Jeff Rosen and Diane Lapson of Dwarf Music, Luc Sante, Jon

Savage, Rani Singh, Henk Tas, David Thomas, Katherine Viner at the *Guardian* in London, and Sarah Vowell.

At Henry Holt, I was lucky to work with Jack Macrae, Katy Hope, John Candell, and Tracy Brown; at Picador USA, Frances Coady was a new friend. At Faber and Faber, Lee Brackstone and, as through six books now, Jon Riley were ideal collaborators; Matthew Richardson of Pentagram provided a superb cover design. My agent, Wendy Wolf, and her assistant, Emily Forland, and her representative in the U.K., Anthony Goff, made me feel very lucky.

Jenny Marcus was the first person to read this book in manuscript; thanks to her it is shorter than it would have been otherwise. But without her I would never have bothered.

> # IMPEACH CLINTON
> ## Franklin
> ## Washington
> ## Jefferson

Sign carried by well-dressed
man in San Francisco financial
district, April 29, 1999

Index